JUN   2018

DATE DUE

SEXUAL
HARASSMENT
ONLINE

SEXUAL HARASSMENT

ONLINE

Shaming and Silencing Women in the Digital Age

Tania G. Levey

LYNNE
RIENNER
PUBLISHERS

BOULDER
LONDON

Published in the United States of America in 2018 by
Lynne Rienner Publishers, Inc.
1800 30th Street, Boulder, Colorado 80301
www.rienner.com

and in the United Kingdom by
Lynne Rienner Publishers, Inc.
3 Henrietta Street, Covent Garden, London WC2E 8LU

Library of Congress Cataloging-in-Publication Data
Names: Levey, Tania G., author.
Title: Sexual harassment online : shaming and silencing women in the digital
  age / by Tania G. Levey.
Description: Boulder, CO : Lynne Rienner Publishers, Inc., [2018] | Includes
  bibliographical references and index.
Identifiers: LCCN 2017036614 | ISBN 9781626376953 (hc : alk. paper)
Subjects: LCSH: Sex discrimination against women. | Bullying. | Social media.
  | Internet and women.
Classification: LCC HQ1237 .L48 2018 | DDC 305.42—dc23
LC record available at https://lccn.loc.gov/2017036614

British Cataloguing in Publication Data
A Cataloguing in Publication record for this book
is available from the British Library.

Printed and bound in the United States of America

 The paper used in this publication meets the requirements
of the American National Standard for Permanence of
Paper for Printed Library Materials Z39.48-1992.

5 4 3 2 1

Contents

Acknowledgments

I wish to thank Lynne Rienner Publishers, particularly Carrie Broadwell-Tkach, for insightful and invaluable advice and support. Former editor Andrew Berzanskis expressed enthusiasm for my research and helped shape the direction of this book. I also wish to thank the editors and anonymous reviewers for their careful and useful feedback.

This book would not have been possible without the support of the Office of Academic Affairs, the Behavioral Sciences Department, and the Sociology Program at York College, City University of New York (CUNY). CUNY and the Research Foundation also provided much-needed financial support in the form of two Professional Staff Congress (PSC)–CUNY grants. I also thank the organizers and copresenters at two sexualities sessions at American Sociological Association meetings for helping this project take form.

I cannot thank Jennifer Marx enough for going above and beyond the duties of an editor, posing questions and suggestions that made the book much stronger. I could not have made it through the writing process without the advice and support of Angela Jones, Kaya Laterman, Dina Pinsky, Josipa Roksa, Christopher Schlottmann, and Robert Talisse. I relied heavily on conversations and support from my friends: Theano Apostolou, Jenell Breitenbach, Bas Elgharib, Erin Goodsell, Tanya Keith, Alyson Palmer, Liz Roseman, Miranda Sidor, Damon Silvester, and Laura Vaillancourt. If I forgot anyone, please know your knowledge and support are in these pages. Finally, I must thank my family: Jason, Marissa, Sandra, David, and Marilyn. They provided constant emotional support and insight on politics, philosophy, language, social media, and popular culture.

1

Gender and Sexual Norms in the Digital Age

The Internet has dramatically reshaped society and social interactions, creating opportunities for self-expression and interpersonal connections that transcend time and space. Social scientists writing in the 1990s predicted not only new ways of communicating, but a transformation in social relationships and ways of exercising power. However, even social scientists writing in the early part of the twenty-first century could not predict the social and political impact of social media platforms such as Facebook, Instagram, and Twitter.[1] On average, people around the world spend 100 minutes browsing social media every day (Global Web Index, 2016).

Given the popularity of social media, it is regrettable that recent years have seen an increase in rampant online misogyny. Bloggers and journalists have documented countless examples of death and rape threats on women's blogs, Twitter accounts, and gaming accounts; the sharing of nude photographs without consent, with some altered to depict violence; and Facebook pages, websites, and forums dedicated to woman hating (Hess, 2014a; Marcotte, 2013; McAuliffe, 2014). As a warning to the reader, this book contains content that includes violent imagery and terms designed to offend. In agreement with Jane (2014), I believe the lack of attention to gender-based online abuse in the scholarly literature is due to the inclusion of words considered uncivil and offensive. I recognize the risks of repeating abusive language and pejoratives but believe doing so is necessary to establish the problem and thoroughly examine the effects of misogynist language. This book does not name abusers as it does not want to give them another platform. However, publicizing the abuse is crucial in order to reframe debates and incite action, as we are seeing with recent high-profile rape and sexual harassment cases.

Well-known cases of online abuse involving contemporary social media sites include blogger Ariel Waldman, who received a flood of tweets[2] calling her[3] a "cunt" and a "whore," as well as a string of threatening tweets that revealed private information in 2007. Writer Cheryl Lindsey Seelhoff was one of the earliest recipients in 2007 of doxing[4] and coordinated rape and death threats through Internet forums such as 4Chan. Beginning in 2014, video game developers, players, and commentators such as Zoë Quinn, Anita Sarkeesian, and Brianna Wu experienced threats of rape and murder in a harassment campaign known as Gamergate.

Recounting online threats against women writers, blogger Amanda Hess (2014a) recalls the following messages: "you are clearly retarded, i hope someone shoots then rapes you," "i hope someone slits your throat and cums down your gob," and "I just want to rape her with a traffic cone." Throughout 2013, journalist and feminist activist Caroline Criado-Perez was inundated with rape threats on Twitter for campaigning for a female figure to appear on a Bank of England note; the threats included "YOU BETTER WATCH YOUR BACK. . . . IM GONNA RAPE YOUR ASS AT 8PM AND PUT THE VIDEO ALL OVER THE INTERNET." Street harassment activist Feminista Jones has been continually threatened for her #YouOkSis Twitter campaign. "Blokes Advice," a private Facebook group, gives advice on how to force women to have anal sex and how to bombard them with porn. Prior to going on a killing rampage in Isla Vista, California, a man participated in online discussions about wanting revenge against women who rejected him. While in no way suggesting that posting online *caused* the violence, this rampage opened people's eyes to the websites and forums dedicated to woman hating. The *Guardian*'s analysis of its own 1.4 million blocked comments since 1999 revealed that eight out of ten were directed toward women writers. Feminist blogger and founder of Feministing.com Jessica Valenti received the most blocked comments of all *Guardian* writers (Valenti, 2016).[5]

Posting online about feminism, rape, sexual harassment, and political representation attracts the worst online abuse. Lewis's Law is named after journalist Helen Lewis's tweet from 2012 that "the comments on any article about feminism justify feminism" (*Geek Feminism Wiki*, n.d.). Valenti (2016) confirms this idea, finding that any online discussion about efforts to establish true gender equality sends some men into a rage. Women who speak about fields seen as men's domains, such as sports, video games, and technology, also receive high amounts of online abuse. Journalist Laura Penny and her family received rape threats after commenting publicly on economic policy. After speaking about immigration on BBC1, Professor Mary Beard was called a "cunt" and had her face superimposed onto a picture of women's genitals on the since closed website *Don't Start Me Off*. Women have been abused even when talking about topics traditionally associated with women. Shauna James Ahern was relentlessly harassed for blogging about cooking and parenting. Melania Trump, who would become First Lady, was inundated with online abuse after her speech at the 2016 US Republican National Convention, with most of the comments having nothing to do with the actual speech. Instead, tweets most often included terms like "bitch" (443), "plastic" (119), "whore" (118), "slut" (99), "bimbo" (77), "tramp" (47), "hooker" (40), "MILF" (29), "cunt" (22), and "skank" (13) (Steinblatt & Markovitz, 2016).

Online sexual abuse has become so widespread and persistent that a UN report (Broadband Commission for Sustainable Development, 2015) calls for a "world-wide wake-up call," offering sobering statistics and recommendations around three areas: sensitization, safeguards, and sanctions. Groups such as the Cyber Civil Rights Initiative (CCRI) and Discourse of Online Misogyny (DOOM) campaign against online sexual abuse. Online harassment is associated with headaches, drug use, social isolation, suicidal thoughts, and diminished school performance and future employment (Poole, 2013; Sinclair et al., 2012). Over the past decade, cyberbullying has been linked to higher rates of suicidal attempts among adolescents (Hinduja & Patchin, 2010), including the sexual shaming of adolescent girls and gay males who committed suicide, such as Tyler Clementi, Megan Meier, and Rehtaeh Parsons.

Some women are choosing to leave Internet platforms such as Twitter to escape abuse. Rampant abuse prompted writer Michelle Goldberg (2015) to title a *Washington Post* article "Feminist Writers Are So Besieged by Online Abuse That Some Have Begun to Retire." Actor[6] Leslie Jones chose to temporarily disable her account after being inundated with sexist and racist insults on Twitter upon the release of the new *Ghostbusters* movie, though she fought back against trolls[7] in a comedy segment on *Saturday Night Live*. Comic book writer Chelsea Cain recently left Twitter after becoming the target of trolls after the cover of the final issue of her comic *Mockingbird* featured the main character wearing a shirt that read "Ask Me About My Feminist Agenda." Valenti says if she could start over as a feminist writer, she would write under an anonymous name.

Online threats can intrude into offline lives through stalking and swatting.[8] Valenti decided to take a break from social media after she woke up to a tweet threatening the rape and death of her five-year-old daughter; Valenti tweeted, "I should not have to fear for my kid's safety because I write about feminism. I should not have to wade through horror to get through the day. None of us should have to" (Chasmer, 2016). Feminist video game critic Anita Sarkeesian and developers Zoë Quinn, Kathy Sierra, and Brianna Wu were forced to change their routines and eventually change addresses due to rape and death threats. A brick was thrown through Wu's window. A Pew Research Center study (Duggan, 2014) found that women who have been harassed were twice as likely as men to find their experience "extremely" or "very" upsetting. The ubiquity of the Internet, unlike the workplace and the street, makes it hard for women to escape harassment, particularly if the Internet is their livelihood. Over time, the burden of avoiding and enduring sexual harassment and assault results in lost opportunities and less favorable outcomes for girls and women. Fear of harassment can cause women to fear entering lucrative technology fields.

Gender, Sexuality, and Social Media

The purpose of this book is to describe the contemporary use of misogynist language in online settings and to understand its relevance for contemporary gender and sexual relations. Through social listening and content analysis, this book examines the various ways in which Internet users use misogynist words on the three most popular social media platforms: Facebook, Instagram, and Twitter.[9] The words examined here appear the most often in stories of gender-based abuse and include "bitch," "cunt," "dyke," "slut," and "whore."[10]

Certainly, sexual harassment existed before the Internet. Sexual harassment in the workplace reminded women not to compete for jobs, and sexual harassment on the streets reminded women not to travel freely. Online sexual harassment can be understood as an attempt to keep women from a major sector of the public sphere. Online misogynist terms can be likened to ambient or passive sexual harassment, in which the harassment is not directed toward a specific person, but is experienced by others and can lead to fear and a hostile environment. Social media made harassment considerably more efficient because these outlets can reach millions of people in seconds and harassers can remain anonymous. Certainly, lack of physical presence may encourage aggression by lessening empathy and emboldening otherwise unaggressive people (CASS Briefings, 2013; Morahan-Martin, 2000).

While not all online abuse centers on gender and sexuality, clear patterns emerge when abusers believe they are targeting girls and women.[11] Though the focus is on abuse directed toward girls and women, I will not be attributing gender of user or recipient unless a gender identity is supplied in the profile or text. Abusers often assume gender based on user name, appearance in photos, and occasionally stated gender identity. In the case of video gamers, gender is attributed based on the character and name chosen, as well as voice if the headset is used. Though the focus is on women, heteromasculine norms are also supported by misogynist terms (Bamberg, 2004).[12] Furthermore, this research is limited by a language that reflects and reproduces binary notions of gender. Rather, gender and sexuality are accomplished through a repeated set of practices and power relations (Butler, 1990, 1993; Connell, 1987).[13] Sexual harassment and abuse are examples of practices that reproduce and reinforce essentialist and binary notions of gender.

Reports from the American Association of University Women (Hill & Kearl, 2011) and the Pew Research Center (2014) find that women are much more likely than men to receive sexually threatening messages. Public shaming on social media took on sexual tones for women, such as developer Adria Richards and publicist Justine Sacco, but not for men, such as writer Jonah Lehrer (Ronson, 2015). Commonly used terms such as *cyberbullying*[14] and *trolling* fail to highlight the gendered and sexual aspects of women's harassment. Mantilla (2015) coined the term *gendertrolling* to highlight the viciousness, aggression, and pervasiveness of trolling against women (pp. 10–11). Barak (2005) uses the phrase *gender-based harassment in cyberspace* to include using gender-humiliating or shaming comments, sending sexually explicit messages, and sending unsolicited sexual content. Jane (2014) uses the term *e-bile* to refer to "sexualised vitriol" targeting women (p. 559). I prefer the use of *gendered online abuse* to convey the severity of online campaigns directed at people perceived as women.[15]

Just as the term *fag* serves as a threatening specter for men (Butler, 1990; Pascoe, 2012), women who go against traditional norms are at risk of labeling as *bitches, dykes,* and *sluts*. They have failed at performing gender, occupying the abject position against which all other women are judged (Butler, 1993). Terms like *dyke, slut,* and *whore* remain feared insults for adolescent girls and women offline as well, serving as powerful disciplinary mechanisms through social control and stigma (Attwood, 2007; Payne, 2010). Pejorative labels mark others as outsiders in the social hierarchy and, therefore, as undesirable sexual partners or even friends. All the terms studied here are united in that they depart in one way or another from hegemonic feminine heterosexuality, or what Nielson, Walden, and Kunkel (2000) call *heterogender*. Violations include being unaccommodating or outspoken ("bitch" and "cunt"), sexually unavailable or too masculine in appearance or behavior ("dyke"), and too sexual ("slut" and "whore," though "whores" have broken additional societal rules such as engaging in commercial sex).

Though ongoing sexual harassment and abuse directed toward a particular person may be more serious and emotionally distressing, analysis of social media reveals more subtle forms of misogyny occur thousands of times a day (Demos, 2016b).[16] By focusing on everyday misogyny, not just the worst cases of abuse, we can observe the general online climate. Many argue that Twitter is particularly plagued by harassment.[17] In a press release to the Centre for the Analysis of Social Media study (Demos, 2016a), researcher Alex Krasodomski-Jones argues that "while the digital world had built new opportunities for public debate and social interaction, it had also built new battlegrounds for the worst aspects of human behavior" (para. 8), adding that though Twitter makes its data most available to researchers, misogyny is prevalent across all social media. Demos (2016a) found that over a three-week period in the UK, more than 6,500 unique users were targeted by 10,000 explicitly aggressive and misogynistic tweets, while internationally, over 200,000 aggressive tweets using "slut" and "whore" targeted 80,000 people.

Labels such as "slut" and "whore" deny women basic human dignity, defining sexual desire as indecent and selfish for women while encouraging it for heterosexual men (Fine, 1988; Nussbaum, 1999). Society reinforces traditional gender and sexual relations by placing girls and women into categories that often reduce women to "good" or "bad," depending on how closely they conform to heterosexual feminine norms. Gender intersects with class, race, and sexuality, resulting in "bad girls" (working-class, black and Latina, sexually active) being blamed for rape and intimate partner violence in the same way that "good guys" who are white and affluent are forgiven.

The themes of women's worth and bodily autonomy online are not arbitrary, but are situated within larger cultural, historical, political, and social processes. Internet communications reflect structural gender and sexual inequality and a culture that normalizes misogyny. Abusers resort to attacks on women's bodies and sexuality because women's social worth is perceived as directly linked to their likability and desirability in a way that heterosexual men's social worth is not. The fact that so many women are threatened with rape and death affirms the societal belief that women do not have control over their bodies. Arguing that online sexual abuse is not a problem because it is so common and ordinary or comes from only a few people suggests that we should accept the denigration of women as a common and ordinary part of our current society. Professor of law Citron (2009) writes, "the online harassment of women exemplifies twenty-first century behavior that profoundly harms women yet too often remains overlooked and even trivialized" (p. 373).

Gender and sexuality intersect with class and race-ethnicity (Armstrong et al., 2014; Hill Collins, 1990). In this book, I examine class, racial, and religious slurs accompanying misogynist terms.[18] African Americans are a disproportionate share of Twitter users (Brock, 2012) and access Twitter four times more often each day than white users (Smith, 2011). Most of the public cases of online abuse refer to white, educated, middle-class women in coveted positions. Women of color,[19] such as writer Malorie Blackman, activist and legal analyst Imani Gandy, actor Leslie Jones, organizer Erica Lee, political analyst Zerlina Maxwell, and anthropologist Robin Nelson, receive a torrent of racial slurs in addition to gender-related threats, though they do not receive the same kind of media attention or public support as white women. Feminista Jones regularly receives racialized and sexualized harassment, though she is more likely to be harassed by white men when she speaks about racism and by black men when she speaks about issues specifically facing black women. Regardless of her harasser's race, the content is similar, such as calling for her to be raped and lynched (Mantilla, 2015).

Hill Collins (2004) argues that black women are already stereotyped as "jezebels," "whores," and "hoochies." Brown's (2016) study of singer Taylor Swift's fan forums reveals that unlike singer Nicki Minaj or actor Camilla Belle, Swift is a "beacon of morality because of her adherence to standards of white heteronormative propriety" (p. 401). Though Swift experienced online sexual shaming when a woman posted a photo of a sandwich on Twitter suggesting it resembled her vagina due to an active dating life, Twitter users jumped to Swift's defense, and the woman who posted the picture received a stream of hateful tweets.

This book contributes to our understanding of the ways in which gender and sexual norms are currently enforced and challenged. Social media sites serve as a public stage for the construction and performance of gender and sexuality. The need for regulatory power and the resultant negative sanction when inappropriate behavior is suspected reveals how gender and sexuality are achieved through online gender performances. Publicly performing heteromasculinity by declaring desire for a "slut," or enforcing femininity by calling a woman a "slut" for displaying sexual desire, reveals a need for the constant realization of gender and sexuality.

Conversely, gender and sexual norms can also be challenged and upended. This book contributes to the existing literature on gender, sexuality, and the Internet by also considering the possibility for Internet users to transform norms surrounding female sexuality through online communications (Brickell, 2012). This book moves beyond stories of victimization to explore the potential for social change through digital technology. While one obvious function of online sexual abuse is to regulate women's behavior, the openness and reach of the Internet creates the potential to change meanings and identities. In the same way that large numbers of anonymous users can log onto sites like Reddit and Twitter to share misogynistic ideas, these platforms can create opportunities to challenge beliefs and ideas. Inductive analysis reveals use of slurs like "dyke," "slut," and "whore" beyond the expected regulatory function, including extension, reappropriation, and direct critiques that carry potential for cultural transformation.

Language and Society

Ultimately this book is about language, albeit a specific kind of language (misogynist slurs) used in a specific setting (social media). Drawing from symbolic-interactionists in sociology (Berger & Luckmann, 1966; Blumer, 1969; Goffman, 1959), language enables society by forging identities, enabling communication and shared meanings for interaction, clarifying norms, and facilitating an understanding of the social world. Words themselves carry no power, but their references to ideas and objects gives them significance. As the stuff of social life, language is crucial for studying social problems (Maynard, 1988). Society and inequality are not composed solely of language; certainly, we must recognize the importance of power structures such as institutions and laws to establish norms around gender and sexualities (Butler, 1990; Foucault, 1978/1990; Rubin, 1992). Nevertheless, language enables much of what occurs in the larger social world, including justifying differential treatment by marking insiders and outsiders.

Trottier and Fuchs (2014) argue that above all, social media is used for communicating and establishing connections. Digital traces left in the form of posts, hashtags, and tweets play an important role in expressing the self, forming identities, sharing information, building communities, and engaging in contemporary social issues. This research is situated within sociology and critical social media studies by analyzing online content in relation to power structures and gender relations. We must consider the way in which larger social and political forces (for instance, a presidential election) and certain mediums (Twitter's 140-character limit) constrain expression. Language on social media is shaped by software, institutional policies, and structural forces such as commerce and law. Sassen (2002) writes, "Power, contestation, inequality, hierarchy, inscribe electronic space and shape the production of software" (p. 366).

Posting anonymously, tagging people without their consent, writing and reading quickly, and the dominance of a few forums can also make social media more conducive to abusive practices. The fact that great debate and concern exist over the influence of social media is important to note. A study by the Pew Research Center finds that 44 percent of US adults "often" or "sometimes" obtain their news on social media (Gottfried & Shearer, 2016). These statistics raise concerns that phony news stories and suppression of certain news stories could influence views and behaviors such as voting. Even with attempts to lessen fake news, research finds people tend to believe and share what they read online (Levin, 2017). In forthcoming research, searches for "rape" on Twitter revealed most tweets reported false accusations and gang rapes committed by immigrant men, leading to a severely distorted view of rape.

The normative and evaluative power of language is seen in the use of pejorative slurs[20] (Ashwell, 2016; Tirrell, 2012). Misogynist language, like classist, racist, heterosexist, ableist, or ageist language, mirrors power relations in society. The study of slurs yields information about attitudes and larger social inequality. Words for women often define women in relation to men (consider "Mrs." and "Miss," which denote women's relationship to men, while all men can be called "Mr."). Objects or forces that are small and graceful like kittens or owned or controlled by men such as boats are called "she," while powerful controlling forces such as God or tigers are referred to as "he" (Richardson, 2004).

Despite claims that language cannot harm us, terms that dehumanize make it easier to inflict harm (Kleinman, Ezzell, & Frost, 2009; Tirrell, 2012). Racial epithets, for instance, stereotype entire groups of people and justify continued oppression. As a colonial project, Europeans renamed and humiliated Africans and outlawed their language (hooks, 1997). According to Camp (2013), slurs are "rhetorically powerful because they signal allegiance to a perspective: an integrated, intuitive way of cognizing members of the targeted group" (p. 335). The purpose of slurs is to denigrate, attach stigma, and establish differences between "them" and "us." Calling women "bitches" and "sluts" both reflects and perpetuates a continued belief in women and men's essential differences, women's inferiority to men, and women's lack of ownership over their bodies. Observing what makes someone receive the label of "slut" on the Internet warns others to avoid the same behaviors. Language on social media influences behavior even when the social media users lack authority or power because social media can be public and long-lasting. Misogynist slurs are important for constructing masculinity as well, similar to the use of "fag" (Pascoe, 2012). Noted by Pascoe, oversimplifying femininities and masculinities must be avoided by recognizing the intersections of gender, sexuality, race, and class. Furthermore, recognizing the relationship between culture and structure, discourse not only reflects patriarchal social structures, but is important for producing and reproducing power structures. Misogynist slurs establish and cement norms around gender and sexuality, reinforcing essential differences and hierarchies. The question remains whether online discourses can transform a misogynist culture and society.

Recognizing that language is not fixed and meanings can change is important. Meaning is created within specific contexts. For instance, slurs are used affectionately or jokingly among people within a racial group or among friends. Almost everyone understands *slut* to be a derogatory slur, but the word is more acceptable in art (as in *Slut: The Musical*) and in commentary (as in Slut-Walks[21]). *Slut* can also have different meanings when used to admonish someone for sexual activity and used to admonish someone for "slut-shaming." Therefore, interpreting tweets within a larger context of a conversation is important. In addition to analyzing misogynist terms such as "bitch" and "slut," I include terms that have been reclaimed or represent resistance to oppression, such as "queer" and "slut-shaming."

Methods

This project uses digital trace data from Twitter, Facebook, and Instagram to examine contemporary misogyny and social change around gender and sexuality. Social Media Management Software (SMMS) includes a feature that allows the collection of data from social media platforms using a process known as "social listening." Much like traditional content analysis, data containing the keywords "bitch," "cunt," "dyke," "slut," and "whore" are gathered from Facebook, Instagram, and Twitter. These data are then examined for themes using the qualitative data analysis software NVivo. This research makes several methodological contributions to the literature on gender and sexuality. Apart from research by boyd (2014) and the Centre for the Analysis of Social Media (Demos, 2016b), most Twitter studies focus on political events. A digital divide exists among researchers who have resources and computational skills to analyze "big data" (boyd & Crawford, 2011; Bruns & Burgess, 2012; Manovich, 2011). Researchers lacking resources in fields such as humanities and social sciences can offer methodological training, sociological understandings of technology, and a concern for social justice to the analysis of big data.

The past decade has also seen abundant research on cyberbullying among adolescents (e.g., boyd, 2014; Cassidy, Faucher, & Jackson, 2013; Kofoed & Ringrose, 2012; Ringrose & Renold, 2010). I depart from previous research by including public interactions among people of all ages in this book. Public misogyny sends a warning to all women, regardless of age, to remain in line with feminine and hetero-sexual norms. Though Tanenbaum (2000) interviews women between the ages of 14 and 66, the book focuses overwhelmingly on high school students and women between the ages of 18 and 24. Although Tanenbaum's updated 2015 book includes the Internet, only a few cases of online sexual shaming are discussed. Furthermore, only one respondent indicates any kind of resistance to sexual shaming, whereas significant resistance is found among social media users.

The Centre for the Analysis of Social Media (Demos, 2016b) conducted a systematic study of the terms "slut" and "whore" on Twitter. That study complements this research because of the differ-ent methodological approaches taken. The researchers relied prima-rily on a computer algorithm to code tweets, which allowed them to analyze millions of tweets. However, they coded data into only three themes, "aggressive," "self-identification," and "other." The induc-tive approach used here did not require identifying themes prior to analysis. Though regulation of women's behavior was expected, the flexible method allowed for new themes to emerge from the data. Human coding revealed a much wider range of themes beyond aggression and self-identification, such as positive self-identification and rejection of the label. This richness of coding permits examina-tion of the power of online content to transform meanings around heteronormative female sexuality.

A computer algorithm may not be able to capture the nuances of meaning, especially given the 140-character limit. Mistakes in cod-ing could be avoided; for example, Hom (2008: 429) offers the example, "Racists believe that Chinese people are chinks," which would likely be coded negatively by a computer. Often sentiment could only be discerned by examining emoji, data in links, photos, videos, and entire conversations. My research also includes more terms, examining silencing ("bitch" and "cunt") as well as sexual shaming ("dyke," "slut," and "whore") as major aspects of a misog-ynistic climate on social media.

Social media researchers argue that more transparency and con-sistency across studies is needed (Bruns & Burgess, 2012; Driscoll &

Walker, 2014). Appendix A provides more detailed information on the methodology, including the sampling method, coding schemes, ethical issues, and limitations. Considering the significance of the medium under investigation, some of the problems identified by boyd and Crawford (2011), Driscoll and Walker (2014), and Rogers (2013) can be avoided by treating social media as a site of research in and of itself, with all its problems and messiness. It is the multiple meanings that emerge around interactions on social media that are of interest. By analyzing the content of tweets, Instagram hashtags, and Facebook groups and pages, we can learn how shaming and silencing terms are used on social media.

Theoretical Framing

This book is framed within sociological and feminist approaches. Eschewing explanations that focus on the personalities of the abusers, online misogyny is interpreted as grounded in the fabric of society. Many imagine online abusers are all socially isolated men who believe women are taunting them. However, criminal investigations into Internet users who have sent death and rape threats reveal a range of personality types, ages, and genders, including adults and teenagers with rich social lives, accompanied by a range of reasons, including anger and revenge, entertainment, and opportunity due to the perception of anonymity. In a 2012 interview on the show *Anderson Cooper 360°*, the man known as the website Reddit's "biggest troll" claimed he was playing to an audience of college-aged men and that Reddit encouraged his behavior by offering prizes to people who drew traffic to their site (CNN, 2017). Writer Lindy West (2015) met her online harasser in person, and he expressed deep remorse and admitted to feeling bored and angry after the loss of a relationship. According to a survey by the National Association of Schoolmasters Union of Women Teachers, teachers are increasingly recipients of online abuse, and more than half of that abuse comes from the parents of their students (Laville, 2016). It is also important to recognize that interactions with public websites are group activities. Though people may be posting alone at home, they are choosing to participate in a social community by sending their message to any number of potential viewers.

Leaning toward what has been called a "sex positive" feminist perspective, this book recognizes that sexual freedom is an important part of women's freedom (Califia, 1994; Queen, 1997; Willis, 1992), while also recognizing that power relations are complex. Women should be free to engage in public discourse and erotic activity without stigma, though I take seriously critiques of views of women's sexual agency offered by what has been referred to as "choice" feminism. Sociological theories recognize that agency is most available to those with the most structural power (Archer, 1995; Giddens, 1984), such as white, middle-class, heterosexual, cis-gender women. Critiques of neoliberal views of agency argue that girls' sexuality continues to be confined through commercialism and displays of agency (Bay-Cheng, 2015a, 2015b). Contemporary media are criticized for hiding a "tidal wave of invidious insurgent patriarchalism . . . beneath the celebrations of female freedom" (McRobbie, 2008: 539). Additionally, a narrow focus on sexual agency and pleasure can alienate women who choose not to have sex (Hills, 2015; Zakaria, 2015). Remembering the distinction between rights and capabilities and the interconnected relationship between structure and agency is important.

Avoiding moral panics is crucial, particularly with respect to adolescent sexuality, remembering that social media has not increased the amount of bullying among adolescents and far more physical assaults occur outside the context of the Internet (boyd, 2014). Concerns over "sexting" tend to focus only on regulating and surveilling girls, reproducing the sexual double standard of girls as innocent and needing protection from aggressive male sexuality (Ringrose et al., 2013; Tolman, 2012). Though genuinely interested in helping women, Tanenbaum's (2015) advice for ending slut-shaming online includes advising women to avoid consuming alcohol, sending semi-naked photos, posting sexy selfies, and dressing in a "sexually provocative[22] manner unless [they] want to be looked at sexually and can handle being reduced to a sexual object" (p. 340). None of the recommendations in the appendixes "Creative Solutions to Eliminate 'Slut'" and "The Slut-Shaming Self-Defense Toolkit" includes recommendations for boys and men or schools. Ringrose et al. (2013) ask what it would mean to live in a world where adolescent girls could take, post, or send images of their breasts without risking sexual shaming.

In this book, I take as a given that gender inequality exists and is connected to other forms of inequality such as ableism, classism, racism, and heterosexism. Social inequality is multidimensional, supported by cultural, relational, institutional, and structural forces around labor, property rights, and reproduction. At the cultural level, gender inequality is supported by misogyny, which is defined here as hatred and mistrust of women. Misogyny maintains that women are inherently inferior, untrustworthy, or worse, evil. Justifications for gender differences in autonomy and trustworthiness are widespread and persistent, stretching from ancient myths, plays, and poems to philosophical writings, contemporary sociobiological and evolutionary psychology research, to contemporary political discourses around sexual assault and reproductive rights (Millet, 1970; Pomeroy, 1995).[23] Theriault (2014) points out that misogynist sentiments are everywhere, ranging from online pick-up artists (PUA) to the constant stream of violence against women by men. In the 1970s, Germaine Greer (1971) wrote that women had very little idea of how much men hated them and, in fact, internalized this hatred.[24] It should be noted that women are as likely as men to use terms like "slut" about other women (Demos, 2016b).

Some argue that misogyny is fought in subtler or softer forms today (Rivers and Barnett, 2015). One could also argue that contemporary attacks on women's rights are not so subtle, including restrictions on women's reproductive rights and severe mishandling of sexual assault and harassment cases. Though acceptance of physical violence against women is declining among women and men (UN Statistics Division, 2015), more men are meeting online on men's rights and revenge porn websites to advance the long-standing belief that men deserve to control women (Marcotte, 2013). Arguments that men's era of dominance has ended (Rosin, 2012) stoke fears that men are losing status and power, resulting in a backlash (Faludi, 1991, 2011). Some characterize the 2016 US presidential election as a widening chasm over awareness and concern for gender inequality. It does not seem to matter that, overall, men continue to occupy positions of authority in the political structure, workplace, and home, and the dominant culture reflects a bias toward men's accomplishments and traits associated with masculinity. In a *New York Times* opinion piece, "The Men Feminists Left Behind," Filipovic (2016) argues that the election period revealed that Trump embodied "masculine power reclaimed," offering "dislocated White men convenient scapegoats—Mexicans, Muslims, trade policies, political correctness—and promises to return those men to their rightful place in society" (para. 10). I would add women to this list, for in addition to xenophobia, misogynist language became a major part of the public discourse during the 2016 US presidential election.

Analytical Framework and Chapter Outline

Analysis of online misogynist slurs reveals two distinct but related types. Chapters 2, 3, and 4 address misogynist slurs that are designed to shame women who deviate from traditional sexual norms, or *sexual shaming*.[25] Tweets, posts, and hashtags include the terms "slut" and "whore" and center on women's sexual behavior and bodies. The question here is how people construct narratives around female sexuality. Women's reputations have been used to keep women in line. A sexual double standard still exists in the United States, in that women are shamed for heterosexual sexual desire and activity. Sexual shaming reinforces hegemonic heterofemininity at the level of the interaction, reminding girls and women to manage others' impressions of them. "Dyke" is included in this category, as it is typically used to enforce heteronormative standards of sexuality, though it may also be used to silence women. Sexual shaming affects lesbians as much as their heterosexual peers. Lesbians are by definition labeled "bad girls," and therefore must distance themselves from sexual agency and desire (Payne, 2010).[26]

Chapters 5 and 6 address the second type of misogynist slurs, what I call *silencing slurs*. These involve tweets, posts, and hashtags designed to silence women's voices and participation in the public sphere, and they include the terms "bitch" and "cunt." Like sexual shaming terms, these terms remind women when they are deviating from expectations for femininity, such as holding strong opinions. These terms reflect the idea that women should be seen and not heard, particularly in "men's-only" spaces (which to some means preventing women from participation in all parts of the Internet). Beard (2014), Nussbaum (2010), and Spender (1991) find a long history of silencing women in public discourses through attempts to dehumanize and discredit.

Each chapter provides a phenomenology of each slur by describing the various online uses, including such themes as promiscuity,[27] friendly terms of endearment, and positive self-identification. Some chapters will include variations on the slur, such as "slut-shaming" in Chapter 2 and "hoe" in Chapter 3, and comparisons to other terms such as "queer" in Chapter 4. The influence of external cultural events will be examined. Additionally, terms intersect and include norms around class and race-ethnicity.

Each chapter follows the same overall analytical structure, organizing the various uses of slurs into three broad categories that emerged from an analysis of themes: regulation, extension, and dissent. Regulation is perhaps the most expected use: misogynist language used to encourage women to behave in ways consistent with gender and sexual norms, such as having few sexual partners, remaining faithful, dressing modestly, and behaving in an accommodating manner.

Inductive analysis reveals a second major function, extension, in which slurs are used in alternative ways. For instance, despite a sexual double standard, the term "slut" might be used to refer to men with many sexual partners or as a friendly term for a friend. "Whore" might reference someone who wants a lot of something, as in "attention whore." Other examples include "bitch" as an intensifier as in "I'm back, bitch" or something difficult as in "This test is a bitch." "Bitch" is often used as a replacement for woman or girlfriend. Here we see opportunity for transformation of language, though the word is used because of its derogatory content (a test is a "bitch" because a "bitch" is bad or annoying).

The third use is dissent, which includes rejection of the label, positive self-identification, direct critiques of the use of misogynist slurs, and information about online and offline collective action, which I am defining as organized acts carried out by groups to achieve social and political goals. This category holds the most transformative potential. However, even when users exhibit agency by denying that they are sluts, it is often because they have had sex with only one person, reinforcing the original meaning of having many sexual partners. Positive self-identification or reappropriation can remove some of the negative content but often depends on the original meaning being desirable as an identity. Direct critiques, education, and organization possibly hold the most transformative potential.

In Chapter 7, I examine whether slurs were used most often to regulate women's behavior or provide alternative meanings and critiques. I will compare uses across the misogynistic terms under examination and look at how fluctuations in use and sentiment vary alongside external social and political events. Why are some words such as "dyke" used in a positive way (reappropriation), while others such as "cunt" are not to the same extent? Why do some external events such as the 2016 US presidential election figure so prominently in online uses of these misogynist slurs? How do uses of slurs also demonstrate heterosexism, classism, and racism? Because rape threats figure so prominently in online abuse of women, I will briefly discuss their use on Twitter, and a full analysis is forthcoming. Like the other slurs, threats of rape serve to dehumanize and silence women through fear. Online activist Mercedes argues that calling for men to lose their jobs is the biggest degradation for men while rape is the biggest degradation for women (Ronson, 2015).

In the final chapter, I explore whether varied uses of misogynist slurs, such as extension and reappropriation, can cause ruptures in meanings, draining slurs of their pejorative power. In addition to regulatory uses, I find high numbers of slurs used in alternative ways, such as "bitch" as an intensifier to make statements unrelated to gender or sexuality more forceful, or "cunt" to refer to men on rival football and rugby teams in the UK. However, these words are deeply embedded in power relations and structural inequality. We might ask whether "bitch" is truly a "neutral" counterpart when used to refer to one's girlfriend, even if used in a complimentary way as in "my bitch looks good." "Whore" is extended to phrases like "attention whore," but still refers to disproportionate desires, and a test can be a "bitch" because it is difficult. Can positive identification with slurs like "slut" and "whore" thoroughly transform their meanings, as my data show with "dyke" and as we have already seen with "queer"? Tanenbaum (2015) believes it is impossible to reclaim words like "slut" or "whore." Positive identification may remove some of the power of the stigma, like we have seen with "nigga," but it does not necessarily change the meaning for people who hold negative opinions or disrupt the good girl/bad girl distinction in the same way that directly admonishing sexual shaming or providing education can.

Debates around the reclaiming of derogatory slurs raise larger questions about the relationship between culture, in the form of online language, and structural gender and sexual inequality. Can supplying new meanings around misogynist terms, for instance reappropriating "bitch" and "slut" to signify women who are powerful or unashamed to pursue their own sexual pleasure, reverberate back to the social structure by supplying new meanings around women's sexuality? For hooks (1997), there is potential liberation in reclaiming speech by creating counterhegemonic speech and worldviews. Others argue that language cannot transform social relations without a complete shift in patriarchal social norms and structural relations (Ashwell, 2016; Butler, 1990). Furthermore, whether social media can be a site of social change has incited debate. Misogyny may be heightened on sites like Twitter due to software choices, anonymity, distance, low threat of punishment, lack of autonomy from state and economic power, and a broad audience. Furthermore, online interactions mirror power relations offline, with educated, white, English-speaking, and male users more likely dominating discussions through abuse, excessive posting, and dictation of the agenda and style of dialogue (Dahlberg, 2001).

However, Internet scholars argue that we cannot rely solely on dystopian views (DiMaggio et al., 2001; Nyboe, 2004). Social media networks create potential for change never seen before (Shirky, 2008). Social media has been described as a catalyst for social movements such as Black Lives Matter (Eligon, 2015; Ware, 2016), Occupy Wall Street (Penney & Dadas, 2013), and the Arab Spring revolutions in the Middle East and North Africa (Howard & Hussain, 2013). Social media users can react quickly, demonstrated by the creation of #MuslimID after Trump called for a database of all Muslims. Facebook users checked into Standing Rock, a gathering of tribes and allies to protest the Dakota Access Pipeline, thus making it harder for law enforcement to use the social media site to identify who was there. Social media can publicize issues the media are ignoring. Sassen (2002) argues that cyberspace can be a more effective site for social struggles than the political system because it allows engagement by previously excluded people and action that bypasses formal systems. Skeptics argue weak ties are compelling people to action (Gladwell, 2010) or point to the ineffectiveness of changing one's profile picture or creating a hashtag, using pejorative terms such as *slacktivism* and *clicktivism* to describe low-effort political activities that have little effect, such as changing a profile picture to express solidarity. Doubt exists that social media transforms people because individuals self-select into groups that match their values and interests.

The Internet also offers opportunities for increased participation of women, and a wealth of feminist work is happening in the form of blogs, magazines, advice for avoiding abuse, and online campaigns such as #metoo, #SayHerName, #hollabackgirl, and #ShoutYourAbortion. "Slut-shaming" has entered the public vernacular, suggesting the possibility for increased awareness around female sexuality. As historical constructs that continually need accomplishing, sexuality and gender are constantly open to transformation. Can social media users create alternative narratives around female sexuality by redefining, reappropriating, and critiquing misogynist slurs? The Internet is complex, having contradictory effects on power and creating spaces for oppression and empowerment (Morahan-Martin, 2000; Spender, 1995). Avoiding determinist theories means the Internet neither solely regulates nor transforms social meanings (boyd, 2014; Cavanagh, 2007). Trottier and Fuchs (2014) argue that social media neither causes nor is entirely unimportant for social movements.

Finally, I examine individual, institutional, and legal attempts to lessen online misogyny and abuse. Institutional and legal attempts to block users or ban certain words are met with concerns over censorship, free speech, and a free Internet. "Techno-libertarians" hold absolutist views on the First Amendment, focusing on the expansion of online voices and the democratization of authority, with power to create a society in which everyone can express themselves freely. However, some users are choosing to leave social media sites such as Twitter because of the abuse. Examining the ideas of political philosophers such as John Stuart Mill raises the question of whose right to engage in human affairs free of coercion takes precedence. Butler (1997) and Foucault (1978/1990) oppose censorship because it tends to have the opposite effect than intended, and they object to the state having the power to determine appropriate speech and behavior. Many victims of severe abuse complain that their cases are mishandled by social media websites and law enforcement (Citron, 2014). I explore efforts to increase awareness of the injury caused by misogynist slurs and whether this awareness can create new norms around gender and sexuality without institutional or legal intervention.

Notes

1. For the purposes of this study, social media includes sites that allow social networking, microblogging, and the sharing of photos, video, and other content. Facebook, the largest of the top three social media platforms, was launched in 2004; Twitter, in 2006; and Instagram, in 2010.

2. *Tweet* is the term for a post to the social media site Twitter.

3. When gender identity is not available, I will be using the singular *they/them/their* instead of the pronouns *he/him/his* and *she/her/hers*.

4. *Doxing* refers to the exposing of someone's personal information (name, phone number, address, Social Security number, familial relationships, or financial history) to encourage harassment from others.

5. Of the eight most targeted women, four identified as white, four identified as black, and one identified as lesbian. The two men out of the ten most harassed writers both identified as black men, one of them also as gay, showing intersections between gender, race, and sexuality (Gardiner et al., 2016).

6. *Actor* will be used regardless of gender identity because it originally referred to all theatrical performers and only later were performers distinguished by gender (Oxford English Dictionary, 2017). In this book, I recog-

nize the assumption of male superiority when generics such as *he* or *man* are used for all people and prefer nongendered words such as *Latinx* to reduce gender bias in language.

7. *Trolling* is defined as making online comments or engaging in behaviors such as disruption with the purpose to upset or enrage others, often for amusement (Mantilla, 2015).

8. *Swatting* means making a false report to the police so that they send a SWAT team to a person's home.

9. As of the end of 2016, Facebook was the most popular social networking site with 1.79 billion regular users, measured as monthly active users (MAU). Instagram, a photo- and video-sharing app, had 600 million MAU. Microblogging site Twitter had 317 million MAU (*Statistica*, 2017). Most of the data will come from Twitter for reasons related to availability of data. Abuse of women has been found on other Internet sites not discussed here, including Reddit, Tumblr, and YouTube (Poole, 2013; Schmitz & Kazyak, 2016).

10. Variations on "whore," including "ho" and "hoe" and the more recent "THOT" (an acronym for "that hoe over there") are included in searches as well, although searches for "ho" and "hoe" return any words with these strings of letters. Though not analyzed fully here, "queer" and "rape" are also included as search terms.

11. Though life stages are socially constructed, the literature tends to distinguish between girls (under 18) and women (18 and over). Adolescent girls are often defined as 12–18 years of age. For simplicity of writing, I may refer to girls and women as *women* unless age is relevant.

12. I will also note when online abuse is directed toward men as well as trans* and queer identities.

13. For further reading, see Kimmel (2000); Lorber (1994); Messner (1999); and West and Zimmerman (1987).

14. I tend to use the term *online,* though *cyber* can be used interchangeably and is preferred by others studying this topic. *Cyberbullying* is defined as "when someone repeatedly makes fun of another person online or repeatedly picks on another person through e-mail or text message or when someone posts something online about another person that they don't like" (Hinduja & Patchin, 2012, p. 2).

15. In this book, I may refer to gendered online abuse simply as *online abuse* or *abuse*.

16. For incredibly thorough examinations of more extreme forms of online abuse, see Citron (2014), Jane (2014), and Mantilla (2015).

17. Humphreys, Gill, Krishnamurthy, and Newbury (2013) argue that systematic analysis of even short everyday writing reveals information about the larger cultural climate, though I am unable to generalize about the frequency of misogyny because Twitter users are not representative of the general population. Instead, I am analyzing the qualitative content, and I will discuss if counts fluctuate relative to external events such as presidential debates.

18. While this research did not directly track racist and homophobic speech, groups such as the Southern Poverty Law Center have been tracking

all forms of hate crimes and harassment in the *New York Times* (2017) editorial "This Week in Hate." Since the 2016 US presidential election, much of the incidents reported include death threats and photos with racial, Islamophobic, and anti-Semitic slurs uploaded to social media.

19. For the purposes of this paper, and in recognition of the social construction of race and ethnicity and the failure of language to capture diverse experiences of groups, *people of color* will be used to refer to people not of European descent. *Black* will be used to refer to people of African descent but who may have diverse ethnic identities such as Caribbean. Some authors use *African American* to describe the identities of native-born blacks in the United States, and I will defer to their word choice.

20. I am defining terms such as *bitch* and *slut* as slurs because they derogate, debase, and disparage a class of people, though I do not think all terms or all uses of each term can be replaced with a neutral counterpart (Anderson & Lepore, 2013). Resisting semantic and pragmatic perspectives, I argue that words are defined as slurs simply because they are prohibited and display disrespect.

21. SlutWalks are protest marches and rallies first organized in 2011 in Toronto in response to victim blaming and slut-shaming as integral parts of a culture in which rape is widespread and normalized.

22. The term *provocative* implies clothing can inherently provoke or incite responses, supporting victim blaming in cases of sexual harassment and violence. I will use *revealing,* though also problematic, to describe data where references to women's clothing are blamed for calling them a "slut" or a "whore," for example.

23. Essentialist psychological theories that focus on fear of women as the basis of misogyny are not as successful at explaining agency and social change, and theories such as womb envy fail to explain misogyny among women.

24. It is important to note that not all women support or identify with other women, particularly across race and class lines. Exit polls for the 2016 US presidential election, though not perfect, revealed slightly more white women voted for Donald Trump than for Hillary Clinton, leading some to deduce they would rather support a candidate who expressed misogyny than a woman for president.

25. I prefer the term *sexual shaming* to the more commonly used *slut-shaming* because women are shamed for any kind of sexual behavior, including refusing sex and experiencing sexual violence.

26. Though I track "queer" to relate to the use of "dyke" in Chapter 4, I am unable to analyze discourses specifically addressing other identities under the LGBTQIA umbrella (which includes lesbian, gay, bisexual, trans, queer and questioning, intersex, and asexual) in this book, though conducting this research is important in the future.

27. I recognize that the concept of *promiscuity* is problematic because it upholds a good girl/bad girl dichotomy by determining an appropriate number of sexual partners for women, but I am using the term because it is the enforced norm.

2

SLUT:
Shaming Sexual Activity

In this chapter, I examine the social media uses of the term "slut" and its variations, including "slutty" and "slut-shaming." According to Demos (2016b), "slut" is one of the most common misogynistic terms on Twitter. Based on Demos's findings that 200,000 tweets containing "slut" or "whore" were sent over a three-week period in April and May 2016, Dewey (2016) estimates someone is called a "slut" or "whore" every 10 seconds on Twitter. In the seventeenth century, *slut* was used as a pejorative for kitchen maids, unclean women, and women of low social classes.[1] Today, "slut" refers to a "'woman who has sex with *more than an appropriate number of partners for a woman*,' or 'woman who has *more partners than she ought to*,' where the number that is said to be appropriate will be fixed by the external social context" (Ashwell, 2016: 235, emphasis in original). The use of "more than appropriate" shows that "slut" is not only descriptive and normative, but also contextual. What is considered appropriate behavior depends on the cultural, historical, and social context; therefore, who counts as a "slut" is open to interpretation.

Despite changing sexual mores, research continues to show "slut" remains one of the most feared slurs among girls and women. A strong double standard exists for acceptable sexual behavior, such as having sex outside of a loving, committed, monogamous, heterosexual relationship (Crawford & Popp, 2003; Kreager & Staff, 2009;

Lyons et al., 2011). The label "slut" serves as a mechanism for labeling and exclusion. Tolman (2002) finds that cultural pressure to be a "good girl" heightens in adolescence, with only adolescent girls worrying about their reputations if they kiss someone or express sexual interest. By college, women are still more likely than men to feel judged for "hooking up" (Kettrey, 2016). The sexual double standard is internalized, with young women believing their gender makes them worry about their reputation and emotional well-being and young men believing their gender makes them have a higher sex drive (Maas et al., 2015). This norm is also enforced through peer acceptance from boys and girls (Armstrong et al., 2014) and occurs even in places like Norway that are considered exceptionally socially liberal (Fjær, Pedersen, & Sandberg, 2015). Demos (2016b) found that roughly half of "slut" tweets came from women. It is argued that adolescent girls use the label "slut" to enhance their status by stigmatizing others, also reflecting class and racial hierarchies (Armstrong et al., 2014; Bettie, 2014; Garcia, 2012). White and middle-class girls cement their racial and class privilege by labeling women of color and working-class women as inferior and tainted.

This chapter argues that "slut" (and "whore" in Chapter 3) are primarily used online to shame women into conforming to heterogender norms. "Slut" has long been used to keep women in line, characterizing women's reputations as valuable but easily lost. Numerous examples in history show the use of women's sexuality to discredit their character and ideas, including English writers, philosophers, and social theorists Aphra Behn, Harriet Martineau, and Mary Wollstonecraft (Spender, 1991). The reputation of one's family and even the entire culture can rest on women's purity. Among Filipino immigrant families, Le Espiritu (2000) confirms that only daughters and not sons who have sex before marriage can bring shame to their families and cultures. Shaming serves to enforce norms and warn people of transgressions by exposing people who deviate (Jacquet, 2015). The Internet simply expands the "public" in public shaming. Cautionary tales, told both online and off-line, reestablish notions of good, moral sex. Even if the person who is using the slur lacks real authority or power, a public post or tweet carries weight by widely broadcasting information that can be taken as true by many viewers.

Although the Internet has dramatically increased the number of people who can observe and comment on women's sexual behavior, it has also created opportunities for competing discourses. Note that the number of "acceptable" sexual partners depends on cultural norms around women's sexuality, leaving it open to revision. Canaan's (1986) interviews show that even "good" girls engage in "bad" practices, suggesting that the line between good and bad is difficult to determine and thus has the potential for renegotiation. On the other hand, the murkiness around what constitutes slutty behavior makes it hard to know when or why someone may be labeled. Competing ideas of cultural acceptability both coexist and clash on the Internet.

Findings

Between January and September of 2016, tweets containing "slut" averaged 37,646 a day, ranging from a low of 23,766 to a high of 89,874 (see Figure 2.1).[2] The number of tweets, 9,110,325, depict the massive volume during this time. A total of 2,430 tweets were coded for themes (see Appendix B for coding scheme and counts). Tweets could contain more than one theme, such as referring to both a woman's number of sexual partners and her appearance. Weekly peaks occured on Sundays during times that correspond to mornings in North and South America and evenings in Europe, reflecting higher Twitter use in these regions. "Slut" tweets increased slightly when tracking informally began in December of 2014, but decreased slightly over 2016, despite a leveling of Twitter use. Several cultural and political events explain the considerable increase in tweets on March 8, 2016, including a heavily retweeted tweet by celebrity Kim Kardashian admonishing slut-shaming. I discuss these external events in detail. A high portion (989, or 40.7 percent) of "slut" tweets advertised pornographic video and webcam sites. Another 154 could not be reliably coded or were irrelevant,[3] leaving a sample of 1,287 tweets. For people with stated gender identities, almost all those targeted identified as women, and about half posting identified as women, consistent with findings by Demos (2016b).

Fifty-three Facebook pages and groups with "slut" in their titles were analyzed. Instagram does not allow photos or videos to be tagged with #slut or #slutty, but included are the top twenty tags containing variations of "slut." Roughly a quarter of Facebook pages including the term "slut" (27 percent) advertise pornography, such as "Slut Girl," "Slut Lovers," and "Night Slut." None of the sites on Instagram were pornographic in the sense that they showed complete

Figure 2.1   Keyword Mention over Time: "Slut" (Twitter)

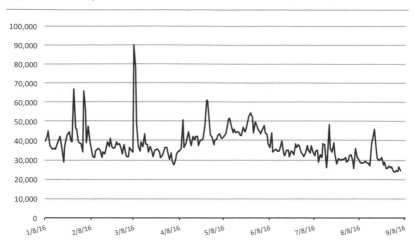

nudity, though roughly half were dominated by pictures of women in revealing clothing. Pornographic advertisements are omitted from analyses because of interest in how misogynist terms are used in non-commercial ways. However, it is worth noting that "sluts" are considered assets in pornography, drawing more traffic to a website.[4]

The analysis of tweets revealed expected uses, such as regulating women's sexual activity and other behaviors. In addition, "slut" was used in ways that extended its meaning, such as applying "slut" negatively to men[5] with multiple sexual partners and using "slut" in friendly ways. Holding even more potential for disruption, people are dissenting from the traditional concept of a "slut" in the form of positive self-identification, direct critiques, and awareness through education and political organizing. Analyses of Facebook and Instagram data will be included throughout each section.

Regulation (751 Tweets)

The term "slut" most often served as a regulatory function used to shame women into conforming to the traditional norms of sexual behavior—virginity, selectivity, controlled desire, passivity, and monogamy. The typical understanding of "slut" refers to a woman with more than the acceptable number of sexual partners, but analysis found tweets also regulated the identity of the partners, what women should do with them, and even what women *might* do sexually. In this last case, we see women labeled as "sluts" even if they have never actually had sex. In fact, even women who conformed to heterosexual monogamous sex risked labeling as "sluts" for exhibiting any form of sexual agency, such as initiating or rejecting sex. Tweets also regulated clothing considered appropriate for girls and women. If a person was named or tagged, the tweet became a public scarlet letter for many to see. Even those not named "slut" are warned; observing what qualifies someone else as a "slut," such as a woman initiating sex, can warn others to avoid the same behavior.

A large portion of tweets fell into the *naming* theme, in which the tweet referenced only a specific person's name or @username (243 tweets). During this period, data included a trending hashtag #WeAllKnowA that was followed by, among other words, "slut" and a person's name or tag. The reason for publicly attaching the slur to someone was not always clear in the text of the tweet or by reading the conversation on Twitter. If there was a reason or the person was called other names such as "dumb," the tweet was also included in another theme. The overarching purpose of naming someone a "slut" is to publicly shame them into conforming to one or more heterogender norms. Tweets are retweeted, expanding the audience for public shaming even further. Targets cannot untag themselves, so the label becomes permanent and takes viewers to their account unless removed by the user who wrote it, the tagged person deletes their account, or the tweet is removed by Twitter for violating their Terms of Service.[6]

- *Melanie Bloom is a slut*
- *@Melissa2494 is a slut*
- *We all know a slut named @Tina_Lee*

Many tweets fell under *generic slurs* (113 tweets). In this theme, tweets included "slut" with no additional information. While these tweets may not have targeted anyone directly, they contributed to a general climate of sexual shaming. The lack of reasons for naming someone a "slut" could lead to even more distress among viewers because the criteria for being labeled are unclear. Common examples include the following:

- *UR A SLUT*
- *Look who's already being a slut*
- *When did you turn into such a slut* 😠😐😶
- **Cough* Slut*

As expected, another category of "slut" tweets referred to more sexual partners than is considered appropriate or a perception of recklessness in selection of partners (84 tweets). Tweets that fell into this theme are coded as *promiscuity*. Again, women were shamed for not controlling their sexual desires and for not choosing partners carefully, so mentions of women "going from guy to guy" were common. Tweets showed fear and distrust of women who can have sex outside of a romantic relationship. Note that women's ability to engage in sexual activity without romantic love makes women deviant from feminine norms even if the person is engaging in kissing only. Men also created tweets claiming to be desperately looking for women who were not sluts, suggesting that they believed women today cannot be trusted. The last tweet was heavily retweeted and summarizes the sexual double standard perfectly:

- *@angelina slut...goes from guy to guy and doesn't care*
- *close your legs you slut*
- *why kiss him if you don't like him fucking slut nope*
- *I hope my future wife isn't being a total slut right now*
- *Kissing 5 girls in a night = legendary. A girl kissing 2 guys in a night = slut. #LoveBeingAGuy*

Many tweets in this theme were expressed as jokes or memes, as in the trending "*I'm not saying she's a slut,*" followed by various endings. Packaging sexual shaming in the form of jokes or memes makes shaming appear harmless, but in fact is reinforcing and normalizing misogyny. Examples included the following:

- *Sorry slut, but unfortunately, there isnt a clear history button for your vagina*
- *I'm not saying shes a slut, I'm just saying if her vagina had a password, it would be 1234*
- *I'm not saying shes a slut, but her favorite shade of lipstick is penis*

Tweets also identified *sex workers* as "sluts" (six tweets). Sex workers deviate from the most important norms of femininity, including monogamy and the need for romance during sexual activity. Chapter 3 will expand on the sexual shaming of sex workers and whore stigma.

- *she's a stripper she's automatically a slut and an attention seeker.*
- *@KoffiMoto awkwrd momnt wen yu screwn slut & u happn to say SAY MY NAME BeBe she says CUSTOMER*

Society considers women to be naturally relational and nurturing, which means putting other people's feelings before their own and preferring monogamy in relationships. Therefore, women were called "sluts" for being *unfaithful*. Tweets included direct accusations of infidelity as well as any appearance of disloyalty (32 tweets). Women were expected to maintain relationships over personal desires; therefore, they must consider friends' feelings and their former partners' feelings even after a relationship ends. Women were much more likely to blame other women for men's infidelity in heterosexual relationships, reinforcing the idea that it is expected for men to be unfaithful in relationships, but the same act is a transgression for women. Calling other women "sluts" also serves to define oneself as the "good girl," showing that misogynist slurs are as much about defining oneself as defining others:

- *I consider a slut someone who messes with someone's man and knows about her. !!!!*
- *If you fuck your friends ex without talking to them first you are a SLUT*
- *you are a nasty slut who has nothing else better to do than to hangout w peoples ex's and skip school lol ew*
- *@PrettyGirl he has a girlfriend, do you know what that means? that means leave him the fuck alone, slut*
- *@angelahey stop flirting with the love of my life #slut #teef[7]*

Because "slut" is a word primarily used to shame women, it is not unexpected to find tweets blaming women for men's infidelity. We see evidence of beliefs in essentialist gender differences in sexuality and the sexual double standard, as shown in these two tweets, the first one heavily retweeted:

- *Once upon a time, there was a boy and a girl who both loved each other. Then a slut came along and ruined everything*
- *Women cheat cuz their slut friends and whore family members encourage it. Men cheat cuz we like pussy*

Other men used Twitter to get back at ex-girlfriends who had cheated in the relationship, sometimes naming or tagging them. Like the other regulatory uses, these tweets send a signal to women to remain faithful or risk public shaming:

- *@kateeee because I'm tired of you posting stupid shit like you didn't cheat on me with 6 guys... Yo is a slut girl admit it*
- *When your ex was already a cheater and a liar and decides to add slut to the list*

Women were labeled "sluts" for desiring *any sex*, including having one sexual encounter or expressing the desire to have sex (24 tweets). Thinking about sex or having a single sexual encounter within a monogamous heterosexual relationship puts women at risk of being labeled a "slut." This theme represents the most extreme form of regulation, denying women any sexual desire even within heterogender norms. Tweets in this theme also mentioned women's use of alcohol, which will be discussed further under the theme *demeanor*. These tweets act to reinforce the idea that women must always maintain self-control and behave modestly. Note the competing discourses regarding female sexuality, showing the ruptures in gender constructions: cheating is not part of women's natures, so they cheat because others encourage them, and women cannot go one second without thinking about sex and cannot be trusted in relationships. The last tweet shows potential for agency by questioning the label, resulting in this tweet also coded as a form of dissent.

- *Females can't go one second without thinking about sex or guys like read a book find a hobby you slut.*
- *Still no period, huh? Bet you wish you weren't a slut on New Year's Eve*

- *ol girl mad she just lost her virginity and that she was being a drunk slut*
- *Slut but I got one guy?* 🔥 *oh damn. Hey Guys I guess I'm a slut because I got someone* 🐚😒💀

Included in this category is a heavily retweeted post showing that women also feel stigmatized for *not* having sex, one of the reasons the term *sexual shaming* is a more accurate description than *slut-shaming*. This heavily retweeted tweet is also included within the extension category because it is presenting a positive view of the attention "sluts" receive: "*so many beautiful girls go unnoticed bc they're not popular or a slut.*" Women retweeting these words are responding to the conflicting information around women's sexuality; women who have sex gain male attention but lose men's respect. Either way, women are defined by their relationships to men. Although lesbians are held to the same sexual norms (Payne, 2010), my sample did not include women referred to as "sluts" due to many romantic or sexual relationships with women (see Chapter 4).

Regulatory tweets remind women of appropriate feminine behavior. A large portion referred to women's *appearance*, primarily attractiveness, weight, and clothing (106 tweets). One tweet included a picture of a woman, creating an even more public scarlet letter than a name or tag. Like naming, this form is public and permanent and could be considered direct harassment. Tweets may also be included in the *demeanor* category because of the use of terms such as "nastiest" and "skank," as well as the slur "bitch" (see Chapter 5). The first tweet is a quotation from the movie *Mean Girls* (2004).

- *This girl is the nastiest skank bitch I've ever met. Do not trust her. She is a fugly slut*
- *Amy Roth is a fugly slut*
- *Last time I try to be nice to fat slut like u* ✌😒

Clothing figured prominently in tweets regarding women's appearance. Women were often called "sluts" for dressing in clothing that showed their bodies, which according to the tweets, determined whether they were deserving of respect. Clothing even inspired aggressive statements and negative comments from people who claim to be against slut-shaming:

- *I know that the sun is out... but its still 30 degrees put some pants on slut*
- *How do you expect boys not to see as an object if you keep dressing like a slut!!*
- *You dress like a slut but expect to find a gentleman? Please walk infront of a bus*
- *let's quit pretending showing your asscheeks in public is okay because coming from the biggest anti-slut-shamer ever, it's inappropriate.* 🙄

Less expected were heavily retweeted references to women's height, reinforcing the idea that anything and anyone is at risk for labeling as a "slut." These tweets suggest that shorter and taller women have to actively seek male attention. Whatever the reason, these tweets imply extensive and widespread regulation of women's bodies as well as a possible weakening of the label "slut" if anyone can acquire it.

- *You automatically a slut with that height*
- *Female height chart: 4'10 – 5'1: Mega Hoe 5'2 – 5'4: Slut 5'5 – 5'7: Harlot 5'8+: Goddess.*

In addition to physical appearance, women were expected to carry themselves in accordance with feminine norms of cleanliness, modesty, and control. These examples are included in the theme *demeanor* (31 tweets). "Slut" often occurred alongside terms such as "dirty," "trashy," "skank," "sleezy," "garbage," "scummy," "germy," and "disgusting," showing the intersections between gender, sexuality, and socioeconomic status as many of the terms imply women of a lower class. Often real names were used, sometimes to broadcast someone's potentially real health issues. Again, women were blamed for losing men's respect, and any resulting bad treatment was blamed on their behavior.

- *@JJanelle Enjoy your STDs, slut*
- *@rogers_natalie it makes you a dirty slut*
- *If you act like a slut, you're gonna get treated like one.* 📷
- *slutty girls are literally so disgusting and if you think I'm slut shaming or whatever i don't care*

Women were also called "sluts" for using drugs and alcohol, suggesting that risk-taking behaviors go against feminine norms of modesty and restraint, particularly those that may cause someone to lose control:

- *If your a girl and you go out every weekend and get smashed then your a slut...*
- *Jesus Christ slut u smoking more meth then anyone I know #lmao*

The slur "slut" was also used to mark women as *unworthy* of being men's girlfriends or wives (83 tweets). These tweets reinforce the distinction between good and bad girls. Tweeters did not always give reasons for marking women as unworthy, though tweets occasionally contained words such as "stupid." Some attempted to lower women's self-esteem, correcting beliefs that they were "hot" or important. The coexistence of another slur, "bitch," suggests that women are not following feminine norms of niceness and agreeability (see Chapter 5). Some women participated in this distinction between good and bad girls, revising the last heavily retweeted tweet to read, "*Fucking on a slut but thinking about me.*" This revision serves to distinguish them from "sluts," reinforcing their superior status:

- *Ima still fuck her just can't get married to dat slut*
- *You're Nothing But A Stupid Fucking Slut Okay So back off*
- *@MikeF579 how to deal with a slutty ass bitch who thinks she is hot*
- *Fucking on a slut and I was thinking about you*

Some tweets contained *threats* of violence or hoped for accidents and illness, serving to control unwanted behavior (29 tweets). Most of the online abuse of women takes the form of rape and death threats, so it is not surprising to find misogynist terms accompanied by threats. However, rape and death threats point to a climate on Twitter and the connection between misogyny and male violence against women. While these data do not show if abusive tweets are ongoing in the same manner as gendertrolling, the fact that women are tagged in most tweets shows an intent to publicly abuse a particular person. The first three examples were from men; the last three were from women, reinforcing the idea that women are divided by competition over males. Note women were physically threatened for talking to or just being near other women's boyfriends, however serious the intent:

- *@Princess-KL you fucking cunt how about I come down...and rape Laura heard she loves out like that the slut*
- *@eve1990 go get cancer. Al tie your mam up and throw her off a bridge fucking slut*
- *@Carrie_K choke on balls slut*
- *@SierraMa go killyourself you're a gold digger that's pathetic I hope u get cancer you slut I will watch u block me cuz you're a pussy*
- *When you see a slut talkin to bae and you tryna decide whether to kill her or not*
- *#ImThatGirlfriend that's not afraid to kill a bitch, Thot, whore, slut etc etc that touches, looks, breathes around you.* 😊😊😊

Seven Facebook pages and groups containing the word "slut" suggested the regulation of women's sexuality, though most posted content had nothing to do with women's sexual behavior or physical appearance. *"Letting a slut know she's a slut by yelling slut at the slut"* and *"Your a Slut, Guys like you because, Your a Slut, No other reason"* included sexual content, such as news about foreplay and photos of girls on Tinder "DTF"[8] interspersed with nonsexual content, such as funny cat videos and collections of autocorrect texts. The reason for the varied content is hard to determine without speaking with the page administrator. Nonetheless, the names of the pages and groups marked women as "sluts" and therefore as unworthy and inferior.

Instagram does not allow users to tag photos with #slut. Among the first twenty hashtags containing variations of "slut," most featured women in revealing clothing, including #sluts, #slutlife, #sluttygirls, #slüt, and #slüts. It is likely variations on "slut" are allowed due to oversight. However, like "sluttyselfie," most contained photos where women tagged themselves in the original post (coded as *self-identification* below). Others such as #slutsofinstagram included photos tagged by others in their comments section. Commenting with a name and hashtag does not require the user's consent. However, posts and comments can be deleted by users, though applying a hashtag immediately collects photos into a category, allowing others to see the #slutsofinstagram label.

Extension (63 Tweets)

The second major category of "slut" tweets can be thought of as extending the word in ways unrelated to the regulation of women's physical appearance or sexual behavior. Extending the meaning has the potential to disrupt the good/bad girl distinction, though some extensions reinforce it. Tweets that were used in novel ways were coded as an *object or state of being* (7 tweets). These tweets included two references to the dance move called a "slut drop" and the tweet *"being broke is a bitch and jealousy is a slut."* A tweet from astrophysicist Neil deGrasse Tyson was heavily retweeted during this period, apparently quoting Jon Stewart calling carbon the "slut" of the periodic table because it bonds with everything: *"Carbon is the slut of the Periodic Table. - @neiltyson on The Daily Show."* While this play on words extends the meaning of "slut" to encompass chemical elements, it is effective because of the belief that "sluts" are considered sexually indiscriminating.

Tweets explicitly calling *men* "sluts" were coded into a separate theme (43 tweets). All referred to men who had many sexual partners, though sometimes interpretation required examining full conversations. Shaming men for multiple sexual partners shows some disruption in the sexual double standard. However, the fact that people had to put the word "man" in front of "slut," as in "man slut," shows that "slut" is still a term strongly associated with women with no current male equivalent.

- *@larry1234 a slut who sleeps with a lot of guys*
- *This is a Public service announcement: Greg Daniels is a slut ass bitch*
- *Gosh what a man slut*
- *@RyanDGallagher so I always have the last word. Public ur fault!!! Don't be a man slut!!! Or boy slut*

When the gender identity and sexuality of the tweeter could be discerned, about half occurred in the context of gay male relationships. Only a few were used in other ways such as a general male insult: *"@glbsatullo what the heck. are you telling me to shut up?*

you shut the fuck off man, you slut." A single tweet was a mix between male shaming and celebratory: "*I reaaaally don't want to because he's such a SLUT .... But I can't help myself* :(." Many had to be removed because during this period a bot posted male celebrity names followed by a rhyme including "slut" as in "*Ryan Reynolds knows a farty slut that jumps bucks.*" It is possible the bot was programmed to include the word "slut" to increase clicks or page visits. Twitter users often retweeted a line from the television show *The Office* where a male character, Dwight, is called an "ignorant slut." Note referring to a man as a "slut" reflects an extension of the word because it applies to a man. However, calling men "sluts" is considered humorous, suggesting a reinforcement of the sexual double standard. "Slut" also is made an acceptable slur by inclusion in prime-time network television.

Tweets using "slut" to identify the submissive individual in sadomasochist (SM) relationships were coded in the *BDSM*[9] theme (10 tweets). Tweets that referenced BDSM are included as extensions of the word "slut" rather than regulatory because SM relationships are primarily loving, consensual, and safe.

- *@submit2pain he is my master I'm his slut he treats me as he likes*
- *Scream through the pain, little slut. #D/s*[10]

"Slut" (much less frequently than "whore" in Chapter 3) was used to show an inordinate *interest in something* (3 tweets). This extension makes sense because "sluts" are perceived as having insatiable desires. Examples include:

- *I'm always a slut for attention*
- *'im a pr slut'- @KathyJones as bill walks by*

Many examples of extensions appeared in Facebook pages with "slut" in their names. Unconnected to the traditional understanding of the word, Facebook had pages for restaurants including "Pizza Slut" and "SlutMunchie." At least six bands with "slut" in their names had Facebook pages, including "The Sluts," "Undercover Slut," and "You Slut!" "Slut" is also a clothing company based in UK whose "About" page references "debauchery" and says the company owners started their endeavors by writing "slut" on their shirts to "get laid." Similar to regulatory "slut" pages on Facebook, the content has changed, with the site now selling basic casual attire. Facebook had several groups with *"truck slut"* in the name. Although this term typically means women who have sex with men with big trucks, the pages primarily featured photos of upgraded trucks. Instagram contained the hashtag #sluttygirls that primarily tagged women in revealing clothing, but like Facebook pages and groups, also included nonsexual photos of men, dogs, and animations.

Dissent (459 Tweets)

Tweets, pages, groups, and hashtags included within the category dissent include the following themes: rejection of the label "slut"; celebratory; positive self-identification or reappropriation; direct critiques of the sexual double standard; education on slut-shaming; and organization and promotion of collective political action around women's sexuality. These uses possess the most potential for disruption of heterogender norms. Sex-positive feminists like performance artist and sex educator Annie Sprinkle and members of the riot grrrl movement[11] reclaimed "slut" to mean something positive. However, cultural theorists debate the effectiveness of reclaiming slurs through the removal of their derogatory content (Butler, 1997; hooks, 1997) and argue that the relationship between derogation and reclamation is more complex (Brontsema, 2004). In this case, it is not always clear whether reclamation of "slut" disrupts the meaning and removes the derogatory content or whether reclaimers even want the derogatory content removed.

Many women *rejected* the label "slut" (40 tweets). Tweeters expressed unhappiness with receiving the label, giving the reason that they never had sex or had sex with only one person. While rejection of labels shows opportunities for self-expression and debate on Twitter, rejecting due to few or no sexual partners reinforces the idea that women who have multiple sex partners are "sluts," offering less possibility of disruption in the meaning. Referencing celebrities, Twitter users defended actor/singer Selena Gomez from slut-shaming, arguing she is in her first relationship years after dating singer Justin Beiber (whose fans are called "beliebers"). Again, rejection of the label may serve only to reinforce heterofeminine norms such as monogamy and the number of years between sexual partners:

- *How can I be a slut if I only slept with one guy?*
- *I'm not a slut because I'm 20 and I've only had one partner*
- *I find it hilarious how beliebers are calling selena a slut when this is her first relationship other than justin since 2010..... Smh*[12]

While many women were disparaged for sleeping around, other tweets expressed desire and appreciation that can be defined as *celebratory* (63 tweets). These tweets were posted mostly by people identifying as men but also a few identifying as women and queer. This use has questionable disruptive power because it revises "slut" to mean something positive ("fun") but perpetuates traditional views ("promiscuous"). As it is impossible to definitively infer intent, one concern is how tweets may be received by other users. The potential for celebratory tweets to disrupt good/bad girl dichotomies will be discussed.

- *I want to sleep with a slut*
- *Retweet if you want a girl who's a dirty #slut*
- *sluts are fun, where can I find one?*

Within tweets and larger conversations on Twitter, analysis revealed that "fun" frequently referred to a woman who was up for sex. A heavily retweeted photo featured a woman carrying a large box on which someone had added the word "condoms," and the tweet read, "*Some people may call her a slut ,but I say she is ambitious,prepared & historically optimistic.*" This tweet removes some of the derogatory content by reframing a highly sexual woman with lots of condoms as ambitious and prepared rather than "slutty."

Another theme under the category of dissent involved women adopting the label "slut" as a *positive self-identity* (42 tweets). By adopting a slur as a positive identity, users attempt to remove its derogatory power by revising it to have a positive meaning. Though I am unable to determine whether the third tweeter is in fact the "school slut," note the contrast between this narrative and the narratives expressed in Tanenbaum's (2000, 2015) interviews where the "school sluts" felt shame. Typical examples of the positive self-identification theme include:

- *I'm proud of being a slut.*
- *I am a slut, but who cares I have fun!*

• *Hey, just wanted to let y'all know that I'm the school slut* 📷
just incase you didn't know 🙈

"Slut" was also used often on Twitter in a *friendly* way, showing affection as a term of endearment among friends (57 tweets). This theme revises "slut" to have positive meaning and is similar to *positive self-identification* where people are reclaiming "slut" for themselves. These individuals also use "slut" in ways both related and unrelated to sexuality. This form of reappropriation might signal a real weakening of the negative content of "slut," with more potential for disruption. The question remains whether rescuing and redefining "slut" can transform larger social attitudes.

• *@Jenny_K I miss ya too slut*
• *happy birthday, ya slut* 🎈🎉
• *Real friends don't get offended when you call them bitch, hoe or slut. They smile and call you something more offensive*
• *@Chloe_Dougherty slut bag you out Saturday!?* 🐚

Most tweets in the dissent category were *direct critiques* of the label "slut" and of the sexual double standard (201 tweets). These tweets possess even greater potential for disruption by pointing out the impossible limitations put on women's self-expression, as even certain body types put women at risk of labeling as a "slut." The following are examples of critiques, with the second and third receiving high numbers of retweets:

• *When will the world stop comparing women? When will the word 'slut' die?*
• *Skinny = anorexic, thick = obese, virgin = too good, non-virgin = slut, friendly = fake, quiet = rude. Society can never be pleased!*
• *Boobs = no ass, Ass = no boobs, Ass & Boobs = ugly face, Sexy Ass, Big Boobs & Nice Face = Slut. You can never win*

Tweets within this theme also directly addressed the double standard:

- *There's no such thing as a slut she just a women who really enjoys sex just like 99% of men*
- *ok so according to society it's okay for a male to post nude but when a female does it she's a slut?*

Critiques focused on the same issues found under regulatory uses: women's number of sexual partners and physical appearance:

- *destroy gender roles and slut shaming 2k16*
- *Slut isn't even an insult anymore. You're no longer a slut for having sex with multiple people, you're a slut for fuckin breathing nowadays; stop slut shaming 2k15*
- *WHY DOES SLUT SHAMING EXIST LIKE WEAR WHAT U WANT SHOW SKIN HAVE SEX WHO FUCKING CARES IDGI!!!!!!*[13]

Some directly confronted people on Twitter for slut-shaming. A tweet *"why don't you teach guys not to slut shame instead of teaching girls not to send nudes"* was in response to another Twitter user who tweeted "slut" below a woman's photo. This language refocused the debate on the shaming behavior rather than blaming women who sent nudes for experiencing disrespect and embarrassment.

Tweets containing "slut" also directly critiqued men for perpetuating the double standard:

- *boys want to be the #1 CHEATER* 😜 *but as soon as the girl cheats* 😐 *she's the hoe, slut, bitch and every word in the book!!*
- *so they'll ask to see your body. but once you show them that image gets sent around & you're automatically a "whore/slut/hoe/thot" like wtf*[14]
- *"Slut chaming" é o qd o menino quer transar com vc e vc quer transar com ele ai vcs ficam e no dia seguinte ele te chama de puta*[15]

Women also addressed other women, particularly ones who identified as feminist. One example pointed out that shaming sex workers is a form of slut-shaming:

- *It's never okay to call another girl a whore or a slut. Especially over social media. Idk[16] the girl but I'm sure she doesn't deserve that*
- *Tragic when you see girls post about how they should support other girls but they slut shame and bring down other females ://///////*
- *never going to understand why girls think calling another girl a whore or a slut is ok? Doing whatever u want with ur body doesnt devalue u?*
- *...@JackieSH is confused as to what slut shaming is. She does it to sex workers with out realizing*

Social media can also be used as an avenue for sharing information and resources, labeled under the theme *education* (41 tweets). Tweets had the goal of educating others on the meaning and consequences of using the term "slut:"

- *The word 'slut' originally referred to a woman who was untidy or who kept a messy house*
- *The idea of being a slut/hoe/whore is a manmade social construct intended to limit a woman's sexuality.*
- *#Whore #Slut, #Tease, #Die #Fat I saw all these comment on one photo of a girl wearing a bikini #weneedfeminism #womensrights #heforshe*

Twitter users harnessed the platform to share information about politics and entertainment. Tweets that occurred in the later months of 2016 focused on women in politics, including Hillary Clinton, Jill Stephenson, and Melania Trump. There were also references to women celebrities Ariana Grande, Kim Kardashian, Khloe Kardashian, Amber Rose, and Taylor Swift. Events inspired many online discussions about "sluts" and "slut shaming." Not shown here, tweets also discussed "slut-shaming" on shows such as CW's *Vampire Diaries* and Netflix's *Stranger Things.*

- *Sure Hillary isn't to blame for the sex act, just the slut shaming and intimidation. #hillaryswaronwomen[17]*

- *Outrage over top female academic Jill Stephenson calling SNP's Mhairi Black 'a slut' Full report in tomorrow's paper*[18]
- *KARDASHIAN ON SLUT SHAMING*
- *MTV's True Life shows slut-shaming in action, and it's nauseating*
- *The Avengers' Black Widow Problem: How Marvel Slut-Shamed Their Most Badass Superheroine*

Feminist websites and women's magazines used Twitter to post links to articles and blogs on slut-shaming. These links were shown to be heavily retweeted by individual Twitter users, greatly expanding their potential audience.

- *Women's health mag: it's time to stop slut-shaming yourself for good http://www.womenshealthmag.com/sex-and-love/sex-shaming*
- *@urbanette: Examining the Motivations for Slut-Shaming https://t.co/shioxoZeOd #LifeasaWoman #sex #sexism#themediaads*
- *IT HAPPENED TO ME: My Boyfriend's Slut-Shaming Led to Our First Talk About My Eating Disorder https://t.co/qlKlNd75kb #bitchmag*

The phrase "slut-shaming" has entered the public vernacular. This phrase gives people language with which to critique restrictive norms around women's sexuality. A separate search for the phrases "slut-shame" and "slut-shaming" revealed an average of 192 tweets crossed Twitter each day.[19] Analysis of 151 tweets revealed common themes addressing school dress codes; contradictory standards regarding censorship of women's bodies, including breastfeeding and menstruation; and the Gamergate harassment campaign. Even though the phrase "slut-shaming" is an English phrase, tweets in languages such as Filipino, French, Italian, Japanese, Portuguese, and Vietnamese included the phrase "slut-shaming." This circumstance reflects a global awareness of issues regarding sexual shaming.

Twitter also provided a platform for addressing racial bias within feminism, raising the question of whether sexual shaming primarily affects white women in North America and Western Europe. For example, a heavily retweeted post by @weneedfeminism was *"Feminism is about more than dress codes and slut shaming so don't say it's not important https://t.co/zwDYcl3OuQ,"* which linked to photos of Indian women who survived acid attacks. There were variations on this tweet, including the first tweet below. Tweets compared slut-shaming to more serious issues facing women around the world, such as sexual assault, intimate partner violence, poverty, and trafficking. These tweets recognize the racial and economic privilege of white women living in affluent countries and the reflection of these problems in many feminist writings and campaigns, including SlutWalks.

- *Feminism is about more than dress codes and slut shaming and free the nipple so don't say it's not important*
- *White feminist journalism be like: "See This White Girl Say Some Basic Things About Slut Shaming & School Dress Code"*
- *I'd love to see a slut walk anywhere in the middle east, feminists.* 😔

Social media can be used to share information about feminist *collective action* (15 tweets). Tweets with the term "slut" included information about slut walks around the world and hashtag campaigns to raise awareness about feminist issues. While debates exist over the effectiveness of campaigns that remain online, these tweets raise awareness and may lead to direct action as seen with #blacklivesmatter. Included below are also examples meant to educate on the connections between slut-shaming, suicide, and rape culture.

- *WHO HAD A BLAST AT SLUTWALK THIS YEAR?! Share your pics with us using #AmberRoseSlutWalk2016 & we'll repost some of our favorites!*
- *Wanna support @SlutWalkMelb, a protest against slut-shaming and victim blaming? Head down to #slutfest on Saturday! slutwalkmelbourne.com.au*
- *I hope your #EveryWoman campaign also covers Mocha Uson no? Regardless of her rep, she's been slut-shamed since who knows when?*
- *#JeSuisFeministeQuand des gens continuent de slut-shamer une jeune fille qui s'est suicidée à cause du slut-shaming[20]*

• *Victim blaming, fault renaming, and slut shaming: Sorry's not enough.* #YesAllWomen #StopRapeCulture #StandWithWomen[21]

People posted dissenting content on Facebook through feminist magazines and news and culture websites such as Feministing.com and Samuel-Warde.com. Examples of educational content included the following: "8 Ways You Were Unconsciously Conditioned to Slut Shame as a Child" by *Bustle Magazine;* "The Feminist Takedown of the Economics of Slut-Shaming" by the news website *Mic;* "Wanting to Have Sex Doesn't Make Me a Slut" by *Cosmopolitan Magazine;* and "Would You Call Amber Rose's SLUT Garb a Feminist Statement?" by news and culture website *HipHopWired*. Facebook interest pages and groups provided information against slut-shaming, such as "Stop Slut Shaming," though none had large numbers of likes or members.[22] A quick look at the Facebook stream in HootSuite showed many writing words of encouragement about bullying and shaming for possessing physical beauty or having sex. The online campaign "I need feminism because . . ." that started in a class at Duke University went viral, showing that Facebook can be a source of political action and support. Another ten Facebook pages advocated political action, such as "Rock the Slut Vote" and pages for SlutWalks in different cities and countries. Pages also showed "slut" used in alternative cultural ways, such as pages for the book *The Ethical Slut* and "*SLUT: The Play*."

Tagging pictures of oneself on Instagram with the hashtag #sluttyselfie can be included under dissent as a form of positively identifying with "sluttiness" by reappropriating the label "slut." Instagram also had many hashtags devoted to ending slut-shaming, including #slutshaming, #slutshamingiswrong, #slutshamingstopshere, #slutshamingisbad, #slutshamingisnotok, #stopslutshaming, #slutwalk, and #slutshamingisntcool.

External Events

Between January and September 2016, March 8 was a peak day for "slut" mentions on Twitter, due to a heavily retweeted post by Kim Kardashian about slut-shaming. This peak shows that while many celebrity women are shamed on Twitter, people with large numbers of followers have the potential to reach large numbers of people. The nomination of Hillary Clinton as the Democratic candidate for president of the United States, a professor calling Scottish National Party member Mhairi Black a "slut," and high-profile sexual harassment cases caused increases in the use of "slut" online.

The high volume of "slut" tweets after September 2016 exceeded limits imposed by the software used, so it was impossible to show if "slut" increased near the US presidential election like the other misogynistic terms. However, the fact that "slut" exceeded the software's limits speaks volumes. An analysis of the Twitter stream after September 2016 showed that the most-targeted person was Hillary Clinton, followed by Melania Trump.[23] Examples included: *"He's doing the work of corrupt slut @HillaryClinton"*[24] and *"@HillaryClinton she's a greedy ass little slut."* Examples of tweets mentioning Melania Trump included *"@melaniatrump is a whore. Sloveian slut. Call girl who wants women to be raped by her husband. She only wants money, gold digging immigrant"* and *"Definitely don't want a slut first lady Melania @SL_WestIndes #Melania can KEEP being a SLUT as YOU say. Just NOT #1stLady ever #Never1stNakedLadyOfUSA THOT."* Note the mention of her nationality and the use of "THOT," which will be discussed in Chapter 3. Sexual shaming serves not only to regulate women's sexual activity but to discourage women from seeking power and participating in the public sphere.

Tweets also pointed out the inconsistency of feminist ideals and slut-shaming, as in *"when the same people calling Trump a sexist, misogynist piece of shit are slut-shaming Melania Trump/First Lady."* Besides Hillary Clinton and Melania Trump, other frequently mentioned public figures included celebrities Azealia Banks, Selena Gomez, Ariana Grande, Kim Kardashian, Megyn Kelly, Amber Rose, and online gamer LegendaryLeaTV. Tweets included the following: *"Enough with this @KimKardashian shit in snapchat news feed. She's a slut stop giving her attention! #KimKardashian #slut"* and *"@AmberRose is such a bitch,us gays struggle everyday,the fucking comment u made about @Tyga was uncalled for,worry about your kid slut!!"*[25]

Intersections

There were not as many references to race-ethnicity as found with some of the other slurs, but 17 tweets included racist and anti-immigrant content. For example, after making a comment that she hates America, Ariana Grande was told to *"go back to Mexico"* and *"@ArianaGrande Please leave America soon, slut"*[26] Other Twitter users commented that a common reaction to "*Selena [Gomez] is smoking*" was "*WHAT A SLUT KYS BITCH UR UGLY YOU FUCKING IMMIGRANT.*" Note that "KYS" stands for "kill yourself," making this also a disturbing and threatening tweet. During the data collection period, anti-immigration narratives proliferated in various sectors, including politics and media. Racism also explains why so many celebrities called "sluts" were women of color. Amber Rose's race was mentioned, including, "'*Is there nothing positive going on with black women?*' ~ *Eldee comments on Amber Rose slut walk.*" The relevance of SlutWalks to the black community has been questioned (*Crunk Feminist Collective*, 2017). This issue will be explored further in Chapter 3.

Seven tweets made explicit mention of the LGBTQIA community, most falling within the theme of *friendly* tweets as in "*Happy birthday my little lesbian* 😀💚 *love you ugly slut* 😏❤.*" However, two were coded as *regulatory*, including, "*Gay marriage is gross. Being a slut is gross and I'm sure Gonzalo Higuain loses his gross income. Nobody wants to hire him now. He is gross.*"[27] Another two were *direct critiques*, including the heavily retweeted "*There's so much 'slut shaming' in the gay community.*" Referring primarily to gay men, slut-shaming shows some weakening of the gendered double standard (i.e., men can be "sluts" too) and raises concerns about reinforcing stereotypes of gay men as promiscuous. However, slut-shaming of gay men represents yet another form of regulation for a community whose sexuality has already been literally policed. Regardless of gender or sexuality, sexual shaming limits expression and prevents equal rights.

Conclusion

Although the typical understanding of "slut" is a woman who has more than an acceptable number of sexual partners, the analysis of findings shows a wide range of themes on social media. Most uses of "slut" on social media were critical of any sexual agency for women, serving as a regulatory and shaming function: engagement in any sex, expression of sexual interest, multiple sexual partners, engagement in sex work, and infidelity. Many women were named or tagged "sluts" on social media, which serves as a public branding on sites such as Twitter. General tweets, such as "*UR A SLUT*," foster a climate in which female sexual agency is discouraged for all women. Other tweets included threats of violence to encourage conformity through fear. The label "slut" was also used to regulate women's appearance and behavior, particularly the wearing of clothing that revealed women's bodies.

Regulatory tweets serve to construct and reinforce essentialist notions of heterofeminine sexuality. Regulatory tweets shame women who transgress from heterofeminine norms, including not just sexual interest in men but the culturally approved degree of sexual interest, as well as traits of caring, honesty, modesty, and self-control. The finding that women also engage in sexual shaming, confirmed by Demos (2016b), reveals the role shaming plays in constructing the good girl image. By calling other women "sluts," the speaker defines oneself as a good girl. The concept of a "slut" then divides women into two categories, good and bad. Using "slut" narratives about women also serves to solidify masculinity (Bamberg, 2004), identifying boys and men as heterosexual, virulent, and more powerful. "Slut" also serves to maintain a class and racial hierarchy, with women using the slur to denote women of lower socioeconomic statuses (Armstrong et al., 2014). Recognizing the privileged position of white, middle-class, heterosexual women in the sexual hierarchy, "slut" can also be used to elevate one's status in the face of racism and xenophobia (Le Espiritu, 2000).

Sexual shaming is unquestionably a feminist issue. Attwood (2007) writes, "whether our focus is the way 'slut' is used to police[28] women's behaviour, the significance of sluttiness in popular culture, or its appropriation in mainstream and subcultural practices, an understanding of the ways it might unite or divide us as women and as feminists is crucial" (p. 244). Shaming women based on sexual activity dehumanizes them by limiting opportunities and self-expression. Shaming women's sexual behavior and clothing reinforces the belief and practice that women's bodies are not their own, but are controlled by spectators. Women who fail to conform to sexual norms of modesty and monogamy were not only publicly shamed, but blamed for resulting bad treatment. Failing to conform to sexual norms can cause women to be blamed for harassment and sexual assault. Public narratives on social media serve to produce and reinforce existing cultural attitudes and ideas. Cultural ideas that women's bodies are controllable form the basis for larger political efforts to limit women's agency through policies regarding health care, reproduction, and sexual assault. The relationship is cyclical, as public policies feed back into attitudes that are publicized and internalized on social media. As public support for misogynist ideas becomes popularized, users of social media feel emboldened to shame women on social media, perpetuating the cycle.

Conversely, a substantial portion of tweets show extensions of the meaning and dissent from the traditional understanding of the slur "slut." The use of "slut" to describe women exhibiting any kind of sexual agency, including desiring sex within a monogamous heterosexual relationship, suggests the concept is capable of change and thus could be watered down to the point that it loses pejorative significance. Tweets, Facebook pages and groups, and Instagram hashtags extend "slut" to refer to men with many sexual partners, despite the presence of a sexual double standard in which men are encouraged to have many sexual partners.

"Slut" was also used in ways that varied or dissented from original meanings. Examples include using it as a term of affection among friends, expressing appreciation of "sluts," reappropriating it as a positive identity, and offering critiques in the form of counterarguments, education, and collective action. While most tweets from men expressed aversion to "sluts," some expressed appreciation, although this appreciation keeps intact the original meaning of "slut" as a woman who has had many sexual partners. Similarly, using "slut" endearingly about a friend refuses the shame but does not necessarily challenge the good girl/bad girl dichotomy.

Calling oneself a "slut" with pride contains more potential different meanings and intentions (Sutton, 1995). Positive self-identification has a history among feminist writers and performers, such as the riot grrrls (Attwood 2007), Califia (1994), Easton and Liszt (1998), and Sprinkle and Beatty (1992) who revise the meaning of "slut" to mean a woman who is powerful and unashamed to pursue her own pleasure. Context is crucial in assessing the ability for "slut" to transform norms; for instance, slurs are generally more acceptable in art and activism such as *Slut: The Musical* and SlutWalks. SlutWalks have been one way to use reclamation in social activism. However, a criticism of SlutWalks is that they reflect the privileged position white women occupy in the hierarchy of sexual purity. In a blog post, the *Crunk Feminist Collective* (2017) critiques the surprise and outrage expressed by white women at being called "sluts," while black women have always been perceived as overly sexual and experience daily assaults on their worth. The intersections between gender, sexuality, and race will be explored further in the discussion of the slurs "ho" and "hoe" in Chapters 3 and 7.

It can be argued that some forms of dissent contain more transformative power than others. Rejection of the label because the meaning of a "slut" does not fit due to a low number of sexual partners leaves the meaning of "slut" intact and reinforces the traditional meaning of someone with more than an acceptable number of sexual partners. Using the example of denying someone is a "kike," Camp (2013) argues that the categorical offense remains standing. Therefore, denying someone is a slut, for instance, "threatens to make us complicit in the bigot's way of thinking, despite our finding it abhorrent" (Camp 2013: 330). Identifying as a "slut" in a proud and positive way does not necessarily change the word's meaning though it may remove the stigma. The greatest potential for real transformation of moral judgements lies in direct critiques of the concept of "slut" and "slut-shaming." Direct critiques of the meaning of "slut" challenge the idea of "bad girls" and restrictions around female sexuality. The creation of the phrase "slut-shaming" also increases chances for disruptive discourses.

If watering down the meaning, or reclaiming it as friendly or positive, succeeds in lessening the stigma associated with "sluttiness," the question remains whether reclamation challenges gender and sexual norms. Canaan (1986) argues:

> By suggesting that females as well as males can have physical relationships without an emotional bond, it makes it difficult to bifurcate females into two moral categories. Since drawing the line between proper and improper sex concomitantly separates good girls from bad girls, erasing moral judgments of females calls into question the segmentation of sexuality on which it is based. (p. 201)

While reclamation attempts can challenge sexuality and power, Ashwell (2016) and White (2002) argue that "slut" discourses cannot be successful until the social norms on which they rest change.

Raising awareness through education and providing information and opportunities for collective action seem best positioned to challenge beliefs. Efforts to increase women's bodily autonomy must be addressed in areas that are directly related, such as reproductive rights; areas that may seem trivial, like school dress codes that define girl's bodies as distractions; and areas not directly related to sexuality, such as economic and workplace policies and structures such as social services, child care, and family leave policies. Additionally, for bodily autonomy for all women, norms and practices that reinforce and reproduce notions of respectability among women of color and working-class women must be upended as well. Chapter 7 will expand on this discussion and address the overarching question as to whether discursive actions reverberate back to the social structure, supplying new meanings around gender and sexuality that create real possibilities for structural change.

Notes

1. For histories of the term *slut*, see Blackwell, 2004; Greer, 1971; Mills, 1991; and Schulz, 1975.
2. It is possible this average would be much higher because I was unable to track "slut" due to the increased volume after September 9, 2016. I could access tweets through HootSuite's streaming function, so thematic coding extends to November 10, 2016. Overall, my concern is with meaning, not frequency.
3. Forty tweets were omitted for being bots or outside the focus of this project (*slut* means "end" in Swedish), and another 114 contained nonsensical text or did not contain enough information to code into one of the themes such as "slut ☺," which could be celebratory, but I tried to be certain in my coding.
4. Future research will analyze the content of pornographic tweets and pages, such as inclusion of race-ethnicity when the actors are black, Latinx, or Asian.
5. Since the slurs studied here refer to women, tweets serving regulatory or shaming functions that are directed toward men are included in the extension section.
6. Users can report a tweet to Twitter, and it will be removed if Twitter considers the tweet against its Terms of Service, which includes "offensive, harmful, inaccurate or otherwise inappropriate, or in some cases, postings that have been mislabeled or are otherwise deceptive" (Twitter Terms of Service, 2016).
7. Urban Dictionary (2017) defines *teef* as "thief" and Jamaican slang for "to steal."
8. DTF is an acronym for "down to fuck."
9. BDSM is an acronym for "bondage, dominance, submission, and masochism," and is more inclusive than SM, which refers to relationships

that involve giving and receiving pain for sexual pleasure. Individuals tagged in tweets predominantly identified as male.

10. #D/s refers to "dominance and submission."

11. Riot grrrl refers to a music, art, and political movement that developed in the Pacific Northwest and Washington, DC, in the early 1990s and addresses issues such as violence against women and female empowerment. It is associated with bands such as Bikini Kill and Bratmobile.

12. SMH is an acronym for "shaking my head."

13. IDGI is an acronym for "I don't get it."

14. WTF is an acronym for "what the fuck."

15. Translated from Spanish by Google Translate as "'Slut-shaming' is when the boy wants to have sex with you and you want to have sex with him, and the next day he calls you a whore."

16. IDK is an acronym for "I don't know."

17. This tweet linked to an article about former president Bill Clinton's infidelity.

18. SNP refers to the Scotland National Party.

19. Search terms contained a hyphen, even though people also write "slut shaming." The phrase "slut shaming" was included in keyword searches for "slut."

20. Translated from French by Google Translate as "I am a feminist when people continue to slut-shame a girl who committed suicide because of slut-shaming."

21. This tweet commented on a *Washington Post* article (Guerra, 2016), "Judge Apologizes for Asking Accuser in Rape Case Why She Couldn't Keep Her Knees Together," in which a Canadian federal court judge apologizes for making offensive and victim-blaming comments during a rape trial.

22. This project is unable to measure the reach of feminist tweets and Facebook pages and groups, though this area is important for future research.

23. Misogynist words are the focus of this research; therefore, I did not calculate counts for individual public figures. Furthermore, given the limitations of the software, I was unable to archive data in NVivo after September 2016, making a count of occurrences of "Hillary" or "Clinton" more difficult. However, given the massive increases in the occurrence of "slut" on Twitter due to tweets about Hillary Clinton, I conducted a search for "Hillary" in the first 70,000 tweets on October 5–6, 2016. Data revealed 153 mentions, 60 of which called Hillary Clinton a "slut," 49 accused her of "slut-shaming" other women, and 18 accused Donald Trump of "slut-shaming." Eight tweets were positive, with people defending Clinton against the label "slut" or positively identifying as "sluts" who support Hillary Clinton for president.

24. This tweet linked to an article about John Kerry and Syria.

25. Tyga is a rapper.

26. It does not change that "go back to Mexico" was meant to offend, but some Twitter users defended Grande by reporting that she was born in the United States and is of Italian descent.

27. Gonzalo Higuaín is an Argentinian professional football player.

28. It is important to point out that using *police* or *policing* in a figurative way does a disservice to men and women of color who are literally policed in ways that result in violence and death. This idea is also true for transwomen of color, who have high arrest rates for suspected "loitering" due to their clothing (Ellafante, 2016). I have tried to use *regulating* or similar words to highlight this distinction.

3

WHORE:
Judging "Bad" Girls

This chapter examines the online social media use of the term "whore" with its variations "ho," "hoe," and the more recent "THOT" ("that hoe over there"). Feminists argue that a good girl/bad girl distinction exists for women, serving as a powerful form of sexual shaming through social control and stigma (Nagle, 1997; Pheterson, 1993; Queen, 1997; Vance, 1992). "Normal" female sexuality is defined as passive and occurring within committed heterosexual relationships. The distinction between a chaste virgin and an overly sexual prostitute is oversimplified, as sexuality intersects with other forms of structural inequality and class and race identities (Hill Collins, 1990; Rubin, 1992). Nevertheless, Griffin (1982) argues that a Madonna/whore dichotomy that contrasts the Virgin Mary (known as Madonna or Our Lady in Christianity) and a prostitute is central to the preservation of patriarchal power.

Along with "slut," "whore" is one of the most common misogynist terms on Twitter (Demos 2016b). Both terms represent women who have had more than the "appropriate" number of sexual partners. However, the concept of "whore" is older than "slut," deeply embedded in ancient and Judeo-Christian thought and carries more stigma owing to its association with prostitution. The contemporary English word *whore* can be traced back to the Old and Middle English *hore*, which means prostitute or harlot. *Online Etymology Dictionary* (2017) suggests that the current pronunciation of this term was influenced by various words for "desire," "filth," "slime," "moral corruption," "sin," "unchaste," and "lewd."

The word *whore* can be found in writings dating back to ancient Greece (Pomeroy, 1995). In the comedy *Thesmophoriazusae* by Aristophanes (411 BCE), women accuse Ancient Greek playwright and poet Euripides[1] of slandering women as whores and adulteresses by calling them "sex fiends," "heavy drinkers," and "rotten to the core" (chapter six, part 3, para. 3). Hippolytus depicts women as a "primal evil," "unceasingly wicked," and likely to "drain the wealth from [men's] households" (chapter six, part 3, para. 7). Hippolytus especially warns against "clever" women who are more likely to commit evil undetected (chapter six, part 3, para. 7). These ideas reflect and reinforce notions of women as inherently insatiable, deceptive, and materialistic.

References to "whores" appear in different translations of the Bible, including the *King James Bible* and the plays of William Shakespeare.[2] Ruether (1974) traces the Madonna/whore duality to Christianity, which relies on notions of female sin, essentialist views of gender, a belief in a gender hierarchy, and a distinction between body and mind. This distinction is based on the idea that women are associated with the body and men with the mind. Conrad (2006) adopts a neoinstitutional perspective in which this mind-body/male-female dualism becomes so simplified and taken for granted that it is considered natural, allowing it to operate as a legitimate myth. The themes of women as inherently insatiable, deceptive, and materialistic persist today, seen in online forums such as "The Red Pill" on Reddit, where users claim women have more power than men and cannot be trusted. Common themes on forums include false rape accusations and unfair custody battles (Gotell & Dutton, 2016).

Additional stigma surrounds "whore" due to its association with prostitution. A hierarchy of stigmatized sexualities exist, with the prostitute occupying the bottom position (Chapkis, 1997; Rubin, 1992). Whereas "sluts" are stigmatized for having more than the appropriate number of sexual partners, prostitutes violate additional norms laid out by Pheterson (1993):

> (1) engaging in sex with strangers; (2) engaging in sex with many partners; (3) as a woman, taking sexual initiative, controlling sexual encounters, and being an expert on sex; (4) asking for

money in exchange for sex; (5) as a woman, using one's energy and abilities to satisfy impersonal male lust and sexual fantasies; (6) as a woman, being out at night alone, on dark streets, dressed to attract male desire; (7) as a woman, being in situations with supposedly brash, drunk, or abusive men whom one can either handle ("uppity or vulgar women") or cannot handle ("victimized women"). (p. 46)

Note the similarities between Pheterson's "whore stigma" and the traits associated with women in *Thesmophoriazusae*. Also important are the number of components within Pheterson's (1993) whore stigma that are prefaced with "as a woman," for example, "as a woman, taking sexual initiative, controlling sexual encounters, and being an expert on sex" (p. 46). Like "sluts," "whores" are decidedly women. The sexual double standard means that women are stigmatized for taking sexual initiative while men are expected to take initiative; nor are men nearly as stigmatized when they are brash, drunk, or abusive. Even within the sex trade, women are much more stigmatized for providing sex in exchange for money than men are for paying for sex.

Empirical research shows girls and women fear the label "whore" while also using it to regulate other girls' and women's sexuality (Armstrong et al., 2014; Eder, Evans, & Parker, 1995; Lyons et al., 2011; Miller, 2016; Reid, Elliott, & Webber, 2011). However, Attwood (2007) shows adoption of a kinder-whore look worn by some punk musicians in the riot grrrl movement, characterized by torn baby-doll dresses and smudged makeup. Research by Renold and Ringrose (2011) and Kofoed and Ringrose (2012) finds some adolescent girls publicly identifying as "whores" on social media. Nonetheless, the label "whore" might be harder to reappropriate since the Madonna/whore dichotomy is so embedded in culture and commercial sex is severely stigmatized. The Madonna/whore dichotomy also seems to be the foundation on which other heteronormative slurs such as "dyke" and "slut" rest.

Results show most people use "whore" to regulate the number of women's sexual partners and behavior. Other common uses do not concern sexual activities, such as "attention whore." Though not explicitly sexual, the phrase "attention whore" exists because it suggests an inordinate interest or appetite for something, reinforced by the ancient view that women are insatiable. Nevertheless, applying "whore" to men and using it to refer to interests other than sex suggests possibilities for disruption. Fewer instances of education and organization are focused on the opposition to the use of "whore." More intersections between gender, sexuality, class, and race-ethnicity exist for terms like "ho," "hoe," and "THOT."

Findings

The term "whore" was tracked on Twitter from January 1, 2016, to December 1, 2016. During this period, "whore" was used over 7 million times. Shortened versions of "whore" (e.g., "hoe" and "ho"[3]) were sampled from January 22, 2016, to July 5, 2016. The more recent acronym "THOT" was sampled between September 26, 2016, and October 4, 2016. *Urban Dictionary* (2017) defines "THOT" as "that hoe over there" and "thirsty hoes out there," and users debate whether it is considered an insult. Tweets including "whore" ranged from 6,544 to 65,947 daily uses, with an average of 21,018 uses a day (see Figure 3.1). A total of 834 tweets were coded for themes, which is lower than the amount coded for "slut" because fewer new themes emerged and data saturation was reached after approximately 500 tweets.

A much lower portion of "whore" tweets advertised pornography compared to "slut" tweets. Twenty-four percent (201 tweets) advertised websites for pornographic videos and webcam models. Very few, if any, used "hoe" or "THOT." It can be theorized that "whores" are less desirable in pornography because of the move to amateur and girl-next-door motifs. Because "hoes" and "THOTs" are associated with cheapness, they also may not make good searchable hashtags for pornography. A total of 31 tweets could not be reliably coded in any of the themes. Only two could have created their own category of neutral identification, but the sentiment was unclear: *"I can't tell if I was just called a whore"* and *"I feel like a whore."* These tweets were unclear even when other information was considered, such as other Twitter users' responses. Four were clearly posted by bots, resulting in a sample of 598 tweets.

Twenty-nine Facebook pages and groups were analyzed. Instagram bans #whore, but 19 variations such as #whores and #whöre were included. As with "slut," it is possible that Instagram administrators have not yet been able to delete all offensive hashtag variations. Explicit content was not found on Facebook or Instagram,

Figure 3.1   Keyword Mention over Time: "Whore" (Twitter)

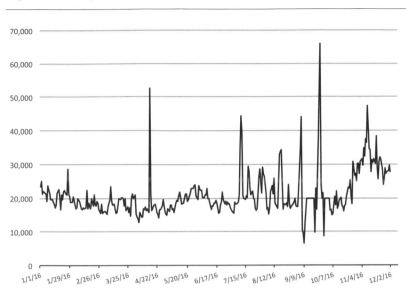

though several Facebook pages ("Attention Whoring in Progress," "Don't feed the Whores," and "Whore Church") posted nonexplicit content such as "drunk girls falling down" meant to draw traffic to external pornographic websites.

Like "slut," use of "whore" increased on Sundays, although peaks often included the entire weekend in North America. The spikes in use of "whore" on dates such as April 4, 2016, and September 24, 2016, are due primarily to external pop culture and political events, and they will be discussed in detail later. An increase in the use of "whore" occurred over time, likely due to the interval leading up to US presidential election. When gender identity was available, about half of users of "whore" identified as women, consistent with the findings of Demos (2016b). Only five people who identified as non-binary used "whore" on Twitter.

As with the other slurs, data were grouped into three major types of uses. The most common and expected use is to regulate women's sexual activity and other behaviors considered unfeminine. Like "slut," extensions of the meaning also emerged from the data, such as using "whore" to negatively label men with multiple sexual partners as in "man whore" or to refer to the disproportionate need for recognition as in "attention whore." Because terms like "slut" and "whore" are decidedly female, references to men are considered extensions of the original meaning. Findings also show dissent in the form of rejection of the label, positive self-identification, and direct critiques. However, not much content raising awareness through education or political organizing was found (see Appendix B for coding scheme and counts).

Regulation (378 Tweets)

Similar to "slut," using the term "whore" on social media serves to remind women to conform to norms of virginity, selectivity, controlled desire, heterosexuality, passivity, and monogamy. The fear of being labeled is heightened when names or tags are used, but the use of the word extends the warning to all women. Because *whore* historically has meant prostitute, new themes of "gold digger" and accusations of engagement in commercial sex were found, representing violations of feminine romanticism more severely than sex with a larger than acceptable number of people. As Pheterson (1993) pointed out, whore stigma contains more components than just having many sexual encounters. Furthermore, the sting of the label was used to silence women in a way that "slut" was not.

A large portion of tweets fell into the *naming* theme, involving a person's name or tag (77 tweets). The phrase "@WeAllKnowA" appeared again often, this time followed by "whore" instead of "slut" and a traditionally female name or tag. Similarly, "*boo you whore*," coming from the movie *Mean Girls*, was heavily retweeted using different women's names, and could be interpreted as representing disappointment among friends. Tweets including the English word "whore" were also found in tweets written in other languages. Some were more aggressive and may be included in other categories. Regardless of the users' intents, targeted people cannot untag themselves and are now publicly associated with the pejorative label "whore."

- *@WeAllKnowA whore named Isabelle*
- *@amanda_rogers boo you whore*
- *@tsktsktsk_ Whore по английски курва*[4]

- *@kristen_v237 FUCK OFF YOU WHORE, YOU'LL BURN IN HELL MOTHER FUCKING BITCH*

Many "whore" tweets were coded as *generic slurs* (66 tweets). No person was specifically named; "whore" was simply used as a general slur. Although no one was named, the slur creates a climate on Twitter that reminds women to avoid behaviors likely to invite the label. Text and emoji helped to clarify sentiment. Naming someone's mother or sister caused strong reactions, suggesting paternalist attitudes. The last tweet was heavily retweeted by other users.

- *Fuckin whore* 😡😡😡
- *Shawty Really a Whore* 😩😡😡😡 *Thts bad* 😡👎👎👎
- *Your mom is a whore*
- *Does your mom know you're a whore?*

As expected, when more information is given, many tweets were related to women's sexuality, including number of sexual partners, selection of sexual partners, faithfulness, and any interest in sex at all. *Promiscuity*, referring to number and selection of partners, was a common theme (40 tweets). "Whore" appeared in the hashtag #FreshmanAdvice, which gives advice, some humorous, on topics such as studying for exams and making friends. Many tweets were written in the form of jokes. Jokes serve to make sentiments seem harmless, but in fact make stigma and discrimination seem socially acceptable while portraying individuals who object as uptight. Note the denial of women's agency and consent in the use of the phrase "passed around."

- *Also stop using the free spirit as an excuse to be a whore. Free and open/ accepting spirit doesnt really mean free & open*
- *@HotBarbara never knew someone can be a whore so much doesn't your mouth get tired from sucking so much d*ck.*
- *#FreshmanAdvice find a whore and pass her around with your boys like a blunt!*
- *Did it hurt? When you fell from the whore tree and banged every guy on the way down?* 😂😂

Because of the connection between "whore" and prostitution, mentions of *sex work* also emerged (18 tweets). Engaging in sex work violates the ideal of feminine romantic love and sexual passivity. This theme includes references to stereotypes that sex workers lack the ability to discriminate among clients and are addicted to drugs. Because of this perceived lack of ability to discriminate among clients, failing to "score" with a prostitute becomes an insult for men. Note also the homophobic slur "faggot" and reference to "useless," which will be discussed further:

- *@NellieNJesse You better thank @realDonaldTrump for not being a faggot, or else a useless whore like you wouldn't make money being nude.*
- *You wouldn't score in a whore house m8*
- *Bald guy sez "if you're gonna finger-fuck a porn whore in public, you should go for it all the way."*
- *My oldest basically likened my hair to that of a crack whore's. Thanks, son*

A major component of feminine sexuality is monogamy. Women were called "whores" for being *unfaithful* (14 tweets). Many tweets identified women as home-wreckers, blaming them but not men for infidelity. Since contemporary society perceives men as having insatiable sexual appetites, it falls upon women to ensure the sanctity of heterosexual relationships. Women are suddenly given tremendous sexual agency and men sexual passivity when engaging in infidelity. Women were slightly more likely than men to post these warning tweets, showing that the good girl/bad girl distinction continues to divide women. Some of the tweets were aggressive. Data included a common tweet, "*We all know a boyfriend stealing whore,*" with and without names and tags. Men were also called "whores" for cheating, but will be included under extensions of whore as the traditional understanding of a "whore" is a woman. Note also reference to men's masculinity in the first tweet.

- *you're a liar, a cheater, and a whore that fucks dudes that wear my sisters sweat pants. that dude is wack as fuck*
- *We all know a boyfriend stealing whore @_eveylyn_eve*

- *She's probably concerned cause your a home wrecking whore. Ha dumb bitch. Die already*
- *The whore finally tells the truth it aint my kid. And I'm fine with that she can take her ass and rot in hell.*

Similar to findings for "slut," any form of sexual agency, labeled *any sex/sexual interest*, can result in women being labeled "whores" (21 tweets). Women were not afforded the same sexual agency as men, who are expected to be the initiators. Women can be shamed for expressing any kind of sexual desire. Tweets mentioned behaviors such as "going all the way" and oral sex, as well as behaviors considered more deviant such as fisting. Even sending texts or nude photographs puts women at risk of labeling as "whores." All of these themes, including promiscuity, faithfulness, romanticism, and passivity, reaffirm sexual desire and experimentation as the purview of men.

- *This girl only wants me for my body. Whore* 😣
- *You as friend... "Can we make out again soon? ...But not all the way, 'cause I'm not a whore... I'm not a whore."...*
- *Who's up and is a whore that wanna send me nudes, atm[5]*
- *I guess praying to God isn't the only thing you kneel down for, you whore*
- *"Two fisting it tonight," means something completely different when you're dating a whore.*

The label "whore" also relates to appropriate heterofeminine behavior. A common theme was *appearance*, particularly clothing and body type (26 tweets). Women were expected to maintain heterofeminine norms of beauty and modest dress. Note that some of these guidelines not only regulated women's appearance, but also linked revealing clothing to weakness and desperation, overlapping with the next section on *demeanor*. Shaming women for showing their bodies or having body types that deviate from traditional norms of beauty removes women as subjects with control over their bodies and defines women in relationship to men. There were many references to television celebrities, including the Kardashian/Jenner sisters and reality TV stars such as Nene Leakes from the program *Real Housewives of Atlanta* (*RHOA*).

- *@angelica_94: Fat whore lol*
- *I'm not saying your shorts should say "Whore" on the bum... but your labia's showing*
- *Your tweets say you're a strong woman. Your avi[6] and posted pics say desperate whore. Congrats on your diversity. Cunt*
- *Kim Kardashian Admits Her Dress Is Too Sexy After Khloe Calls Her A Whore*
- *Nene DEF WAS flirting with Peter and NO ONE called that moose a whore*

In addition to appearance, women were called "whores" for acting in ways considered unfeminine, labeled *demeanor* (43 tweets). A common theme was that "whores" are dirty or trashy, lacking respectability and behaving in an improper manner. Classism and racism intersect with this theme, noted in the use of terms such as "white trash" and "ratchet." *Ratchet* is a newer term defined by various entries on *Urban Dictionary* (2017) as predominantly African American women from low-income neighborhoods who appear trashy and loud. The intersection of class, race, and sexuality with respect to "whore" and its variations will be explored further under "Intersections." Further reducing women's agency, women and men alike admonished women who posted photos featuring their bodies. While feminist debates exist over the current commodification of female sexual agency, admonishing women for revealing their bodies reinforces the idea that women are not allowed to express sexiness or sexual desire. Again, we saw the hashtag #Freshman Advice and references to Kenya Moore, a cast member on *RHOA*:

- *@msmaddie fuck you whore you white trash*
- *This bitch ass whore be coming next Friday 🐮 ratchet ass skank & shit. 💇🔫💅*
- *#FreshmanAdvice if you're gonna be a whore, keep it lowkey*
- *If your friends post pictures of you naked, or in your panties and you laugh about it with them, you're a whore. Nothing for the imagination.*
- *Kenya stfu bitch your dress was only $30 but you "own" a Bentley LOL #rhoa dumb whore @KenyaMoore*

The stereotypical view is that women must always be in control and act modestly, so the word "whore" also occurred with accusations of drug and alcohol use. The reference to "crack whore" again shows the connection between "whore" and "prostitute" and the stereotype of sex workers as drug addicts. The use of alcohol and drugs was cited as a cause for a lack of relationships with men, and some women were named or tagged. The use of the relatively new term "fuck boy" is also significant in that a slur emerged to admonish men who sleep around and lead women on, suggesting this behavior is no longer so accepted and warrants a label.[7] Examples included the following:

- *Oh looks like cuntface got too fucked up again no one likes a sloppy whore*

- *Maybe if you weren't an alcoholic druggie whore, you'd find the right guy. But a non fuck boy doesn't want a girl that gets drunk every night*

- *@marialawson I DIDNT CALL U FAT I CALLED U A CRACK WHORE THERES A DIFFERENCE*

Like "slut," "whore" is used to deem women as *unworthy* (43 tweets). The line between good and bad women was drawn often on Twitter; a revealing example was the distinction between a "lady" or "wife" and a "whore." "Whores" were deemed unworthy of respect or long-term relationships. When gender identity was provided, about half identified as women and half as men. Some directly named or tagged women and were clearly aggressive. Once women were labeled as "whores," it was argued they were "nothing more" (this last tweet was heavily retweeted).

- *Fucking whore ass piece of shit 🐷 @Tinaissweet*

- *Don't be mad that he wants a lady and not a WHORE!*

- *so basically you decided to be a whore! Round of applause for you not respecting yourself! You win*

- *Can't turn a whore into a housewife*

- *Once a whore you're nothing more*

Tweets relating to unworthiness also contained references to women's lack of intelligence. Hillary Clinton was mentioned often and will be discussed further in the "External Events" section:

- *@_fatima dumb whore*
- *@tstyla no! YOURE FUCKING BRINGING IT UP! FUCKING STOP CAN YOU NOT SEE IM STRUGGLING JUST IGNORE ME YOU STUPID WHORE!*
- *@HillaryClinton ur a dumb fucking whore ive never seen anything in 50 yrs like you trying to run this country if i end up back in combat.*

Two new themes emerged from the data that were absent in "slut" tweets, coded separately here. Based on stereotypes about prostitutes, "whore" was applied to *gold diggers*, a derogatory term for women who are suspected of only being interested in a man's money and not love (6 tweets). As with the other behaviors above, dating individuals for their money severely violates romantic notions of femininity. Examples included:

- *@jennyfergirl she's a golddigging fake whore with collagen lips and fake tits and fugly face*
- *@PacificCal calvin curren is a superdick has a kid with a whore who already had a kid just wanted his gold*

The term "whore" was also used to *silence* women, a theme that was absent in tweets containing the word "slut" (6 tweets). The effort to silence women will be discussed in tweets containing "bitch" (Chapter 5) and "cunt" (Chapter 6). "Whore" carries more stigma than "slut" due to its association with prostitution, so it serves as a more powerful silencer. Again, a reference to Kenya Moore, a cast member on *RHOA* appeared. Examples included the following:

- *@Debbi4690 you shut your whore mouth*
- *Wow your the biggest shit talker ever Janelle so shut up whore* 😈😈😈
- *@KenyaMoore and you wonder why you're called a whore, have a seat Kenya Moore Whore with your old tired self!*

Tweets containing "whore" were found to be angrier and more aggressive than tweets including "slut." Threats of violence and wishes for illness and accidents are included under the theme of *threats* (18 tweets). In trying to examine conversations more fully on Twitter, it was noted that several accounts had been suspended, showing that Twitter is responding to some complaints of abuse. Slightly more men were responsible for making threats online (only the last one below is from a woman). Several specific references were made to religion, which will be discussed in the "External Events" and "Intersections" sections:

- *@phillie420 Imma kill you and that whore of a girl Jessica, you fucking asshole motherfucker*
- *@Will_Matthews54 is no better than ISIS, an American Taliban terrorist. Christian sharia law lover. I hope the whore gets his ass kicked.*
- *I hope you get an STD and die stupid whore*
- *I'M GOING TO MAKE YOUR LIFE LIKE A LIVING HELL! #Whore #Bitch*

"Hoe" and "THOT" were most frequently used in regulatory ways to refer to women who were considered promiscuous and indiscriminating. Note the lack of agency and unworthiness of respect or relationships due to sexual activity. A spike in the use of "THOT" on Twitter occurred due to a tweet requesting guests for *The Jerry Springer Show*, which suggested "THOTs" are not only unworthy but problematic:

- *Yo hoe get passed around* 💦
- *wifey material don't come around often so u better recognize when u have yourself a rider before u end up with a hoe my g*
- *Can't be no sucka for no thot* ✖
- *@SpringerTV: Is there a #THOT in your life causing trouble? Call Jovan at 1-888-321-5358 to confront them on #Jerry Springer*

"Hoe" and "THOT" were much more likely than "whore" and "slut" to include black slang and references to class.

- *Y'all Niggas Be ready to leave a girl cuz she's not easy like a typical hoe..Y'all niggas should want somebody with standards*
- *RT[8] if your girl a hoe be honest nigga.*
- *They wear cheap and revealing clothing: I know this hoe is not wearing spandex at blinn.... sos*
- *YOU SO IN LOVE WIT YO BD[9] BUT HE BROKE HOE*

While men warned one another about "hoes" and "THOTs," women distinguished themselves by putting down other women, reinforcing their good girl status. Women also used the stigma attached to "hoe" to discourage women from disrupting their relationships. The first tweet was heavily retweeted:

- *The best girls are always gonna be the most difficult, so deal with it or get yourself a basic hoe*
- *if you're gonna be a hoe can you at least have some type of morals to only try with single niggas*
- *jeneanefoster90 smack me hoe, I'll beat ya ass :) again*

Only two Facebook groups fell into the regulatory theme. "MEME WHORE" was a closed Facebook group that asked users to "Please post the best memes you have. Looking for memes that are sexist and racist." "THE MAD SEX AND WHORE HOUSE!!!" was a closed group for posting pictures of women in revealing clothing, but rather than encouraging sexist and racist content, it included a statement about showing respect through not posting racial slurs, sending unsolicited sexual content, or engaging in sexual harassment or trolling.

Instagram had removed all content that included the hashtag #whore (33,497 posts removed). Users tried variations, but during data collection, posts were removed from the following hashtags as well: #whores, #whöre, and #whoresonfiles. Overall, Instagram hashtags are more difficult to classify since many people with differing motivations can attach a hashtag to a photo. Combinations of the two categories (*regulation* and *dissent*) were used in the coding of the hashtag #whoresbelike. Photos included women who tagged themselves, often dressed up and out with friends. Also included were similar regulatory themes seen on Twitter: women cheating, engaging in too much oral sex, partying too much, and looking trashy.

Extension (153 Tweets)

The second major category of "whore" tweets can be thought of as extending its meaning in ways unrelated to the regulation of women's sexual behavior or physical appearance. Many more extensions of "whore" occurred than of "slut." Some extensions have the potential to disrupt the Madonna/whore distinction, and some reinforce it. The largest extension meant an inordinate interest in something, the most common example being "attention whore." Other extensions included using "whore" as an insult for men and referring to the submissive individual in an SM relationship.

The most common theme under extension included phrases indicating more than a socially acceptable *interest* in something (79 tweets). Most tweets referred to "attention whores," people who behave in exaggerated ways simply to attract attention. Social media may, in fact, increase the need to attract attention. In a Pew Research Center Report, Madden et al. (2013) quote a 15-year-old female defining "like whores" as people who desperately need likes on social media, influencing what and when they post content. This theme was not gender specific and referred to many different interests. The phrase "attention whore" even appeared in other languages, including Filipino, French, German, and Spanish. Although "attention whore" may differ from the traditional meaning of "whore," it makes sense as a device because the cultural image of the "whore" is a woman who is desperate or has an inordinate amount of desire.

- *Because I'm a selfie whore.* 😈
- *I feel like a YouTube video whore this evening*
- *I must say, Tinder always comes in clutch when I wanna be an attention whore @SpringMady*
- *Wer hätte das geahnt, Attenttion Whore Kate hängt sich an Attenttion Whore Ken*[10]

"Whore" can apply to an inordinate interest in anything, not just attention, even to the point of becoming a problem:

- *@bettygeorgegfy I fucking Love winona ryder shes the Reason im a film whore fuck*
- *see, this is why I lost my followers they're sick of my attention whore bullshit*
- *NEVER DATE AN ATTENTION WHORE*

This inordinate interest can result in compromising oneself for gain or "whoring" oneself out. Again, this result arises from connection between "whore" and "prostitute," given that many incorrectly characterize prostitutes as "selling their bodies" (Queen, 1997). The data referenced individuals who compromised themselves for any kind of gain—not just financial, but also status and power. The first tweet refers to actor and talk show host Stacey Dash. The last tweet in Spanish included suicidal thoughts, but was no longer available so I could not see if people responded:

- *Why whore yourself out to the conservative right @REAL-StaceyDash? Be the Dee from Clueless I know you have the potential to be*
- *Hillary is a whore who's been sold out to Saudi 💰. Every decision revolves around donations to Clinton Foundation*
- *Pano nyo madedefine na fame whore that means you're fame whore as well*
- *parezco una att whore pero es que me quero morir*[11]

When gender identity was available, a sizable portion of tweets referred to *men* (61 tweets). Note the examples that were preceded by "man" (as in "man whore") show the general understanding of a "whore" as a woman. Slightly more women were posting about men, but men also called other men whores. By examining additional data from the conversation threads, some of the men confronting other men as "whores" indicated they were involved in sexual relationships.

- *@techmanbobby man whore*
- *My cousin is a man whore!*
- *@brandnew95 i fucking hate you you whore*
- *When Simons not being a man whore he's just being a whore* 💀💀💀

Women also called men "whores" by name, and there were a few examples of men recognizing their potential to be "whores." These examples suggest some weakening of the sexual double standard, in which men are perceived as naturally nonmonogamous:

- *@JPCooper shut up cheating whore*
- *Lmao @LarryG_777: the trash gets picked up tomorrow, be ready, whore.*
- *I've been a good joe the past few months. Haven't slept with anyone and in a way I'm glad I'm not a whore. Shows my intuition for loyalty*

Public figures were mentioned as well, including then president Barack Obama, singer Justin Beiber, and footballer Dejan Lovren. Note using the term about men may only challenge the gendered aspect of "whore" while keeping its meaning as an insult intact. The phrase "son of a whore" has become less common than "son of a bitch" today, but historically served as a great insult for men by calling their mother a prostitute and defining them as illegitimate:

- *@MrMUSA: This is leadership. At least someone is calling out Obama for the son of a whore he is*
- *Justin beiber still my little white whore he so fine*
- *Take Lovren off. Bolasie is destroying his ass like a 20$ whore*

Like "slut," "whore" was also used on Twitter to denote the submissive individual within a relationship, coded as *BDSM* (13 tweets). Omitted are tweets that directly advertised BDSM websites or webcam models, though it was difficult because much of the mainstream porn advertised on Twitter describes scenes of women passively and violently penetrated, most often anally, by several men. Consequently, the text accompanying mainstream porn and BDSM on Twitter are converging. A perfect example is the first tweet from a man, which included language virtually indistinguishable from tweets accompanying pornographic advertisements. This tweet is included in the sample because it was not accompanied by pornographic website links, photos, or video. Most expressed appreciation for the submissive individual within a dominant/submissive relationship. However, again, using "whore" to demean submissive individuals makes sense because "whore" is considered derogatory, and the association with prostitution depends on the stereotypical view of a woman without agency or ownership over her body.

- *The result..the same as anytime I'd make @Babe_Lisa my anal whore. Her ass'll be sore dripping cum and gaping.*

- *@ETaylor32 can I be your slutt slave whore miss*

- *@tomayers your a fucking slutty fucking whore tom i can not believe my eyes lmao wow my slave good boy tom*

Most Facebook pages and groups used "whore" in alternative ways. The names suggest a regulatory use while an investigation of the content shows extensions. One explanation is that "whore" is used to attract attention or imply edginess. While potentially originally related to sex, the following pages and groups posted general comical content such as cat videos and text message pranks as well as friendship advice, celebrity gossip, and inspirational quotations: "Awe, That's Cute You Cheating Whore"; "Dont shake the whore tree"; "Have A Bitchtastic Day You Fucking Whore"; "~My Inner Child is a Drunken Whore~"; and "Raging Whore-moans." Several pages named "You're a whore" were about comedy. The use of "whore" is significant because many "whore" tweets were told in the form of a joke. Hashtags on Instagram also showed extensions of the use of "whore." Several hashtags including "whore" contained sexy selfies as well as pictures of men, cats, and humorous memes: #whorelife, #whorehouse, and #whoreable. #Whoreindrawer featured photos of Barbie dolls.

Like Twitter, many Facebook groups and pages used "whore" to mean excessive interest or to sell oneself for something. "Boo You Whore" was a public group for fans of the movie *Mean Girls* and "Star Whores!" was a public group for fans of the movie *Star Wars*. "Atheist Whores" was a closed group for making atheist friends; "Gore Whores" was a closed group about serial killers and true crime stories; "Guitar Whore Groupies" was a closed group to "post, discuss, and say silly shit about guitars"; "Obsessive Book Whores" was a public group promoting books; and "Softball Whores" was for selling and trading softball bats. Furthering the allusion to prostitution, "Obsessive Book Whores" used "pimping" in their description to refer to self-promotion. Similarly, the "About" section for "Atheist Whores" reads, "Feel free to whore yourself for new friends!" Many Facebook band pages contained "whore" in their name, suggesting again that slurs are less offensive when used in art and commentary. Examples of band names included Whore, Whores, Whore's Mascara, and Iron Whores. However, it is likely the choice of "whore" was due to its derogatory content, giving the bands a subversive and controversial image. Some tried to distance themselves from the "whore" connotation, for example "Wheel Whores" a closed group, included "Wheels and Tires Posts only!" in their description.

Dissent (108 Tweets)

Feminist and sex work activists have recognized the damage of "whore stigma," some calling for its reclamation (St. James, 1987). Content that challenges "whore" stigma is included in this section. Dissenting themes have the most potential for transformation of heterofeminine norms around "whore." Data show "whore" has not yet been reappropriated to the same extent that "slut" (Chapter 2) and "dyke" (Chapter 4) have, although there were examples of agency through rejecting the label, celebratory uses, reclaiming "whore," and using it affectionately among friends and in direct critiques. The same online education and activism were not found as those surrounding the concept of "slut."

Tweets *rejecting* the label showed that social media provides opportunities for self-definition even around a deeply stigmatizing word such as "whore" (27 tweets). Women expressed relief that they were not "whores" and rejected the label for similar reasons that women rejected the label of "slut," suggesting similarities between the terms. Some defended other people from the "whore" label, but note below that one user thinks "sweetness" is the farthest thing from a "whore," showing that "whores" possess a wider range of negative traits than just promiscuity. Though these tweets allow for agency, they ultimately uphold the Madonna/whore dichotomy:

- *At least I'm not a whore*
- *Question: how can I be a whore if I'm a virgin*
- *but in all seriousness how could i be a slut@or@a whore like ive never kissed anyone or had a boyfriend/girlfriend or anything*
- *@baller1579 @helen_durand funny cause Helen can't play games she's too sweet. Farthest thing from a whore Matthew and you know it.*

In contrast to tweets disparaging "whores," *celebratory* tweets expressed desire or admiration for "whores" (14 tweets). There were fewer celebratory tweets including "whore" than "slut," likely due to the stigma attached to prostitution. While celebratory tweets may remove some of the pejorative content, they do not disrupt the concept of "whore."

- *Angelina is a fine Hispanic whore with curves that loves to shake that ass!*
- *I DONT WANT A GOOD GIRL I'LL JUS TAKE A WHORE*
- *@Abbyutube ahahahaha omg. You look like the village whore... but I love it* 😳
- *A fuckboy and a whore. Now that's a power couple.*

Another theme included under dissent is *positive self-identification*, where women reclaimed the label "whore" (23 tweets). However, Twitter data did not reveal as much reclamation of "whore" as of "slut." Some tweets, like the first tweet below, were heavily retweeted:

- *@yoifeellike: a whore*
- *I'd rather be considered a whore and/or a harlot*
- *I'm a whore I'm a cunt I'm a slut I'm a bitch*[12]
- *when i told my mom i was a whore. she bought me a skinny vanilla latte and said "welcome to the club."*

Again, there were references to Kenya from *RHOA* "owning" the label "whore" during a reunion episode:

- *Kenya Said "That Was The Best God Damn Whore There Ever Was. That Bitch Did That!"* 😂😂😂😂

Using "whore" in a *friendly* way between friends has more potential for disruption (24 tweets). Sentiment was made clear by text and emoji. When gender identity was stated, all but one exchange was between women, reinforcing the idea that slurs can be used by members of an in-group (in this case, the in-group includes women). Data also included examples of "hoe" used in friendly ways:

- *@ImEveTorres I'll miss you much more whore* 😩😷😔
- *@GamerMaddy* 😊 *im your skanky whore*
- *Happy birthday hoe!! Hope your day is great day* 😻💙💃 *@fannyglam*

Examples of *direct critiques* of the term "whore" demonstrated that Twitter can also be a site of resistance and agency (19 tweets). Most tweets critiqued sexual shaming and directly challenged the sexual double standard. Some used sarcasm to make their points. Others, such as the last tweet below, used "whore" as part of the "I Need Feminism Because" online campaign started by Seidman (2013). One definitive critique of the slur "hoe" was found. The 140-character limit and need to rely on existing data meant sentiment was not always clear, so I was unable to definitively include the following tweet as dissent, but thought it important to make available to readers: "*Women: 'Men so disrespectful.' Men: 'No we not bitch you just a hoe.'*"

- *the words slut and whore are incredibly misused and we continue to throw them around and it's only making things worse.*
- *A man who is open about his sexuality is a hero and a woman who is open about hers, is a whore. #Society*
- *So I get pregnant at 16 and then left to raise the baby alone and the dad can date whoever but if i talk to a guy im a whore?? Ok got itt* 👌
- *Being a "freak hoe" with ya man is totally acceptable* 😜😻🙊🥒[13]
- *I need feminism because I can't talk about sex openly without getting called a whore but boys can.*

Women's frustration with sexual shaming was clear in these tweets:

- *Men that use whore, cunt and love you all in one sentenced, can go fuck themselves...* 😒 *#stalker #leavemealone #fuckingdrunk*
- *Why are you so mean? Does it make you feel like a bigger stronger man to call a woman a whore? You are pathetic*
- *So far this morning I've been called a c**t, a b**ch and a whore by the good folks on twitter! (And it's 730 am) Happy Labor Day everybody!!*[14]

Tweets called men out for hypocrisy regarding their views of so-called "whores." Some also highlighted the lack of agency afforded to women who are called names when rejecting the advances of men. The second tweet was heavily retweeted:

- *100% of men.....if asked if they were a girl, would they be a whore?.... would say, Absolutely*
- *drunk boys: *hits on u and then calls u a whore when u turn him down* drunk girls: *compliments ur eyebrows and gives u a hug**

Only one tweet offering *education* about "whores" was found although it is unclear if the tweeter was choosing to challenge the concept: "*Nell Gwyn: King Charles II's "Protestant whore" http://t.co/RZbWtmmUWu #history.*" It is included here because Nell Gwyn is quoted as identifying as a whore, once telling two men, "I *am* a whore. Find something else to fight about," and after being mistaken for a rival, saying "I am the *Protestant* whore." No hashtags emerged from the data designed specifically to lessen whore stigma other than the "I need feminism" tweet quoted above. Links to political action dedicated to ending "whore stigma" were not found either. However, considering the similarities between "slut" and "whore," it is possible that events against slut-shaming will carry over into awareness of the double standard reinforced by the slur "whore."

Facebook, due to its greater opportunities for personal expression, may possess more potential for dissent than Instagram or Twitter. Some Facebook pages were directly dedicated to challenging gender and sexual norms: *Whore! Magazine* described themselves as "Fast, Feminist, and Feminine," posting articles and photos of women who are "opposed to what traditional society has dictated they should be." The Facebook page also included an 1872 quotation by American suffragist and business person Tennessee Claflin: "We have tried to make 'rake' as disgraceful as 'whore.' We cannot do it. And now we are determined to take the disgrace out of whore."[15] Similarly, the Facebook pages "Have a Bitchtastic Day you Fucking Whore" posted about self-empowerment and "You're a Whore, You Own that Shit" gave women life hacks. "The Culture Whore" page (where members also referred to themselves as "ARTSLUTS") described themselves as "a community of artists exploring queerness in all its forms by creating ephemeral spaces and permanent platforms that cultivate connectivity, inclusivity, free expression, and pleasure." Again, we see less offense when derogatory slurs are used in cultural contexts. On Instagram, #Whorebag contained photos in which women tagged themselves, often out with friends and accompanied by hashtags commenting on their physical attractiveness.

External Events

Over the data collection period, several cultural and political events heavily influenced Twitter activity through retweets. Throughout 2016, Hillary Clinton was named most often in "whore" tweets by women and men. The random sample only included four tweets referring to Hillary Clinton as a "whore," followed by three tweets referencing women on the television show *RHOA*. However, a search for "whore" on Twitter to explain spikes in the use of "whore" on July 10, 2016, and September 6, 2016 (see Figure 3.1), revealed that part of the increase was due to an increase in pornographic tweets, but came primarily from an increase in tweets referring to Hillary Clinton as a "whore," as in the "whore of Babylon"[16] after the FBI announced no wrongdoing with respect to her e-mails. The increase on November 9, 2016, the day following the US presidential election, was due almost entirely to Twitter users calling Hillary Clinton a "whore." We see similar increases in tweets about Hillary Clinton on November 9, 2016, including the slurs "bitch" and "cunt." A heavily retweeted example was, *"Hillary is a whore who's been sold out to Saudi . Every decision revolves around donations to Clinton Foundation."* Others included, *"Hillarys a whore. And can't handle top secret info what makes you think ah can run our country"* and *"@HillaryClinton Not everybody think you are good. You speak like you have a dick, and campaigning like having a vagina is an issue. Whore!"* Some tweets explained Donald Trump's win, including: *"I think it was the fact that she is a lying conniving corrupt political whore."* Commenting on misogyny during the election, many people retweeted after the results of the election were announced: *"Welcome to the 1950s ladies, if you're not married you're a whore. Enjoy your president, he's not mine."*

Trump was also called a "whore" on Twitter, including the heavily retweeted *"Fuck you whore !!"* accompanied by a picture in the style of his campaign but reading "FUCK DONALD TRUMP

MAKE AMERICA GREAT AGAIN" and *"Low-rent piece of crap/ media whore @realDonaldTrump was a big fan of Pelosi/Reid/Obama before he was against them. #tcot."*[17] Other male politicians such as Newt Gingrich and Paul Ryan were also called "whores" for reversing their positions on Donald Trump, alluding to the act of "whoring" oneself out (for political gain, in these cases). Although most tweets referred to men as "whores" for having a lot of sexual partners, using words like "whore" to insult men adds extra injury because it associates them with women, similar to calling men "bitches" (Chapter 5). No third-party candidates in the 2016 presidential election were referred to by misogynist slurs in the sample, though it did not include all tweets that occurred near the election. Tweets referred to President Rodrigo Duterte of the Philippines calling former president Barack Obama a "son of a whore." There was an increase in mentions of Melania Trump, including: *"We literally replaced our best POTUS and FLOTUS with a pimp and a whore. #NotMyPresident"* and *"Am I the first to find out trumps wife was a whore* 😒*?"*

The spike in "whore" tweets on September 24, 2016, was due to tweets about model and actress Gennifer Flowers, who was invited to a presidential debate by Donald Trump. Tweets included, *"The whore Gennifer Flowers is coming to the debate. The biggest mistake in debate history. What an idiot Trump is."* Tweets also included reactions and Bernie Sanders' apology to a speaker's use of "whore" to describe certain Democrats at a Bernie Sanders rally on April 14, 2016: *"@NPR: Sanders Denounces Surrogate's 'Corporate Democratic Whores' Comment At Rally."*

Mentions of celebrities also caused peaks in the use of "whore" on Twitter. On April 14, 2016, Amber Rose and two of the Kardashian sisters were mentioned often in this popular retweet: *"Amber Rose calls Kim Kardashian a 'whore' in clash on Twitter with sister Khloe,"* accompanied by links to news articles. Recognizing it as slut-shaming, Amber Rose later apologized on Twitter. *Variety Magazine* tweeted that actor Chris Evans also apologized for calling Scarlett Johansson's character in the movie *Avengers* a "whore." Rapper Azealia Banks also appeared fairly frequently; for example, in response to *"Whats going on with Azealia Banks?"* a woman responded: *"in short: attention whore."* Reality television star Kenya Moore was also mentioned often. Besides Hillary Clinton, the next most frequent women labeled "whores" and "hos" were women of color, showing the intersection between gender, sexuality, and race.

The importance of race-ethnicity will be analyzed further under "Intersections" and in Chapter 7.

Intersections

More references to class and race-ethnicity were made in relation to "whore" than "slut" on Twitter. Seventeen references to race-ethnicity emerged from the data, including "nigga," "black slang" that has been reappropriated by the African American community, which was virtually absent in "slut" tweets. For example, *"Your new nigga know your old nigga & your old nigga know your old nigga . . . Yall whore we fuck everybody bitches."* Several tweets included lyrics from hip-hop songs using "ho," "hoe," and "THOT" such as *"don't trust a hoe"* by 3OH!3. Hess (2014b) argues that, like "hoe" and "ho," "THOT" is more about class and race than it is about sex, writing the following: "The fantastical nightmare of the thot is a woman who pretends to be the type of valuable female commodity who rightfully earns male commitment—until the man discovers that she's just a cheap imitation of a 'good girl' who is good only for mindless sex, not relationships or respect" (para. 5). Hess argues that THOT is the black counterpart to the "basic bitch," a typically white woman who has ordinary suburban tastes. My data did not include friendly uses of "THOT" that Hess reports.

"Whores" were also described as behaving in "trashy" ways, such as talking loudly, using drugs or alcohol, or wearing cheap clothing. This reveals a socioeconomic component to the idea of a "whore," likely persisting because of the association with prostitution, of a woman who is perceived as lacking money and therefore morally degraded. The assumption of the good girl as affluent explains a new theme that emerged in tweets including "whore" but not "slut:" "gold digger." Again, the association of "whore" with "prostitute" means that "whores" are perceived as superficial and lacking a romantic orientation to sex, which means they cannot be trusted.

This sample included one anti-Semitic and homophobic tweet: *"@carlmmatthews go suck off you faggot kike bernie or rim your whore hillary, trump did nothing wrong."* In this case, anti-Semitism and homophobic slurs were used to add insult but do not show strong support for an association of Judaism or LGBTQIA identities with the concept of the "whore." More common was the use of "whore" to express Islamophobia, as seen in these tweets: *"Come on, the whore is showing her arms, neck and face. She's practically begging to be raped. #IslamIsTheProblem"* and "*@Saleem_23 I piss on your whore mother and shit on the Quran.*" The second tweet was accompanied by a link to a picture of a battered woman on a Christian website titled "'Your Daughter Is A Cute Blonde Whore' Muslim Students Beat Up And Try To Rape Teen Girl At School." The blond white woman is presented as a sympathetic character in the effort to demonize men of color, particularly black and Muslim men. Though an entire chapter on mentions of "rape" on Twitter is not included, tweets reveal that most mentions included claims of women making false accusations and fabricated news stories of immigrant, refugee, and Muslim men raping white women. Almost no mention was made of the most common occurrences of rape, which are unreported and by someone known to the victim.

The inclusion of racist and classist terms in online sexual harassment reveals the assumption of whiteness and economic affluence in normative constructions of heterofemininity. Class and race are integral parts of the ideal chaste woman (Hill Collins, 1990, 2004). White middle-class women are assumed pure unless actions, often extreme or obvious, indicate otherwise, while a blog by *Crunk Feminist Collective* (2017) recounts the frequent use of terms like "ho" within the black community in Western settings. Hillary Clinton was targeted most in "whore" tweets for attempting to reach the highest political position in the country, while the next most frequently mentioned women, Azealia Banks, Kenya Moore, and Amber Rose, are African American women who were targeted for expressing public opinions, appearing untrustworthy, and showing their bodies in public. Affluent non-European and immigrant women were not exempt, as seen with Melania Trump, the Kardashian sisters, and the cast members from the *Real Housewives*, showing the significance of race and nationality in the construction of the good girl.

Conclusion

The lower daily use of "whore" compared to "slut" (21,018 compared to 37,646) on Twitter is driven primarily by the lower rate of pornographic advertisements. These figures also suggest that "whore" has not been as incorporated into mainstream culture and that its uses are not as varied, other than the common extension "attention whore." The 2016 US presidential election figured prominently in the use of "whore" on Twitter. Hillary Clinton was the most referenced public figure, characterized by attacks on her as a woman and as someone perceived to be untrustworthy.

The small number of cases prevent generalizing to all social media users, but qualitative analysis shows that "whore" is used on social media in similar ways to "slut"—that is, a woman who has had more than an acceptable number of sexual partners, who does not choose partners carefully, who is unfaithful, and who has expressed any sexual agency. Women were called "whores" for simply desiring sex. However, it is clear from the analysis of tweets, Facebook pages and groups, and Instagram hashtags that when used as a slur, "whore" carries more aggression than "slut." If there is a scale of deviation from heterofeminine norms, "whore" seems worse than "slut," as demonstrated in this tweet: *"You're lost somewhere between slut and whore* 😒*."* The association with prostitution adds another layer of stigma, such as seeking money in exchange for sex. While at times prostitutes have been revered, contemporary sex workers are heavily stigmatized and structurally oppressed by socioeconomic factors, law enforcement, and government regulations (Ditmore, 2011; Sanders, 2004). The connection between "whore" and prostitution makes "whore" a preferred pejorative label for women perceived as dishonest or interested in money.

"Whore," then, was used to shame as well as silence women, particularly women of color, from appearing in public, deviating from heterofeminine norms, and exerting control over their bodies. "Whore" was used to refer to Melania Trump for modeling nude and Kim Kardashian for wearing a revealing dress. Attacks that target women's bodies, revealing clothing, and online photos mean that women's online behavior is continuously scrutinized and shamed. Women who do not conform to heterofeminine norms are deemed unworthy, particularly of male attention. Again, women's worth is defined in relation to men.

While both "slut" and "whore" refer to women who have had more than the culturally appropriate number of sexual partners, the association of "whore" with "prostitute" adds an additional moral violation. Women who desire money are considered corrupt, unfeeling, immoral, and therefore not feminine. This connection is also seen in tweets about places and things: *"@nationalpost 'performance bonuses' or payoffs, hush money, undeserved 'rewards'; Toronto is a really, really dirty diseased whore"* and during the election, television network CNN was called a *"ratings whore."* "Whore" was also used to silence women in a way that "slut" was not. This difference may be due to the greater strength of "whore" as a slur, though both slurs were included in threats of violence.

"Whore" carries class connotations, and more recent variations such as "ho," "hoe," and "THOT" also carry racial connotations. Racial slurs and slang were more likely to accompany tweets containing "whore" than "slut." The heteronormative ideal is white and middle-class. Women of color, particularly black women but also Latina and Asian women, are stereotyped as overly sexual and untrustworthy (Armstrong et al., 2014; Bettie, 2014; Garcia, 2012; Le Espiritu, 2000). The labels "hoe" and "THOT" have been used most often to refer to African American women from low-income neighborhoods (Hess, 2014b). "Hoes" are described as cheap, failing at attempts to make themselves attractive, and behaving in unsophisticated ways, rendering them unworthy as girlfriends or wives. Through labeling, women of color are then excluded not only from ideals of sexual purity but also from self-worth and respectability. The Madonna/whore or good girl/bad girl is less a dichotomy than a precarious position located in intersecting axes of essentialist identity categories and oppressive structural forces.

Some uses of "whore" show the ability for the meaning of language to change, even words imbued with stigma. "Whore" has been extended to mean an inordinate amount of interest in or desire for anything, not just sex. The most commonly used phrase was "attention whore." Public social media platforms are ideal for people who desire attention. Posting to social media generates attention in the form of "likes" and responses. "Whore" was added to any object or topic someone likes, as in "shoe whore" or "book whore." This reason may be why many of the Facebook groups and pages included "whore" in their titles. It may be theorized that not only does the word attract attention, but it makes the interest sound cool and edgy, similar to the use of "porn" to talk about getting pleasure from looking at things (such as "architecture porn" to describe the pleasure some people get from looking at homes). Men were more likely to be called "whores" than "sluts," though the increased labeling of men was likely due to the use of "whore" as an inordinate interest or desire for something. For instance, men were called "attention whores," "money whores," and "video game whores," all consistent with hegemonic masculinity. Using "whore" in this way upholds the idea that people should keep their desires in check. However, extending words like "whore" and "porn" to ordinary nonsexual uses may water down their meanings so much as to make them meaningless and to reduce their associated stigma.

There were few celebratory uses of the term "whore," likely due to its association with prostitution (Pheterson, 1993). This usage may also explain why "whores" were called "gold diggers" while "sluts" were not. Presumably "sluts" are in it for the sex while "whores" are in it for the money. Women seeking financial gain, not love, violate romantic essentialist views about women. Feminists such as Wollstonecraft (1792/1988) and de Beauvoir (1949/1989) recognized long ago the limitations of the romantic image of women. When men were called "whores" for sleeping with many partners or for cheating, the term was often "man whore." This term showed potential for changing views about the sexual double standard (also shown in the new use of "fuck boy"), while at the same time reinforcing the idea that "whores" can be women only.

Rejection of the "whore" label showed that social media provides opportunities for self-definition. However, denial that one is a whore because one does not have many sexual partners perpetuates the Madonna/whore distinction. A much lower portion of "whore" tweets reclaimed the term in the form of friendly terms of endearment and positive self-identification, perhaps due to the greater stigma associated with prostitution. Direct critiques were found of classifying women based on where they fall on the Madonna/whore continuum and the sexual double standard that stigmatizes women, but not men, who exercise sexual agency. Only one case of education was found, though the sentiment was not clear. No examples existed of organizing online or off-line, as seen with "slut walks" and other anti-slut-shaming campaigns.

It is possible that the lower occurrence of online dissent stems from the fact that "whore stigma" has not entered the public vernacular in the same way that "slut-shaming" has, creating fewer opportunities for feminist writings and activism. However, sex workers and sex work theorists have long illuminated "whore" stigma (Pheterson, 1993; Queen, 1997; St. James, 1987). Sex workers have unique issues relating to safety and criminalization; it is time for feminists to see the connections between criminalization and stigmatization of sex workers and broader female sexual agency. Laws and attitudes regarding women's participation in the sex trade must change for women to exercise full bodily agency. Recognition of the classist and racist dimensions of sexual agency must be addressed through education and far-reaching structural change through policies addressing women's health care, gag rules, law enforcement, voting rights, and international humanitarian efforts. As with all the slurs included in this book, Chapter 7 will continue this discussion and address whether extensions of slurs and dissent carry disruptive power in the sense of supplying new meanings about gender and sexuality, the role of language in transforming attitudes about gender and sexuality, and structural change around gender inequality.

Notes

1. While there is debate over Euripides' personal attitudes toward women, the concern here is not with the truth of the statements but rather with the expression of misogyny in particular cultural milieus.

2. Male versions of these words appear as well. In the *King James Bible*, "whoremonger" is variably translated as any sex outside of marriage or general immorality. Besides often using "whore" in his plays, Shakespeare uses "whoreson" similar to "bastard," though it can be used jokingly or as an insult.

3. It was more difficult to analyze tweets with "ho" since searches yielded any tweet containing the string of letters "h-o." "Hoe" was more effective, but did not always refer to sexuality and yielded words in other languages.

4. Translated from Bulgarian by Google Translate as "English whore."

5. ATM is an acronym for "at this moment."

6. AVI is short for "avatar," and here refers to Twitter profile pictures.

7. On Halloween 2016, pictures of two women dressed as "fuckboys" went viral. They wore shirts inscribed with texts they had received from men, including the following: "Hope you find someone better than me. I laugh cause there's no way that's possible. Goodbye. Your life was meaningless to me." And "I just fuck you when I'm bored."

8. RT is short for "retweet."

9. BD is an acronym for "baby daddy."

10. Translated from German by Google Translate as "Who would have guessed this, Attention Whore Kate is attached to Attention Whore Ken."

11. Translated from Spanish by Google Translate as "I look like an att whore but I just want to die."

12. Apart from "dyke," this tweet incorporates all the misogynist terms studied in this book.

13. The eggplant emoji is used to represent a penis.

14. This tweet was posted by journalist and broadcaster Soledad O'Brien.

15. A *rake* is defined by *Online Etymology Dictionary* (2017) as "debauchee; idle, dissolute person, 1650s, shortening of rakehell."

16. The "whore of Babylon" refers to a woman in the Book of Revelation in the *Bible* associated with the Antichrist and Beast of Revelation.

17. TCOT is an acronym for "top conservatives on Twitter."

4

DYKE:
Enforcing Heterofeminine
Standards

The misogynist slurs discussed in previous chapters relate primarily to heterofeminine sexuality and behaviors. Implicit in the regulation of female sexuality and behavior is the assumption of heterosexuality, with acceptable heterosexual behavior associated with the "good girl" (Payne, 2010). The current chapter examines the uses of "dyke" on Facebook, Instagram, and Twitter to further expand the analysis of misogynist slurs. "Dyke" is considered by many a disparaging or offensive term for lesbians. The origins of the term are debated. The *Online Etymology Dictionary* (2017) finds sources using *dyke* as slang for vulva in 1896 and as a short term in 1921 for *bulldyker*, meaning to engage in lesbian activities. Other origins include the shortening of *morphadike*, a variant of *morphodite* derived from *hermaphrodite* in the 1930s; a shortening of *morphodyke*, a blend of *morphodite* and the preexisting *dyke*; a shortening of *bulldike*; and a variant of *bulldagger*.[1] Its connection to *dikes*[2] as in "ditches" is questionable.

Polls show a continued existence of homophobia[3] and laws against same-sex sexual and marital relationships around the world (Adamczyk, 2017). Despite increasing public support for the LGBTQIA community in countries such as the United States, Worthen (2014) finds that lesbians continue to be excluded from social networks. Additionally, women continue to be stigmatized for not conforming to feminine styles and rejected for exhibiting too much attraction or emotional investment in other women. Homophobia consists of a complex set of attitudes that support and are supported by discriminatory institutions and policies and are strongly linked to misogyny through traditional gender views. Homophobic attitudes are related to gender attitudes: Men who hold traditional views of masculinity are the individuals most likely to perpetrate antigay behaviors ranging from name-calling to murder (Franklin, 2000). To provide a sense of volume, the website NoHomophobes.com found "faggot" was tweeted over 26 million times, "no homo" 7 million times, "so gay" 7 million times, and "dyke" 2 million times between July 5, 2012, and June 5, 2014 (Worthen, 2014: 146). The gender-specific terms "fag" and "dyke" have replaced "queer" as the most common homophobic slurs used (Brontsema, 2004; Pascoe, 2012).

Research uncovered the shaming of people who deviate from traditional gender and sexual norms, including people who identify or are perceived as lesbian, gay, transgender, and/or queer (Payne, 2010; Thurlow, 2001). Homophobic pejoratives constitute one of the most common categories of abusive language among adolescents, which is when identities and social location in groups are formed. Sinclair et al. (2012) found that LGBTQIA youth, students of color, and boys were more likely to experience homophobic name-calling, while female and white students were more likely to experience cyber harassment. Gender non-conformity for males and females is also a risk factor for bullying, exclusion, and name-calling (Collier, Bos, & Sandfort, 2013).

Early radical feminist thought considered heterosexuality as institutionalized male sexual dominance and female sexual submission, serving as the linchpin of gender inequality (MacKinnon, 1989). Rich (1980) referred to this institutionalization as "compulsory heterosexuality." Queer theorists extend this argument to show that heterogender, the intersection of gender and sexuality, is the basis of inequality (Fuss, 1991; Warner, 1993). Expressing concern that lesbians will be as constrained by identity categories as heterosexuals, Butler (1991) and Foucault (1978/1990) argue that identity categories are instruments of regulatory regimes. For resistance against oppressive structures such as heterosexuality, gender and sexual identity are recognized as imitations of imitations, achieved through internalized scripts and performances. The intersection of femininity and heterosexuality, or heterofemininity, means that women's bodies and practices serve primarily to attract males.

Interviews with cisgender late adolescent girls found that half of the rumors circulating about girls in school described nonheterosexual actions or orientations (Miller, 2016). One of Miller's interviewees is quoted as saying, "If we heard a rumor that a girl was bisexual in my high school, we considered them a whore. Because we felt like they just . . . wanted both worlds, they were a whore" (p. 729). Rather than focusing on too much heterosexual sex, as seen with "slut" and "whore," rumors often focused on the "wrong" kind of desire. Messerschmidt (2011) finds that both adolescent girls and boys engage in the monitoring of adolescent girls' bodies.

High school and college students experience high levels of verbal harassment when perceived as gay or lesbian or gender nonconforming in terms of appearance, mannerisms, and activity. This harassment results in long-term negative effects on mental and social health (Collier et al., 2013; Sinclair et al., 2012; Thurlow, 2001).[4] Due to harassment, LGBTQIA youth are at increased risk of physical assault and suicide-related behaviors (Center for Disease Control, 2014). Emotional effects can be more damaging for youth who experience other kinds of bullying, teasing, and physical assault at school (Centers for Disease Control, 2014). Silverschanz et al. (2008) have found evidence of subtle forms of heterosexist harassment in college, defining heterosexist harassment as "insensitive verbal and symbolic (but non-assaultive) behaviors that convey animosity toward nonheterosexuality" (p. 180). Public degradation serves to maintain the invisibility of the LGBTQIA population and perpetuates the belief that their feelings are inconsequential (Armstrong, 1997). Being called a "dyke" to one's face counts as a personal, directly targeted act. Ambient harassment consists of experiences that take place in an environment, such as overhearing homophobic jokes.

This chapter examines the ways the label "dyke" is used in perhaps the most public setting, the Internet. The primary use of "dyke" is theorized as a form of personal direct or ambient harassment that, like "slut" and "whore," uses public shaming to encourage women to conform to heterofeminine norms. Like the "slut," the "dyke" is positioned as a transgressor in that she fails to align her body and behaviors to men's desires (Payne, 2010). By refusing to participate as an object of male desire and embodying "masculine" characteristics, such as an athletic female body and loose-fitting clothing, the "dyke" not only challenges feminine norms but also men's exclusive hold on masculinity through athleticism and female attention.

That being said, "dyke" has been reclaimed by in-group members. Since the 1990s, the homophobic pejorative "queer" has been reclaimed as active, inclusive, and political. Like "bitch" and "cunt," "dyke" may have originally referred to women's genitalia, but its origin is less clear, whereas the original meaning of "queer" meant strange or unusual objects, things, or people (*Oxford English Dictionary*, 2017). Only later did queer become associated with sexuality, referring to "any disruption of the male/female and heterosexual /homosexual binaries" (Brontsema, 2004: 4).[5] For decades "queer" was used as a pejorative, particularly for gay men. Questions about the ability for pejorative slurs to be reclaimed and their effects on larger issues such as inequality and human rights will be continued in Chapter 7.

Findings

The keyword "dyke" was tracked on Twitter from January 23, 2016, to December 1, 2016 (see Figure 4.1). During this time, "dyke" was used a total of 853,980 times. Use of "dyke" on Twitter was much lower than "slut" and "whore." Tweets including the term ranged from 634 to 6,933 a day, with a daily average of 2,720. This number is similar to the daily December average found by NoHomophobes.com (2016). As a comparison, a random two-week period from October 2, 2016, to October 14, 2016, showed "queer" occurring at a higher rate, averaging 10,119 times a day on Twitter.[6]

The sample for analysis included 966 tweets. Eleven tweets could not be validly or reliably coded due to the ambiguity of meaning or lack of information, and 54 tweets advertised pornographic websites. Note the much lower rate of pornography for "dyke" compared to "slut" and "whore."[7] A fuller examination of all slurs was needed to determine if the term is used to refer to sexuality. Another 110 tweets containing the word "dyke" were unrelated to sexuality or behavior, such as the surname "Van Dyke." For this reason, counts in Figure 4.1 should be interpreted with caution. A total of 791 tweets were coded for themes (see Appendix B for coding schemes and counts). Though the use of "dyke" on Twitter did not increase during the period sampled, spikes in use indicated other uses of the word. For example, the

Figure 4.1   Keyword Mention over Time—"Dyke" (Twitter)

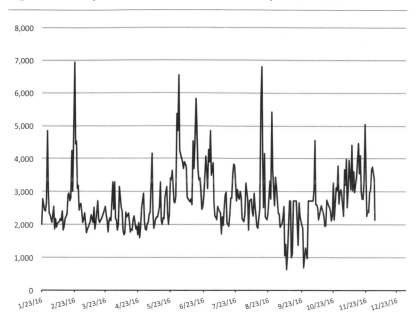

spike on January 28, 2016, was caused by an increase in posts about media executive Greg Dyke. Spikes in use of "dyke" on February 22, 2016, May 31, 2016, and August 16, 2016, were due to mentions of actor Dick Van Dyke, including his endorsement of Bernie Sanders, the announcement of a new *Mary Poppins* movie, and a video of him singing at a Denny's restaurant. At times, additional information was needed to code sentiment. Neither of the following tweets could be coded without examining visual content and other tweets that formed a conversation: "*Your dyke aunt bringing her much younger girlfriend to dinner*" referred to a picture of two Kardashian sisters, and "*no she's a dyke now lol*" was a response to a heavily retweeted photo asking, "*do you still see the person you lost virginity to?*"

Regulation (636 Tweets)

Payne (2010) finds that sexual shaming affects lesbian youth as much as their heterosexual peers. Lesbians are already labeled "bad girls" who must distance themselves from sexual agency and desire to avoid stigma. Tweets serving regulatory uses include naming and tagging someone as a "dyke" and labeling women who fail to adhere to feminine norms regarding appearance and behavior as "dykes." More emphasis was placed on feminine appearance and behavior than on sexual activity. Two new themes not found with the other sexual shaming terms emerged, including unavailability or rejection of men and lesbianism as a sin or as immoral. There were also examples of the casual use of "nigga" with "dyke" in tweets, suggesting the adoption of "dyke" as slang within the African American community.

A portion of tweets were coded as *naming* someone a "dyke" (124 tweets). The label "dyke" has undergone a reclamation among members of the in-group, meaning that naming may not indicate a regulatory use. Since it is difficult to determine whether tweets were posted by in-group members, the number of tweets included under the "naming" section should be interpreted with caution. Nevertheless, the short format provided by Twitter means that simply tagging someone and including the term "dyke" leaves room for interpretation by others and could have harmful consequences for people whose sexuality is not public. Given that tweets included here are public, users often included more text or emoji to clarify sentiment. For example, "*@orphanA bye you dyke* :" and "*@carrie_benjamin you're a dyke* 😒💜 " convey different sentiments. The following are representative tweets including "dyke" plus a name or tag:

- *@lilizhang dyke*
- *Amelia Albe ur a dyke*

Coding "dyke" as a *generic slur* was also not simple due to the reclamation of "dykes" as a positive identity (38 tweets). Nonetheless, it is debatable whether or not using a reclaimed term publicly means others will take it as positive. When more information was available, such as other slurs or a response to a tweet, a regulatory intent was clearer. Still, roughly half of the tweets in this category should be interpreted with caution given a lack of evidence regarding sentiment.

- *absolute dyke*
- **calls everyone a dyke* okay maybe they're not a dyke but still*
- *Faggot dyke bitch*

The following are three examples of testimonials that were difficult to code, though it is likely that the tweeters felt negatively about receiving the label "dyke" based on the phrasing and emoji:

- *@jacksamuels I think you called me a dyke*
- *She keep saying I'm a Dyke* 🙄😒
- *I got called a dyke for the first time today*

A theme clearly intended to regulate behaviors relates to women's *appearance* (95 tweets). Almost all were negative comments about femininity and attractiveness, often referencing short hair, clothing, and body type. The purpose here is to impose feminine characteristics in the service of heterosexual male attraction.

- *Why would you kiss caroline she's a nasty dyke — Uh*
- *I hate how bitches think getting the dyke chop as a haircut is cute like nah im not tryna date you with that haircut*
- *Typical ugly feminist dyke..*[8]
- *The more ecko unlimited she owns the stronger the dyke she becomes*
- *She got a neck tattoo. She gone be a dyke for life* 😩😩[9]

The most commonly cited public figure was Hillary Clinton, who will be discussed further under "External Events":

- *@chriscquinn @cher @HillaryClinton two disgusting fat dyke fags. You ate shit on CNN....honey. Owned by the basic blonde bitch. You Fat pig*
- *@pol_4_Infinite4 @katz_oversight @FoxNews I feel like puking just looking at progressive @megynkelly fake nose,dyke haircut*
- *"Shrill, Inaccessible, Difficult, Frumpy" Nazi Dyke Lena Dunham spits up: https://t.co/7BiXNK5TxN #NaziDykeLenaDunham #PoliticalCorrectness*[10]

Related to appearance, women were often labeled "dykes" for behaving in ways that are inconsistent with femininity. Tweets referencing behaviors are included under the theme *demeanor* (185 tweets). When more information was available, such as a photograph or response, often the women labeled as "dykes" were considered athletic, imposing, and assertive. These cases suggest "dyke" means "manly" behavior. For "slut" and "whore," activities focused primarily on women's sexual behavior. In contrast, activities associated with the label "dyke" placed greater emphasis on women's gender performance, though all three words show intersections between gender and sexuality. Note references to binary and essentialist views of gender and the use of reclaimed black slang:

- *She had her days when her ugly ass wanted to be feminine* ☺ *so not WHOLE dyke* 😖
- *I hate when women basketball players walk around actin like dudes. get your dyke ass on somewhere else*
- *Lmao this dyke rapping about getting her "dick" sucked. I'm confused*
- *& some guy told me he loved my energy & i was adorable and then said no homo so idk if he was gay or i was jus giving off strong dyke vibes*[11]
- 😊 *if your a dyke your still a girl you just basically dress and got the mentality of a nigga*

Included within the *demeanor* theme are 11 tweets that differed in that they regulated appropriate lesbian behavior, demonstrating conflicting pressures to conform to either traditional femininity or traditional masculinity:

- *so is keke palmer like partially dyke? her last two videos confuse me*
- *Bitches love playing dyke until a real dyke show up*
- *"If you're not gonna eat pussy, you're not a dyke." -Sex & the City*
- *Shoutout to the dyke bitches that still wear pretty panties*

There were fewer instances of using "dyke" to indicate *unworthiness* than seen with "slut" and "whore" (18 tweets). These included accusations of unintelligence and inauthenticity and aversion to "dykes" as sexual partners and even roommates. This aversion to "dykes" reflects homophobic attitudes and compulsory heterosexuality. Tweets also suggested essentialist views of male and female sexuality (i.e., only someone with a penis can attract women). The last tweet was heavily retweeted:

- *@seanhannity @ErikWemple she's just another worthless liberal Dyke*
- *Dyke Bitch: I pull more hoes than you and I'm ah female. Me: At least I got ah dick dumb bitch*
- *Only way I'm fuckin a dyke if I'm homeless*
- *Woaaaaaaah I'm dorming with a dyke* 😾😾😾😾
- *When a dyke say she hate fake niggas* 😐 *Sis, you is a fake nigga* 😑

Two new themes emerged from the data, including *women who reject men* (24 tweets) and lesbianism as a *sin* or *immoral* (5 tweets). As passive objects, women who reject men are violating hegemonic femininity, which maintains that women should not only be attractive but also available to males. Men are also judged on their ability to attract women. Losing a woman to a lesbian then is a serious failure of masculinity:

- *I hate seeing a beautiful ass dyke*
- *I walk up in the club and women get extra hype...you walk up in the club and women turn extra dyke*[12]
- *@anniellee @realDonaldTrump What do you call a dyke who hates men?*
- *this nigga salty as fuck cuz my girl @PattyL94 curved his fuckin ass for a lesbian dyke* 😺😳 [13]

Proscriptions against sex with someone of the same gender are pervasive, supported by some doctrines found within religious, medical, and psychological institutions. Members of the LGBTQIA population are considered more deviant than those committing other "sins" such as heterosexual adultery. Furthermore, tweets contained misinformation and fake news stories about the effects of gay and lesbian parenting:

- *@WBCSaysRepent: Taking the Lord's name in vain means using God's name to promote vanity and sin. "The Lord led me to my dyke lover."*[14]
- *Dyke's moaning while getting a strap sucked on = mental illness*
- *Would you trust this creepy Leftie dyke near your children? #Auspol*[15]
- *DEGENERATE DYKE COUPLE FORCE SON INTO FAGGOTRY*

Finally, "dyke" was frequently used as an insult in the context of *threats* of violence and expressions of conflict (142 tweets). The suggestion was that if "dykes" want to act like men, they should be prepared to fight men. Note also the common use of the slur "bitch" (Chapter 6) to intensify conflict and aggression:

- *@MamaDebbie Fuck off you fucking dyke*
- *It be them dyke bitches that think they can't get they ass beat by 4 5 niggas* 😁😁😄
- *dyke bitches get beat up too*
- *@Lee_Chante hey you dyke daddy issues lookin ass bitch ... You doneeeeee*

No Facebook groups or pages containing "dyke" in their titles used it as a slur. Discussed in more detail later, all uses were celebrations of lesbianism in different ways. The same was true for Instagram. The hashtag #dyke had over 680,000 posts. An examination of the top and most recent posts showed that people were tagging themselves in photos, showing the hashtag was not used to regulate appearance or behavior through shaming but rather as a positive reclamation, to be discussed further.

Extension (83 Tweets)

The second major category of "dyke" tweets included using it in ways that extended its meaning beyond the regulation of women's behaviors and appearance. This category includes the use of "dyke" to refer to men and one example of using "dyke" as a replacement for "woman" or "girlfriend." While these usages have the potential to disrupt the meaning of "dyke" by removing some of its derogation and changing its definition, they also have the potential to reinforce the idea that men must conform to heterogender norms.

As with "slut" and "whore," "dyke" was also used to *insult men* who were not performing masculinity effectively (82 tweets). Some of the reasons for nonconformity encompassed physical body (including size of genitals), hair, clothing, and toughness. The findings here are consistent with the use of "fag" in Pascoe's (2012) ethnographic research. Note the high use of "nigga." The most mentioned celebrity in this category was Yung Joc who caused a strong reaction on Twitter due to a permed hairstyle, which may account for the higher portion of tweets directed toward men than occurred with "slut" and "whore." In addition, the term "dyke" was used to regulate gender performance more than sexuality.

- *When you a dyke but yo momma make you go to prom as a girl*[16]
- *@YoungIAm* 😭😭 *u look like more of a dyke then I do*
- *Girls out here going for guys that dress like a dyke on Easter #FOH*[17]
- *Pussy ass nigga shoulda been a dyke man*
- *Because if you're a grown ass man with a small dick, you're a dyke anyways* 😂😂😂[18]

Only one example of "dyke" emerged from the data as a counterpart for "wife" or "girlfriend" (1 tweet). A counterpart for girlfriend or woman was one of the more common themes for "bitch" (Chapter 6), a slur also included in this tweet:

- *I wanna ask my dyke bitch but she b crankin it up on me*

"Dyke" was not used in alternate ways on Facebook or Instagram. All groups, pages, and hashtags are included in the next section on dissent.

Dissent (326 Tweets)

Though "dykes" fail to support heterofemininity, this term has been more successfully reclaimed on social media by members of the lesbian community than "slut" and "whore." Alison Bechdel's (2016) comic *Dykes to Watch Out For* has been a "countercultural institution among lesbians and discerning non-lesbians all over the planet" since 1983. "Dyke marches" for instance are held in cities around the world to resist oppression, express dissent, and build community through occupying public spaces (Currans, 2012). The choice of "dyke" over "lesbian" signals confrontational politics through the reclamation of a term used to denigrate women who do not conform to heterofeminine norms. Although some uses of the label, online and off-line, continue to contain pejorative power, many more tweets were declarations of positive self-identification. Positive self-identification is often referred to in the literature as reappropriation or reclamation. "Dyke" was also used in a celebratory way, an expression of affection, direct critiques of compulsory heterosexuality and gender norms, and awareness-raising through education. Only one example of publicizing collective action appeared.

Evidence emerged of women *rejecting the label* (28 tweets). One Twitter user expressed humor at being called a "dyke," adding "lol" (laugh out loud). Several tweets commented on clothing, an aspect of femininity heavily regulated by the slur "dyke." Women convinced others of their heterosexuality by claiming experience and success with men. Roughly a third of the tweets involved someone defending someone else against charges of being a "dyke." These tweets made it clear that "dyke" still carries offense, threatening women who do not conform to heterofeminine norms.

- *Im NOT A DYKE. Im NOT A DYKE. Im NOT A DYKE. Im a woman & I don't have to explain SHIT to ANYONE about why I dress the way I do*
- *lol im not a dyke* 💀💀💀 *i know how to switch up dudes*
- *y'all thought I was a dyke in the 8th grade but I'm currently out here stealing ya man so where my apology @?!!!*
- *@TOPDOGGG honeyislux isn't a dyke btw*

In contrast to uses that disparage lesbians or lesbianism, the following tweets can be characterized as *celebratory* (81 tweets). When gender identity was available, slightly more than half of tweets came from those identifying as women or nonbinary/queer (44 out of 81 tweets). Celebration for "dykes" also came from men as it did for "slut" and "whore." While holding disruptive potential, celebratory tweets may reinforce traditional notions of beauty and men's sexual prowess (as in they can "turn" a dyke). Celebratory tweets may also reinforce the idea that lesbians are acceptable if they are considered attractive and exist for men's pleasure. Men's celebration of "dykes" also suggests that all women are available as potential sex partners. Additionally, these tweets contain black slang and slang for women's genitals ("pussy").

- *I dont care if she a lesbian, she'll get this pipe, yes! I'm dutch so it's only right i can make a dyke wet* 😏🍆
- *My nigga said he got head from dyke, she sucked the life force out of him...he hasn't been outside in days* 😂
- *I'll do anything for a blonde dyke*[19]
- *Like a thief in the night I take anything but some pussy.She got that head like a dyke,she got that head that I like*[20]

The most common form of dissent was *positive self-identification* or *reclamation* (115 tweets). Extending Brontsema's (2004) analysis of "queer," "dyke" may be embraced to "mark distance from the alleged exclusionary and assimilationist *gay* and *lesbian*" (p. 4, emphasis in original). In other words, "dyke" became a symbol of pride in the difference between lesbians and heterosexuals. These examples of dissent can be considered forms of reappropriation, removing the derogation and reclaiming "dyke" as a positive identity. Most were simple tweets as in, "*I am a dyke,*" while others claimed authenticity or identified other lifestyles. The first tweet was heavily retweeted:

- *Be all the dyke you can be. Namaste*
- *I don't really give a fuck Ima dyke*
- *NOT HALF! A WHOLE DYKE*
- *when the dyke in you thinks you have a dick*
- *Goth dyke for daaayyyyyssss*
- *Please, I just didn't win the Oscar because there is no the category "best dyke."*[21]

Like "slut" and "whore," "dyke" was used on Twitter in a *friendly* way (31 tweets). Friends referred to each other affectionately, evidenced by phrasing and emoji, such as the heart and face throwing a kiss. Like reappropriation, using "dyke" in a friendly way removes the negative content:

- *@carol_bennet you're a dyke* 👤💜
- *@tarynskala love you ya dyke* 💜
- *@respkp happy birthday friend your my favorite dyke*
- *eva fav dyke* 😬 *@aweawedee*

Direct critiques of "dyke" came from two different perspectives (40 tweets). One perspective objected to the use of the word, considering it offensive and homophobic. Note again references to feminine appearance and attractiveness to men. The other perspective did not consider the term "dyke" offensive and thus disagreed with objections to its use. During the data collection period, Twitter heavily weighed in on a debate over slurs after a comedy troupe called a Scottish Member of Parliament "dykey-D" at a rally. This use of "dyke" was defended by a politician, who struck back at the BBC for having previously used the term "jock," which is considered by some a pejorative for people of Scottish descent. The debate was not over the offensiveness of the terms, but whether terms should be banned. In Chapter 7, I will address censorship further. Note the recognition that context matters in the following direct critiques. For example, slurs were considered more acceptable when uttered by members of the in-group:

- *2016 and people use the word 'dyke' to insult someone* 🙄
- *The slurs "faggot", "dyke" "tranny" and "queer" have to stop. It's offensive and it's gross*
- *@anhbraz you just referred to a lesbian as a dyke while trying to defend her from a rapper using homophobic terms, idiot*
- *hair is so unimportant and the fact that people are saying I look like a "dyke" or a "little boy" is disgusting and ridiculous.*
- *I love when a woman who doesn't appeal to men instantly becomes a dyke/lesbian*

- *ya'll other lesbians can keep that word "dyke" .. don't call me that shit. i take it as disrespect*
- *lesbians be using tf outta the word "dyke" but wanna get offended & upset as soon as a straight mf[22] call em one* 🫢
- *When i used to get called fat, gay and Scottish at school i had no idea i could whip up so much outrage as we've seen over #dyke and #jock*

People also used Twitter for *education,* primarily to raise awareness of issues affecting the lesbian community (30 tweets). Tweets served to educate the community about slurs and labels, such as the differences between "studs," "bull dykes," and "baby dykes." Some tweets about the "dyke" and "jock" debate are included here, particularly if they linked to sites discussing the issue. In addition, social media users posted information about news outlets and cultural events. A few also challenged attitudes within the lesbian community:

- *Lesbians, please know the difference between Stud and Dyke.*
- *FRIDAY, welcome back The @shayshay Show! Join us for educational queer realness ft Lick Von Dyke, Polly Amorous...[23]*
- *@OurDailyQueer: https://t.co/NYOH0GRnAY || Queer HIV+ Rapper Mykki Blanco Wants "Dyke for President, Fag for VP"*
- *Woman identified: I've gotten mad off topic, but we gotta get better as a dyke community about reaching down and teaching up. Now you can still get roasted...*
- *Carol Monaghan - Jock is a racist slur The SNP ladies and gents*
- *Cuz you're a dumbass if you're a dyke and make fun of another dyke for wearing a fuckin skirt. You're literally doing what straight ppl do*

There was only one example of *organizing* around "dyke" in the Twitter sample even though "dyke" was more reclaimed than "slut" and "whore" (1 tweet). We will see Facebook groups and pages and Instagram hashtags dedicated to building community and organizing events. Note the reference to race, as Slut Walks and other events around sexuality have been criticized for focusing on white middle class issues and white women receiving the most media coverage:

• *So this Saturday, Chicago's Dyke March celebrates 20 years —
lots of people not recognised by standard (white) left will
be there*

Forty-five Facebook pages and groups including "dyke" in their
name celebrated lesbianism in different ways, including creating
communities around common interests and publicizing activities and
collective political action. As with searches for "ho" and "hoe," some
groups referred to other uses of the term—for example, Dyker Heights
in Brooklyn, New York. Consequently, it was important to look for
mentions of sexuality in the group description, which all 45 groups
here did. Most were closed groups, but profile pictures were visible.
The most common pages and groups were "Dykes on Bikes," "Dyke
Marches" from various cities and years, and groups for dykes from
different cities and countries. There were also groups for "Dykes
with Dogs" and dykes who identify as butch, femme, senior, and
trans. One page, "What Dykes Look Like," attempted to dispel myths
by including pictures of feminine women, but in doing so, reinforced
heteronormative ideals of feminine beauty. A quarterly called *Dyke*
and a public art group called Dyke Action Machine (DAM) had
Facebook pages. Groups and pages on Facebook show the reclamation of "dyke" and the greater acceptance of slurs when included in
artistic or academic commentary.

Eighteen Instagram hashtags included "dyke" in over 1,000
posts,[24] and almost all could be considered positive self-identification
(reappropriation). These posts consisted of selfies and people tagging themselves and friends with hashtags such as #dyke, #dykes,
#dykesofinstagram (the three with the most posts, #dyke has over
680,000), #dykeswag, #dykelife, #dykelyfe, #dykeofinstagram, and
#dykesofinsta. These forums were for pride, not shaming. User pro-
files contained identities such as lesbian, tomboy, butch, femme, boi,
and queer. While most pictures were selfies, photos also included
statements such as "*dykes rule*" and depicted women kissing. The
hashtag #dykesbelike contained humorous photos, including a picture of a military buzz cut with the caption "*when a blond dyke get
a hair cut.*" The rest included photos of women who, while eschewing long hair and feminine clothing, continue to conform to heteronormative ideals of notions of beauty in terms of body types and
facial features. Some hashtags such as #dykestyle showed more
diversity regarding body types, race-ethnicity, and age. For instance,

#dykehair featured selfies with hair in current fashion, including shaved sides, pompadours, and bright shades of blue. The hashtag #dykefashion featured women in bowties and vests as well as athletes in active wear.

Other hashtags such as #dykesonbikes, #dykesonspikes, and #dykeball (the latter two referring to softball) created community based on common interests. Two publicized collective organizing: #dykemarch and #dykepride. Both featured pictures from various dyke marches around the world. The hashtag #dykepride included photos, some selfies, from pride marches around the world; #dykesoverdudes suggested celebration and pride as well, but was dominated by one user as were some of the other hashtags with fewer than 2,000 posts (#dykeofinstagram, #dykelyfe, #dykefashion, and #dykehair). Related hashtags (hashtags that appear alongside the hashtags identified here) include #butch, #gaygirl, #lesbianpride, #lesbiansofinstagram, and #lesbianlife.

External Events

Aside from cultural references unrelated to sexuality, such as Dick Van Dyke and the Black Dyke Band, Hillary Clinton received by far the most individual mentions among public figures (5). As we neared the 2016 US presidential election, searches on days with spikes in use of "dyke" were due to increased mentions of Hillary Clinton, most relating to her appearance and accusations of greed. Examples include: "*@HillaryClinton @realDonaldTrump Dear dyke that tweets for Hill the Cunt, why do you make up lies and/or ignore her DEPLORABLE past*"; "*@chriscquinn @cher @HillaryClinton two disgusting fat dyke fags. You ate shit on CNN....honey. Owned by the basic blonde bitch. You Fat pig*"; and "*So Glenn Beck thinks Trump is pure evil but has no problem cozying up to a Marxist dyke.*" Searches also revealed mentions of rapper Yung Joc (see the earlier discussion of reactions on Twitter to his hair).

Intersections

Hegemonic femininity and masculinity assume whiteness and economic affluence. There were more uses of black slang such as "nigga" in relation to "dyke" than for "whore" and "slut," though less so than for "hoe" and "THOT." "Dyke" may be more reclaimed in the African American community. Examples included *"Pussy ass nigga shoulda been a dyke man"* and *"Nigga Kayla said I need a dyke that look like young ma* 😎😎😎*."* Even when the sentiment may have been negative, "nigga" seemed to be used in the appropriated rather than racist form: *"nigga said 'step dyke'* 💀💀*."* When racial identity was made available, most uses of "nigga" were by Twitter users who identified as black or African American, though the debate continues over whether words can be appropriated even by members of the in-group (Anderson & Lepore, 2013). When used to describe men, it was clear "dyke" was used in a similar way to "fag" (Pascoe, 2012). However, only a few cases of "fag" or "faggot" were found, such as the tweet included under generic insults *"Faggot dyke bitch."* Incidentally, this person's account was suspended as of January 1, 2017. One example referring to Islam included the following: *"@DanielleBarbets Now go tell your dyke friends about how the Hijab is actually liberating."* Intersections between gender, sexuality, class, and race-ethnicity will be explored further in Chapter 7.

Conclusion

Like the other slurs studied here, "dyke" is used in a variety of ways on the social media platforms Facebook, Instagram, and Twitter. Though the exact origin of "dyke" is debated, it carries a negative connotation referring to lesbianism, particularly to identify those who did not conform to feminine norms. LGBTQIA youth have faced high rates of bullying and harassment in high school and college (Payne, 2010; Thurlow, 2001). Climates of homophobia negatively influence educational and mental health outcomes (Centers for Disease Control, 2014; Collier et al., 2013; Sinclair et al., 2012) and deprive the LGBTQIA community of basic human rights and dignity. While this research has not examined other homophobic slurs such as "fag" and "gay," it is evident that a movement to reclaim "dyke" is well underway on social media. Although Twitter exerted regulatory uses particularly around gender expression for women and men, members of in-groups used the word "dyke" about themselves with pride or in affectionate reference to someone else. All Facebook groups and pages and Instagram hashtags exhibited celebration and positive self-identification.

The low use of "dyke" as a generic slur is likely due to its recla-mation, given that this term does not carry the same derogatory power that "fag" or "bitch" possesses. However, this sample contained many instances of people named as "dykes" on Twitter. Though it is unclear if all are in the service of regulating gender and sexuality, public nam-ing on Twitter can have disastrous consequences, putting individuals at risk of rejection at home or harassment at school. Furthermore, given the lack of legal protections regarding workplace discrimination for the LGBTQIA community, naming someone a "dyke" on Twitter could affect the individual's economic livelihood.

Violating heterogender norms puts one at risk for labeling as a "dyke" on Twitter. Violations of heterofemininity include being sex-ually unavailable (a new theme not found in analysis of "sluts" and "whores," who were criticized for being too sexually available), excelling at male-dominated activities such as sports and politics, and appearing unattractive in the eyes of the heterosexual male. Con-sistent with data from Messerschmidt's (2011) interviews, adolescent girls and boys regulated women's appearance and demeanor. Details within tweets revealed that short hair, baggy clothing, and taller, heavier, or athletic body types failed to meet heterosexual male stan-dards of beauty. Rejection of the label "dyke" also showed a belief that women who appear "masculine" must be lesbians.

A disturbingly large portion of threatening tweets used "dyke." Again, numbers should be interpreted with caution due to the limited sample size, but it appears that women who identify as "dykes" are expected to physically fight men, almost as if they must because they dare to appear masculine. This idea is consistent with Lucal's (1999) realization that being perceived as a man in public meant she had to be ready to defend herself from physical aggression from men who felt challenged. Charges of immoral or sinful behavior was another new theme emerging from Twitter data on "dyke." Homophobia is not just a personal attitude held by some people, but has also been bolstered by structures and institutions such as law and religion and can be seen in contemporary debates about discrimination and "gay conversion therapy." Fewer themes represented extensions of the word "dyke" compared to other slurs studied here: as an insult to men and as a replacement for "woman" or "girlfriend." Using "dyke" to insult men enforces men's conformity to hegemonic masculinity through appearance and behavior, reinforcing essentialist and binary views of gender and compulsory heterosexuality.

Among the dissenting uses, rejecting the label "dyke" allows for agency on Twitter, but reinforces the derogation. Celebrating "dykes" has disruptive power because celebration refuses to accept the derogatory content. Holding the greatest potential for disruption of gender and sexual norms is the high rate of positive self-identification, evidence that "dyke" is being reclaimed on Twitter. Furthermore, all the Facebook groups and pages and Instagram hashtags that were analyzed provided examples of positive self-identification and celebration. Rather than people tagging other people's photos with "dyke" as an insult, data revealed people using the word about themselves in an active and positive way. Further evidence of dissent from the original negative meaning is how "dyke" was also used in friendly and educational contexts. These uses do not mean that all women who identify as lesbians approve of the label "dyke"; some still find the word offensive and do not want it reclaimed. These data do not allow for further investigation into why someone might reclaim or reject the label, though, like "queer," it may be partially generational and reflect the diversity within identity groups. Generally, uses of "slut" and "whore" on Facebook, Instagram, and Twitter were more about sexual activity, while "dyke" showed a greater emphasis on gender performance, though all show intersections between gender and sexuality.

During the data collection period, several external events increased the use of "dyke" on Twitter, including the previously mentioned debate in Scotland regarding the use of "dyke" and "jock," the nomination of Hillary Clinton as the Democratic presidential nominee, and photos of a male rapper Yung Joc wearing a hairstyle deemed nonmasculine by the Twitterverse. These examples show that gender norms and gendered language are still arenas of disagreement and potential change. The Scottish debate revealed a belief that concern over language comes from ultraliberal circles.

While gender norms may be relaxing, social change around gender and attitudes toward homosexuality are not evenly distributed across all sectors of society or parts of the world (Adamczyk, 2017). Change often comes up against resistance from people who want to return to traditional gender norms. Certainly, reappropriation of derogatory slurs helps to remove some of the negative content and increases agency among the members of the target group. The question remains as to whether reclamation forever eliminates the pejorative content, preventing the heterosexual and cisgender public from using it to express contempt, or whether the group wants the derogatory content to be removed, for it is this content that gives "dykes" distance from assimilated lesbians.

It is important to move beyond the realm of language when considering if the reclamation of "dyke" signals a growing acceptance in society and support for women who exhibit "masculine" traits such as assertiveness and athleticism. The unwillingness to accept so-called masculine traits in women results in barriers to positions of power in politics and business and even equality in the home. Currently, laws allow institutions to discriminate based on gender identity and sexual orientation, and institutions such as schools fail to provide safe environments for transgender youth. Can reclamation of language affect the high rates of violence and harassment affecting LGBTQIA populations? In Chapter 7, I discuss what needs to happen concerning language and social structures to create real transformative change around gender and sexuality. I also address debates around censorship and the use of black slang accompanying "dyke" on social media.

Notes

1. Encyclopedia.com (2017) defines *bulldagger* as a very masculine lesbian, used more commonly among African Americans during the 1920s.

2. As with all the slurs, analysis is limited by common spellings of words. The more accepted spelling is "dyke," and analysis of "dike" for three days during this period did not yield any new themes.

3. Though I am using *homophobia* to remain consistent with the literature, I prefer *homonegativity* because "phobic" suggests fear whereas most people who oppose homosexuality hold negative and hateful views. Additionally, *homohysteria* considers micro and macro level processes relating homophobia to gendered behavior (Worthen, 2014, pp. 141–142).

4. The fact that Collier et al. (2013) did not find independent effects of gender and same-sex attraction on psychological distress after controlling for homophobic name-calling and other negative treatment by peers does not necessarily mean hypotheses regarding same-sex attraction and gender must be abandoned as same-sex attraction and gender may be the mechanisms through which distress occurs.

5. When "queer" first became associated with sexuality, it referred only to the least stigmatized within the gay community—masculine middle-class men (Chauncey, 1994).

6. Numbers should be interpreted with caution since qualitative analysis of the uses of "queer" was not conducted, and I have no way of determining

if uses related to gender and sexuality. Furthermore, external events could have affected frequency during this two-week period.

7. Further investigation could examine whether the content of pornographic advertisements containing "dyke" privilege the male gaze.

8. This tweet linked to a picture, but the account had been suspended so I was unable to see who or what was referenced.

9. This tweet was in response to the question, "*What if young ma stops being a dike*," referring to rapper Young M.A.

10. This tweet linked to an article about Lena Dunham wanting to ban words in the election, accompanied by comments criticizing liberals for sensitivity and censorship.

11. This tweet was posted by a user who identifies as a "boi," a young biological female who presents in a boyish way.

12. Variation on lyrics to a Rick Ross song.

13. "Salty" in this context meant "irritated, unhappy, or upset." "Curved" is slang for rejection.

14. This tweet originated from the Westboro Baptist Church's twitter account.

15. "Auspol" is short for "Australian politics."

16. Heavily retweeted photograph of rapper Yung Joc. Note the gender play in using a picture of a person who identifies as male to reference "dykes" trying to appear feminine.

17. This tweet was accompanied by a picture of men in jackets, bowties, and colorful Bermuda shorts; "FOH" means "fuck outta here" as in "get out of here," when something is hard to believe or intolerable.

18. This was tweeted by a person who identified as a gay male.

19. Heavily retweeted song lyric by Kanye West.

20. Heavily retweeted song lyric by Young Thug.

21. This heavily retweeted tweet was attributed to the actor Sarah Paulson's Twitter account.

22. TF means "the fuck." MF means "motherfucker."

23. "Lick Von Dyke" was chosen as a stage name because of its double use as a name and sexuality, playing on Dick Van Dyke and "lick" and "dyke." "Ft" means "featuring."

24. As of December 14, 2016, the search for "dyke" under Instagram hashtags yielded 35, though some were unrelated to sexuality, as in the New York neighborhood #dykerheights.

5

BITCH:
Controlling Gender
Performances

In this chapter, I examine the online use of the first of two misogynist slurs that serve primarily to silence and discredit women. Like the previous slurs discussed, "bitch" has sexual origins. The origins of *bitch* is the Old English word *bicce* for female dog, which *Online Etymology Dictionary* (2017) traces to the Old Norse *bikkjuna* for female of the dog as well as other animals, including the fox and wolf. During the early Middle Ages, Caputi (2004) argues, *bitch* served to suppress the worship of femininity in the form of Greek/Roman goddess Artemis-Diana, who was often in the company of dogs or appeared as an animal. The phrase *son of a bitch* was used by Christians to denigrate men who followed the goddess. Perhaps reflecting a growing need to control women, Hughes (2006) finds that *bitch* became a derogatory word for women during the fifteenth century, referring to women's sexual depravity and promiscuity, similar to female dogs who enter heat and have large litters of puppies. By the eighteenth century, *bitch* was solidified as an insult directed toward women.

Today, "bitch" (and "cunt") have less to do with sexual shaming. Instead, these words are used to demean women who fail to adhere to feminine norms of agreeableness and accommodation. "Bitch" describes a woman who is insensitive or has done something someone resents (Kleinman, Ezzell, & Frost, 2009). Similarly, Ashwell

(2016) argues that the word *bitch* suggests a woman who "is disposed to be more boisterous, more assertive, more self-concerned, and so on *than is appropriate for a woman/than a woman ought to be*" (p. 235, emphasis in original). These definitions point out that "bitch" refers specifically to women. Traits that are considered appropriate for women include warmth, kindness, and sensitivity to others (Ridgeway, 2001). The "bitch," however, displays coldness, meanness, and a lack of concern for others' feelings.

Slurs such as "bitch" can be understood sociologically as rooted in a patriarchal society that subordinates women and girls, expecting them to behave in pleasing and deferential ways, consistent with white, middle-class, heterosexual norms. These norms reflect the idea that women should be seen and not heard, particularly in male-dominated spaces. Women have been long excluded from public discourse through attempts to dehumanize and discredit them (Beard, 2014; Spender, 1991). Women who display traits defined by society as masculine are not only considered unlikable, they are evaluated differently in institutions because of proscriptive views of how women should behave (Heilman, 2001). Research finds that many people do not want to work with women who display assertive or authoritative styles, even if they view them as skilled and competent (Bowles, Babcock, & Lai, 2007; Eagly, Makhijani, & Klonsky, 1992; Gregory, 2016; Rudman & Glick, 2001).

"Bitch" entered the mainstream in the late 1990s and early 2000s, appearing frequently in popular culture including music, clothing, and visual media. Although gender norms are deeply entrenched, the sociological view of language recognizes the importance of context: who is speaking and how. Rap music has received the most attention by censors and the media, but the word "bitch" is included in songs by a range of musical artists such as the Rolling Stones and Elton John (Schneider, 2011). Other examples include Meredith Brooks's "Bitch," Ludacris's "Move Bitch," Metallica's "Ain't My Bitch," N.W.A.'s "A Bitch Iz a Bitch," and the Prodigy's "Smack My Bitch Up."

Since the 1960s, feminists have celebrated independence and assertiveness, reclaiming the slur "bitch." Jo Freeman (1968) wrote the following in "The BITCH Manifesto": "Bitches refuse to serve, honor, or obey anyone. They demand to be fully functioning human beings, not just shadows. They want to be both female and human" (para. 12) and "We must be strong, we must be militant, we must be dangerous. We must realize that Bitch is Beautiful and that we have nothing to lose" (para. 31). In *Bitch: In Praise of Difficult Women* (1998), Elizabeth Wurtzel argued her "bitch philosophy" meant doing and being whom she wants to be and answering to no one. Meredith Brooks's song "Bitch" states, "I'm a little bit of everything/All rolled into one," including a "bitch," "lover," "child," "mother," "sinner," and "saint." Rapper Lil' Kim called herself "Queen Bitch." In "Bitch I'm Madonna," entertainer Madonna positively reclaims "bitch" in the lyric "cause I'm a bad bitch," and "bitch" serves as an intensifier in the title. Intensifiers add emphasis or force to statements. Similarly, Britney Spears opens her song "Gimme More" with "bitch" as an intensifier: "It's Britney Bitch; I see you, and I just wanna dance with you."

At the same time that women were reclaiming "bitch" to mean a powerful woman, "bitch" continued to be used in other ways, including a noun for something bad ("that test was a bitch"), an adjective for something good (the 1980s-born term "bitchin'"), and a verb for complaining ("stop bitching"). "Bitch" appeared on network and cable television shows such as *Entourage* and *The Office*. Kleinman, Ezzell, and Frost (2009) point out that "bitch" is not defined as obscene, indecent, or profane by the Federal Communications Commission (FCC). You can watch compilations of the character Jesse Pinkman from *Breaking Bad* saying "bitch" on YouTube, showing "bitch" used in a multitude of ways. "Bitch" was used as a counterpart[1] for "woman" or "girlfriend" in songs such as Kanye West's "Perfect Bitch" and Lil Wayne, Drake, and Future's "Love Me." Rapper Jay Z uses "bitch" in a variety of ways, ranging from the traditional use in "Bitches and Sisters" to a counterpart for girlfriend in "That's My Bitch" with Kanye West to supposedly writing a poem after the birth of his daughter in which he vows not to use the word.[2]

The wide use of "bitch" in literature, music, and visual media raises the question of whether it is losing its derogatory power. Analysis of Twitter reveals many of the same uses seen off-line. Often content on Twitter, Facebook, and Instagram expressed hostility and criticized women for being mean, distrustful, dominant, and unworthy. On Twitter, Hillary Clinton was called a "bitch" more than any other public figure after her nomination as the Democratic presidential nominee in the 2016 US presidential election. Melania Trump was called a "bitch" 443 times during and within six hours after her speech at the 2016 US Republican National Convention (Steinblatt & Markovitz, 2016). Using "bitch" to demean women in the public spotlight suggests that despite its reclamation, "bitch" is still intricately tied with patriarchal power structures and misogynist cultural views. However, the meaning of "bitch" was also expanded to serve as an intensifier, a replacement for women, and a derogatory term for men, although labeling men "bitches" reinforces heteromasculine norms by insulting men by comparing them to women. I also found examples of dissent where "bitch" was reclaimed as a positive identity and a term of endearment.

Findings

The keyword "bitch" was tracked on Twitter during two separate periods in 2016.[3] The first period lasted two weeks, from January 8, 2016, to January 22, 2016. During this time, "bitch" was used an average of 489,080 times a day. The keyword "bitch" was tracked for another three and a half month period from August 16, 2016, to December 1, 2016, for a total of 44,212,922 times, with an average of 417,773 times a day. The total average for all days collected in 2016 is 418,665, with a low of 130,650 and a high of 938,060 (see Figure 5.1). These statistics makes "bitch" the most commonly used misogynist slur studied in this book. While the period in January had a higher average use than August to December, Figure 5.1 shows a relatively stable use of "bitch" over time, with a significant increase on November 9, 2016, reflecting the US presidential election.[4] Only one tweet in my sample used "bitch" to refer exclusively to a female dog. The rest of the sample fell within three general uses: regulation, extension, and dissent (see Appendix B for coding schemes and counts).

The total tweets analyzed for content were 1,150. Of these tweets, 56 were unclear and could not be coded validly or reliably, and another 54 advertised pornographic websites, leaving a total of 1,040 tweets. The low rate of pornography is likely due to the image of a "bitch" as unaccommodating. However, including a "bitch" hashtag to advertise pornographic sites worked for scenarios involving dominant women, as evidenced by the higher rate of BDSM pornographic content.

Figure 5.1   Keyword Mentions: "Bitch" (Twitter)

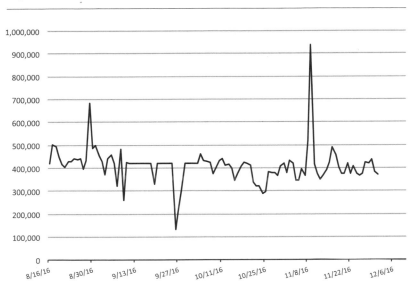

Regulation (442 Tweets)

A range of themes was associated with regulatory uses of "bitch," relating to appearance, domineering and unpleasant attitudes, promiscuous and untrustworthy behaviors, and general unworthiness. The primary use of "bitch" is interpreted as a warning to women who deviate from norms of sensitivity and agreeableness. Women were simply labeled "bitches" or other information was supplied, such as calling women "bitches" for such things as not getting along with a man, talking to another woman's boyfriend, and making negative comments online.

Tweets were included in the *naming* theme if women were labeled "bitches" but no other information was given (49 tweets). By examining other text, emoji, and entire conversations on Twitter, it was clear the intent was to denigrate rather than compliment. By including a name or a tag, the person was labeled as a woman who failed to perform femininity correctly. Again, we see the "we-all-know-a" meme and references to public figures such as Hillary Clinton, who received, by far, the most "bitch" labels:

- *@Heather_nope She a bitch*
- *@louisa_marcalla: This what you get BITCH* 😒
- *@WeAllKnowA: We all know a bitch called Briana*
- *Hillary Clinton lied like a female dog aka a bitch*

Tweets fell into the *generic slur* theme in which no person was named, but the content was clearly meant to regulate traditional feminine behavior (57 tweets).[5] Examples included:

- *why are u such a little freaking bitch*
- *I lost a bunch of followers the same hour I posted this lol bye bitch*
- *Like bitch needs to GO*
- *I can't stand a bitch that truly act like a bitch*

The label "bitch" had less to do with *appearance* than the previous slurs examined (11 tweets). Again, most tweets mentioned attractiveness and weight. Most often, the intent seemed to be to insult and silence the woman:

- *Beer belly having ass bitch* 🐷
- *Bitch this conversation is over, no one invited your ugly ass, leave my mentions.*
- *@DudleyS stop you fat bitch i was in a good mood*

Women were frequently called "bitches" for being *untrustworthy* (117 tweets). Most tweets referred to women as "fake" and "phony." "Bitch" may have been used just to add sting to the insult, though part of hegemonic femininity is displaying honesty and loyalty, as noted further down when a woman's smile is perceived as insincere. In these cases, the content was not about sexual faithfulness, as with "slut" and "whore," but more generally about untrustworthiness. The theme of untrustworthiness can be linked back to early myths of women, such as Eve and Pandora, as the source of all evil.[6] The first four of these tweets were heavily retweeted:

- *SHE'S NOT REAL BITCH*[7]
- *Hilary: Trump is trying to hide something with his tax returns Bitch how about them 30,000+ emails you're hiding. Bye*
- *we have to stop calling women bitches. not because they aren't, but because "bitch" means female dog and dogs are loyal*
- *I only trust a bitch as far as I can throw her*
- *NON SO SE CREDERE CHE ELLA UNA FAKE ASS BITCH COSI SPUDORATAMENTE DICENDO COSE SU DI ME*[8]

Within the *untrustworthy* theme, a portion (29 tweets) referred specifically to infidelity. Though "bitch" may be used as a replacement for woman, these tweets cannot be considered neutral counterparts. The tweets suggest that women are expected to be considerate of former partners' feelings even when they are no longer in the romantic relationship. As with previous slurs, women were referred to as the "other woman" and blamed for men's infidelity and breaking up relationships, showing a connection to the previous theme in which women are considered inherently devious and untrustworthy and reinforcing essentialist notions that men are naturally nonmonogamous.

- *A girl KNOWS when a bitch likes her boyfriend ????*
- *Nobody Likes A Home Wrecking Ass Bitch. Stay In Your Lane* 👍
- *I don't even think any female could get my boyfriend's attention but that doesn't mean a bitch won't try*
- *he loves me bitch, he ain't gonna ever stop loving me bitch*

Two new themes regarding behavior emerged for the misogynist slur "bitch." The common understanding of a "bitch" is an *unpleasant* woman, referring to behavior that is disagreeable and displeasing (62 tweets). Many of the tweets in this category referenced women's bad moods, suggesting women must always behave in an agreeable manner. Words used to describe women in this category included terms such as *demanding, hateful, heartless, nasty, rude, unhappy,* and *venomous*. Women were accused of making insincere faces and pretending to be sweet. This theme gets to the heart of the misogynist view of women as inherently unlikable.

- *ur just a rude bitch*
- *i hate it when people take advantage of your niceness like fuck you bitch*
- *dgaf[9] if you're havin a horrible day, week, life ....if I'm not the cause of it don't toss me your attitude bitch*
- *"I'm always in a bad mood." "No, you're always just a bitch."*
- *This reporter who yelled "thanks a lot bitch" is already the star of tonight's debate[10]*

The second new theme that emerged referred to "bitches" as overly *domineering* (21 tweets). Gender identity was available for all the tweeters and recipients, revealing that every tweet in this theme was tweeted by a man about a woman. Women are expected to be available to men and display deference and submission in relationships. A heavily retweeted post explained the difference between a "bitch" and a "slut:" a "slut" submits to men while a "bitch" does not:

- *There's a difference between a slut and a bitch... A slut will sleep with anyone. A bitch will sleep with anyone... But you*
- *This bitch hung up on me*
- *I'm Fenna[11] Get My Act Together Because It's Embarrassing When You Can't Control Yo Bitch*

Other types of behavior defying traditional feminine norms, including acting in ways considered trashy or crazy (13 tweets), were included under the theme *demeanor*. Women are expected to be modest, clean, and in control of their emotions. Accusations of emotionality are effective insults, as traits associated with women are devalued relative to traits associated with men, such as rationality. A general belief, shown in the third tweet, posits that a woman's sexual desirability is positively correlated with supposed craziness:

- *@realbelle bitch you stink*
- *Emotional bitch!*
- *Good pussy does come with a crazy bitch attached to it lol*

Like other misogynist slurs, "bitch" was used to deem women *unworthy* (46 tweets). Misogynist slurs like "bitch" attempt to maintain a hierarchy in which women are devalued relative to men, though other forms of inequality such as class, race, and sexual orientation intersect with gender.

- *F*ck you! I'm done with Yo ass bitch!!*
- *Run that lame shit on a lame bitch*
- *the bitch literally commented on every post blowing up my damn Twitter. Don't you see I couldn't care less*

Roughly half of the tweets relating to unworthiness were accompanied by insults to women's intelligence:

- *stupid bitch*
- *Have you ever wasted your time on a dumb bitch*
- *You little dumb ass bitch I ain't fucking with you*

To a lesser extent than the previous slurs ("dyke," "slut," and "whore"), "bitch" was used to shame women for *promiscuity* (14 tweets). Tweets referenced too many sexual partners and choosing partners indiscriminately. References to racial slurs and slang will be discussed in the section "Intersections."

- *Bitch STFU[12] guys only talk to you because you're easy*
- *U riding niggas dick like a bitch*
- *Stress bout a bitch tha''s for everybody ? That's some I won't do* 😒💯
- *lmao bitch you got me fucked up if u think I like you witcho 70% of every existing std havin ass take a nap smh[13]*

As emerged from analyses of the previous misogynist slurs, a portion of tweets containing "bitch" made *violent* threats or wished for injury and illness (52 tweets). Among tweets where gender was identified by the user, half of threatening tweets were made by men. The first tweet below made mention of knowing where the target lived and has since been deleted from Twitter. Even when the tweet did not name someone, it was often in response to a tweet that revealed the target's identity. While we hear about online threats of women in the public eye, threats against women occur daily on Twitter, though Twitter is attempting to delete and block abusers quickly.

- *bitch tf[14] u should delete this i know where u live*
- *Slap that bitch*
- *i cant stand when bitches act hollywood bitch ill smack da fuck outa u*
- *@HillaryClinton crooked Hillary* 😡 *you a bitch you pretty much a dog show some tricks or Donald J. Trump will bitchslap you to the floor* 😡

Since starting this project, the only Facebook group or page that included "bitch" in a regulatory way was the following page: "A slut will fuck anyone, a bitch will fuck anyone but you." At the time of writing, this Facebook page had been removed due to Facebook's stricter Community Standard policies around disagreeable or disturbing content or lack of interest from the page's administrators. Note the similarity to the heavily retweeted tweet, *"There's a difference between a slut and a bitch... A slut will sleep with anyone. A bitch will sleep with anyone... But you."* These posts reinforce the definition of a "slut" as someone who has more than the appropriate number of sexual partners. In contrast, "bitch" defines a woman as mean, uncooperative, and unyielding. This aspect of the slur "bitch" may in fact make it an appealing term for reclamation by feminists, which will be discussed later under the category *dissent*.

Among the top ten Instagram hashtags, only four suggested misogynist attitudes, while all contained a variety of photos and reasons for attaching the tag. The hashtag #bitch had over 4.3 million posts, and the top photos included comedic photos and photos of women and some men tagging themselves. Only one photo could be coded under the *unworthy* theme: a man giving the middle finger with the caption *"whatever bitch."* The hashtag #bitchesbelike contained over 2.6 million posts that were overwhelmingly humorous and about relationships from women's points of view. The hashtag #bitchbye (61,000 posts) again involved people tagging themselves, but were used to reject someone as unworthy, and #bitchesaintshit

(52,000 posts) also suggested unworthiness, but the tag was attached to a range of photos. These posts consisted of women calling other women "bitches," men humiliating exes, and women admonishing other women for using the word "bitch."

Extension (474 Tweets)

The slur "bitch" was often used on Twitter in ways that extended its meaning beyond assertive and self-concerned women. For decades, we have seen "bitch" become a neutral counterpart for woman or girlfriend as in the statement, "My bitch is coming over later." Whether this use is neutral will be debated further. Kleinman, Ezzell, and Frost (2009) argue that even though the music video for the Prodigy's "Smack My Bitch Up" had a surprise ending with a woman committing the violence and the band claims that their use of "bitch" was to add intensity, the song and lyrics glorify and capitalize on violence against women. "Bitch" was also used often on Twitter as an intensifier as in, "Bitch please"; as a place or a state of being as in, "Life is a bitch"; and as a verb for complaining as in, "Stop bitching; everything will be fine." In addition, results showed the use of the common insult for men, "son of a bitch," and the more recent phrase "resting bitch face." In one example, a man used the term "bitch" in a friendly way about another man, which is considered an extension of the traditional use: "*@atrpatel shit that was 'sweet' HAHAHAHA YOU BITCH 😭😭 I'm not drunk bro 😭 it's a stay home birthday 🍻 see you nigga 😭.*"

A major theme that emerged from Twitter was "bitch" serving as a *male insult* (188 tweets). Analysis of the text of tweets revealed men were called "bitches" when they acted in ways considered inconsistent with hegemonic masculinity, consistent with the use of "fag" in Pascoe's (2012) ethnographic research. This use carries the potential to remove the feminine connotation of "bitch," while, at the same time, creating a way to regulate masculinity. Only tweets directed toward people who identify as men were included here.[15] The references to gossiping, acting, and athleticism show the importance of the rejection of femininity and performances of strength for the presentation of masculinity (Kimmel, 2000; Messner, 1999).

- *When he's actin like a lil bitch*[16]
- *@chuck_allen wow what a bitch ass*

- *when he's 10 inches big and u scared but mama aint raise no bitch so u take it all*[17]
- *Never trust a Nigga that Gossip like a Bitch*
- *You cant be a professional athlete and be a whiny bitch. It doesnt work. You get paid millions to do what little kids do every day for fun*

"Bitch" was often used as a neutral and sometimes positive counterpart for *woman or girlfriend* (109 tweets). Consider the tweet, "*There are some fine bitches over there.*" It is clear the sentiment is positive, but the question remains why "bitch" was used instead of girlfriend. Kleinman, Ezzell, and Frost (2009) argue that "bitch" is considered a slur because it is not neutral, unlike the generic term "you guys."[18] Anderson and Lepore (2013) and Ashwell (2016) consider the example of the sentence, "A bitch ran for President in 2008," which could now be updated to 2016. "Bitch" can only be considered neutral if we can always substitute "bitch" with "a woman," resulting in the sentence, "A woman ran for President in 2008." However, this would imply all women are bitches, hence "bitch" is not a neutral counterpart to "woman." Note also the inclusion of the reclaimed black slang "nigga" as a counterpart for men or boyfriends.

- *they see me with my new bitch and start missing the good life*[19]
- *luv my goth bitch she call me up before bed time tell me spooky stories*
- *When u remember u ain't got no bitch so yo phone don't ring* 😩😥
- *I miss having a ride or die bitch*[20]
- *idk why bitches stress over niggas that ain't there's anymore like, stop he got a new bitch & he don't want yo ass no mo*

The slur "bitch" was commonly used as an *intensifier* (101 tweets). Like adding the word "really," "bitch" is a device that adds force or emphasis to the speaker's intent. For example, drug dealer character Jesse Pinkman from the television show *Breaking Bad* practices sounding forceful by repeating statements such as, "Where's my money bitch" or "Bitch, I said sorry!" The gender of the person hearing the phrase does not matter. The first tweet from a Britney Spears song was heavily retweeted:

- *It's Britney Bitch*
- *Just posted a photo @ South Beach, Miami (Bitch!)*
- *BACK TO 335 6 REPS BITCH*
- *SHE IS THE QUEEN OF THE QUEENS, PLEASE BITCH*[21]

Within this category, "bitch" was also used to intensify expressions of unhappiness or exasperation, as in the common phrase "Bitch, please."

- *i hate when ppl say "who hurt you" like BITCH EVERYBODY WHY*
- *Nothing I hate more than when I ask a customer how they're doing and they just start ordering. BITCH ANSWER MY DAMN QUESTION*
- *João Dória no rádio dizendo que começou a trabalhar com 14 anos. BITCH PLEASE*[22]

"Bitch" was also used as a noun for an *object or state of being* (48 tweets). Two-thirds of these tweets were negative, referring to something bad or unfair. Even when used as a noun (e.g., "That test was a bitch" or "I made that test my bitch"), the thing or event referred to is clearly difficult and meant to be dominated (Kleinman, Ezzell, & Frost, 2009). These heavily retweeted examples suggest at the very least that "bitch" stands for things that have the potential to dominate or cause distress:

- *Hope's a bitch*
- *Karma is such a bitch*
- *Payback is a bitch*
- *That hurt like a bitch*

A third of tweets used the slur "bitch" to refer to neutral or positive things or states of being, including Twitter itself:

- *Sit on this bitch all day subtweeting with yo broke ass*
- *Just put a down payment on this bitch*[23]
- *dear payday, hurry up bitch*
- *I'm higher than a bitch right now* 🌀🌀🌀🌀

"Bitch" also meant a verb for *complaining* (12 tweets). The association of "bitch" and "complain" likely comes from the association of "bitch" with women. Calling complaining "bitching" can cause even greater insult when used to describe men's complaining. It is perceived as a worse insult for men to be called names associated with women, as we will also see with "cunt" (Chapter 6).

- *If you vote I don't wanna hear you bitch*
- *My job thinks that they can make me work when I requested off a month ago and all and bitch me out???*
- *@cuddleee You want boring ass neighbors who bitch about street parking and unleashed pets? WE GOT EM*
- *Irony is when the ppl who are offended by Kaepernick's refusal to stand are the same ppl who bitch about the pussification of America*

Two colloquial phrases emerged from tweets containing "bitch" (16 tweets). Six tweets involved the phrase "son of a bitch," which has existed for centuries as an insult to men's mothers or lineage. However, it has become so commonplace that it can be used about oneself or just as an exclamation like "damn." While the increase in misogynist slurs around the 2016 US presidential election were overwhelmingly slurs against Hillary Clinton, there were also tweets directed toward Donald Trump:

- *When you know your body would be A1*[24] *if you just worked out but you're a lazy son of a bitch* :(
- *@realDonaldTrump you're a worthless son of a bitch!!!!!*

Ten tweets included the phrase "resting bitch face." This phrase refers to women who appear angry even when they do not intend to. The phrase has been around since the early 2000s but became popularized in 2013 (Barrett, 2013). The concept of a "resting bitch face" likely developed out of the belief that women should always appear cheerful. The first tweet became a heavily retweeted meme that often appeared captioning a picture of actor Vivian Leigh.

* *She is beauty and she's grace. She's got resting bitch face*
* *Resting bitch face no matter whattttttttttttt* 😊

Facebook pages and groups used "bitch" in alternative ways that extended the meaning. "Have A Bitchtastic Day You Fucking Whore" primarily featured celebrity gossip. Though the title contained "fucking whore," the inclusion of "bitchtastic" lessened the derogation by combining "bitch" and "fantastic." "Bitch Sesh" was the official fan page for the *Real Housewives* comedy podcast. "BITCH please" was simply an entertainment page. Another page—"Bitch, please"—was a page dedicated to "those moments where someone you're talking to thinks they know it all and the only thing on your mind is 'Bitch, please.'" Most posts to both pages were comedic and not gender-related. "Life Is A Bitch So Lets Rant" is a closed group for women 18 and older who want to rant and rave, but the group calls for no "bullying or nastiness please." "Bitch you can have my ex" included posts about love and romantic relationships. "I love my bitch" allowed users to "post anything [they] want." Dozens of more Facebook pages and groups used "bitch" in alternative ways. Facebook had fan pages for groups such as "Bitch Magnet," "Side Bitch," and "Bitch n' Dudes." These names may not challenge the traditional meaning of "bitch," but using a slur in a cultural context is considered more acceptable than using it to insult. Furthermore, as the word becomes mainstreamed, it may just add a slight edge to the names of groups and pages. No Instagram hashtags used "bitch" in ways that extend its meaning beyond the traditional understanding of a mean or insensitive woman.

Dissent (147 Tweets)

Despite the high usage rate of "bitch" on Twitter, not as many varying forms of dissent were found as for the other slurs. Women rejected the label, people celebrated "bitches," women positively identified as "bitches," and women used "bitch" in friendly ways among friends. Data did not include direct critiques of the use of "bitch" by defending a woman's strong demeanor as normal. The lack of direct critiques may be because "bitch" has already been normalized. Cultural institutions did not use "bitch" to educate on Twitter, although this theme was found on Facebook. No evidence emerged of feminist organization either online or off-line. Despite its incorporation into mainstream culture, some feminists consider "bitch" derogatory. More nuanced attention is paid to words that are more commonly used in evaluations of women in the workplace, such as "bossy," which Sandberg and Chávez (2014) call "the other B-word."

Like "slut" and "whore," the "bitch" can be thought of as possessing masculine characteristics (aggression, defiance, and independence). Consequently, women who embody these characteristics are labeled deviant ("bitches") to maintain the naturalness of these traits in the hegemonic male (Schippers, 2007). One question to consider is the following: What effect might dissent such as reclaiming the label have on essentialist views of gender? Kleinman, Ezzell, and Frost (2009) argue that reclaiming can keep the negative connotations intact, providing users with a sense of false power.

Women tweeted, often in the form of stories, to directly *reject the label* "bitches" (31 tweets). In this way, Twitter allowed its users to express public online narratives about themselves. As found with previous slurs, this use tends to reinforce rather than disrupt the concept. Nevertheless, self-definition is an important part of agency. Not all tweets presented here are ideal examples of direct rejections, but they do display humor or unhappiness with the label "bitch." Note that two tweeters were apparently called "bitches" by their mothers. The last tweet could be considered a critique, but is included here because it rejects the idea that women should be mean to each other. Furthermore, this tweet is an example of expressing one's opinions on interactions among girls on a public forum. However, it also suggests that being a "bitch" could be acceptable if someone has done something to deserve it.

- *@NateBlue just because I do not feel the same doesn't mean I'm a bitch or two faced Nate it means I can't help how I feel*

- *Not letting NO ONE treat me like I'm some wack bitch . Do you not know who tf I am? Nigga you must be smoking dickarettes*

- *My own mum just called me a stupid bitch for listening to Kpop25 and said I'm not normal. Thanks mum love you too*

- *Mom: "You're so pretty" Me: "No I'm not, I'm not even wearing any makeup. Why do you think I'm single?" Mom: "Because you're a bitch!"* 😂😭
- *Girls that are rude to other girls for no reason are trash, like being a bitch to someone who did nothing to you isn't cool*

Like previous slurs, "bitch" was used in a *celebratory* manner (25 tweets). Celebrating "bitches" offers more disruptive power, although the meaning is not dramatically changed. Only one tweet praised men (*"Greg_GGG u a bad bitch"*); the rest were posted by women and men about women. The inclusion of "bad" as in "bad bitch" makes "bitch" positive, defined by *Urban Dictionary* (2017) as a woman who is attractive, loyal, smart, strong, and successful. Again, we see one of the terms used in the "we-all-know-a" meme, this time, however, serving as a celebration:

- *That bitch is fab af*[26] 😭👹
- *@WeAllKnowA: We all know a bad bitch named Shaniqua*
- *Bitch be representin' #XFactor*
- *smoke good weed with a bad bitch*
- *Naomi Campbell is the bitch with the baddest walk. all the other girls are SHOOK!*[27]

For decades, women have been reclaiming bitch as a *positive label* (75 tweets). Freeman (1968), Wurtzel (1998), and celebrities such as Lil' Kim, Madonna, and Britney Spears have reclaimed "bitch" as the image of a powerful and independent woman. Similarly, Twitter users have reclaimed "bitch" to refer to themselves as honest, passionate, independent, and strong. Furthermore, they present an attitude of not caring about how others think of them (as shown in the first heavily retweeted post), putting them outside of regulatory power.

- *It's so joke when ppl try and insult me by calling me a bitch???? I know I'm a bitch I love it thx for the reassurance tho*
- *Don't be scared to be a bitch*
- *@tracie_ray i needa be a bad bitch from now on*

- *If not taking people's shit makes u a bitch, be a bitch. At least they'll know you're not the one to fuck with*
- *how i sleep knowing I'm a bitch*[28]

Like previous slurs, "bitch" was used as a *friendly* term among friends (16 tweets). This usage also has the potential to remove the derogation from the slur, although, again, it is possible "bitch" works as an edgy term of endearment because of its association with meanness and toughness. Even the cable network MTV tweeted "bitch" in a friendly way. The last tweet was coded as friendly once an examination of the thread showed an amicable conversation.

- *@MTV: @joanneprada see you at the #vmas, messy bitch* 😊
- *One post wasn't enough !! HAPPY BIRTHDAY! HOPE U GET LIT TONIGHT BITCH* 🎉🍾😊💜 [29]
- *@michellee this is gr8 & SEE U IN 5 DAYS BITCH!!!!!!!*
- *@sshhhhjeanie FaceTime me back BITCH*

Most of the Facebook groups and pages used "bitch" in dissenting ways through positive self-identification, education, and direct critiques. A Facebook page for the magazine *Bitch Media* described itself as a "feminist response to pop culture." As with "slut," slurs were more acceptable when used in art or commentary on stigma. Rockaway Bitch is an all-female Ramones tribute band whose members described themselves on their Facebook page as composed of "four badass bitches." Rockbitch was a British mostly female metal band that incorporated nudity and sexual acts into their performances. Other Facebook pages include "Bitches gotta eat" (described as a blog about anything) and "Borderline Bitch" (described as a blog about bipolar disorder, anxiety, and depression).

Facebook groups reclaiming "bitch" with over 1,000 members included the closed group "Anti-Bitch Alliance," which described itself as "Sick of cat fights in girl groups. Sick of the admins being bitches..." This group invites people to post about the following: "a nasty ex, annoying partners, that girl who purposely rammed a trolley into you at the supermarket, how good your butt looks in lingerie, your cat being cute, and how your nudes have your partners drooling at the mouth. Everything is welcome here." Others reclaiming "bitch" included the closed Facebook group "Bitches United," where users can post anything they want. The closed group "Like Minded Bitches Drinking Wine" embodies the reclamation of "bitch" in its description as "badass bitches who make stuff happen," offering support to "like-minded entrepreneurial bitches." "Speak the Truth 'Bitches'" described itself as the original "STTB" (speak the truth bitches) group. This group allows females over the age of 15 to post content of any type and to be "blunt, and brutally honest, without being rude OR nasty!" Note these ideas reflect feminine norms that women should refrain from being honest or blunt. Facebook also saw the widespread reclaiming of "nasty" in response to Donald Trump calling Hillary Clinton "such a nasty woman" during a US presidential debate on October 19, 2016.

Most of the hashtags containing "bitch" on Instagram were also examples of reclaiming the word as strong and positive. Each of the following hashtags showed evidence of women tagging themselves with captions and other hashtags indicating feelings of attractiveness and power. The first two also included photos that regulated women's behavior: #bitch (4.3 million posts) and #bitchesbelike (2.6 million). The following hashtags were almost entirely women tagging themselves in humorous ways: #bitchplease (500,000); #bitchface (278,000), which referenced the idea that women are not supposed to look unhappy or unpleasant; #bitchimmadonna (200,000), which mostly included pictures of Madonna, and was meant to show her fierceness; #bitchwhere (70,000), which was used to challenge someone's comment or possible comment; #bitchmode (55,000), which included captions about looking great and "not taking any shit"; and #bitchcraft (52,000), a play on witchcraft that contained pictures of women and gender nonconforming individuals and cis-men demonstrating the "art of being a bitch." Content of photos suggested that the "art of being a bitch" meant displaying fierceness and power.

External Events

Tweets including the slur "bitch" increased after each of the 2016 US presidential debates and significantly on election night, resulting in the highest daily average occurrence during the period studied. Though counts do not identify people's positions on political events, an examination of the content of tweets showed that Hillary Clinton topped the list of public figures named in the random sample (5 tweets). Other words often appearing in these tweets included "cold," "dumb," and "liar," serving as reminders for women to display warmth and honesty and to refrain from expressing opinions in public. Tweets included, "*WTF! Are you hiding bitch @HillaryClinton,*" and "*@HillaryClinton crooked Hillary* 😡 *you a bitch you pretty much a dog show some tricks or Donald J. Trump will bitchslap you to the floor* 😡." Note the incitement of violence in the variation "bitch slap." A search of Twitter on spike days revealed that Hillary Clinton was referred to most often as a "bitch" as was the case for all of the other misogynist terms. Only one tweet in the sample referenced Green Party candidate Jill Stein, but it served as a negative comment regarding Hillary Clinton: "*@FoxNews @HillaryClinton @realDonaldTrump @GovGaryJohnson @DrJillStein not happy that corrupt bitch still in lead. Sickening!*" Melania Trump also received tweets using the slur "bitch" (Steinblatt & Markovitz, 2016). The political sphere is considered a male space. Attacks on women's character, either through discrediting or sexual shaming, are attempts to exclude women from positions of power within these spheres. During the presidential campaign, t-shirts printed with the slogan "Trump that Bitch" were sold on Amazon.com.

After the 2016 US presidential election, there were also tweets directed toward Donald Trump and his supporters, showing an extension of the traditional use, but reinforcing the idea that the worst insult for a man is to be called a woman, including "*@realDonaldTrump are you sick, bitch?*" and "*If you vote for trump then you a dumb ass bitch.*" Twitter users called into question boxer Floyd Mayweather Jr.'s masculinity by calling him a "bitch" for taunting fighter Conor McGregor, including high numbers of retweets of this tweet and variations: "*Mayweather needs to stop being a bitch and just fight !!!*"

Intersections

Although data do not often include information on the race-ethnicity of the targets of tweets, we might expect words like "bitch" and "hoe" to be attached more frequently to black women than white women due to stereotypical portrayals of black women as domineering and overly sexual (Hill Collins, 2004). Data do reveal that "bitch" was more likely to be accompanied by black slang than the previous misogynist slurs. The sample included only one instance of the racist slur "nigger" and 64 instances of the reappropriated "nigga" as in "*Stop being the right bitch for the wrong nigga*" and "*Bitch I been doing me lately and it's* 👆

👍 *nigga pay me* 🐝🐝." The extensions of "bitch" on Twitter as a noun, verb, and intensifier show widespread use as slang. While debates ensue over whether rap music contains more misogyny than other kinds of music (Schneider, 2011; Williams Crenshaw, 1993), the word "bitch" became normalized in mainstream culture, including in rock and popular music. However, most tweets were of lyrics in the rap genre, including lyrics by Nicki Minaj, Yo Gotti, and Young Thug: *"Look at y'all bitch ass niggas stop lyin' on your dick ass niggas"*; *"Fuck A Bad Bitch Street Nigga Need A Real Bitch* 💯🤮👢👃"; and *"You ridin niggas dicks like a bitch."* Like music, discourses on Twitter reflect available cultural images and slang that reflect the intersection of gender, race, and sexuality. "Bitch" was also used as an insult in tweets that called out racism, as shown in these examples: *"bitch you're white stfu using that word"* and *"Wait a minute bitch u white delete dis shit @kristinfame."*

Conclusion

"Bitch" is the most common misogynist slur used on Twitter, consisting of 938,060 tweets on a single day, November 9, 2016—more than double the average occurrence of 418,665 on Twitter. This figure shows that "bitch" is still used to regulate women's gender performances, particularly when women venture into positions of power in spheres ascribed to men, such as politics and the workplace. When used to regulate, "bitch" tweets commented on women's untrustworthiness, unpleasantness, unworthiness, and domineering demeanor, reminding women to observe traditional feminine norms at the level of the interaction and particularly within heterosexual relationships (Connell, 1987; Kimmel, 2000; West & Zimmerman, 1987).

Unlike what was seen with "dyke," "slut," and "whore," the analysis of uses of "bitch" on Facebook, Twitter, and Instagram shows more extended uses, including as a replacement for "girlfriend" or "woman" and as an insult for men. However, these extensions did not necessarily disrupt gender norms. "Bitch" can be considered a neutral counterpart when we replace "woman" or "girlfriend" with "bitch" in sentences like, "I'm taking my bitch to the movies." However, why is "girlfriend" not used in this sentence? Ashwell (2016) points out that using "bitch" for women in phrases (e.g., "my bitches") assumes one has power over women. Consequently, this use of "bitch" is not neutral.

More disruptive power appears in uses that have less to do with gender performance, such as using "bitch" as a verb to complain or as a noun to identify something bad. These uses still carry negative connotations and suggest ownership and domination. Thus, using "bitch" as a verb or noun is not a neutral use of this slur in a feminist sense. Similarly, the extension of "bitch" to men may extend its meaning, but to replace "man" with "woman" in the sentence would be insulting to a man. Consequently, this use is also not neutral in the feminist sense. Men are called bitches for not successfully performing in a masculine manner, reinforcing gender norms. The use of "bitch" as an intensifier, as in "bitch, please," is least connected to gender, although it still is used to express irritation and disbelief.

The most disruptive power lies in the dissenting uses, such as using "bitch" as a term of endearment among friends and reclaiming "bitch" as a positive identity. On its website under "About Us," *Bitch Media* (2015) writes:

> While we're aware that our magazine's title, and the organization's name, is off-putting to some people, we think it's worth it. And here's why. The writer Rebecca West said, "People call me a feminist whenever I express sentiments that differentiate me from a doormat." We'd argue that the world "bitch" is usually deployed for the same purpose. When it's being used as an insult, "bitch" is an epithet hurled at women who speak their minds, who have opinions and don't shy away from expressing them, and who don't sit by and smile uncomfortably if they're bothered or offended. If being an outspoken woman means being a bitch, we'll take that as a compliment. (para. 6)

Actors Tina Fey and Amy Poehler consider the use of "bitch" a feminist act, saying that "bitches get stuff done" in a 2008 Weekend Update sketch on *Saturday Night Live*. Again, the question might be, why not just use "feminist"? As affluent white women, they also have a greater ability to freely adopt the label "bitch."

Positive identifications on Twitter show that a "bitch" can be reclaimed to mean a strong woman. While not directly studying the slur "bitch," following Brontsema's (2004) argument, it is the very derogation that makes "bitch" an effective term for reclamation by women who value agency and strength. Furthermore, a "bitch" may be edgier and lack some of the negativity attached to the label "feminist." Kleinman, Ezzell, and Frost (2009) remind us that reclaiming suggests there are only two options, domination or subordination, which divides women into two categories: honorary men who use language like "bitch" or doormats. They argue that using "bitch" does not challenge men who believe all women are bitches, nor does it provide women with real power. Dissimilar to words like "feminist," the slur is not tied to a movement for social change that challenges patriarchy. Social media data showed no connections between the reclamation of "bitch" online to off-line campaigns challenging the concept of a "bitch," though there have been similar off-line campaigns to stop using the word "bossy" to describe girls and women (Sandberg & Chávez, 2014).

In Chapter 7, I discuss the ability for social media to create new meanings around "bitch," a word that has served as a derogatory term for women for centuries. The mainstreaming of "bitch" in popular culture, its common use as an intensifier, and its reclamation by strong, powerful women holds promise to deprive it of its pejorative content. However, the increased use to refer to Democratic nominee Hillary Clinton during the 2016 presidential election shows "bitch" continues to possess significant derogatory power. Despite its mainstreaming, "bitch" is rooted in a patriarchal society that expects women to be pleasant and hidden from public discourse (Beard, 2014; Spender, 1991). Moving beyond the realm of language, I address the possibility for changing discourse around "bitch" to lead to real structural change, particularly given spheres such as business and politics that reward styles associated with masculinity but penalize women who deviate from feminine norms.

Notes

1. Whether replacements for woman such as "bitch" can be considered neutral counterparts will be discussed.

2. The meaning of *bitch* in the song "99 Problems" ("I got 99 problems but a bitch ain't one") is often interpreted as a neutral counterpart for women, though Jay Z claims it refers to a drug-sniffing dog.

3. I did not search for variations, such as "biatch" and "beeyatch," though this important work for the future could yield additional insights into contemporary uses of "bitch."

4. I cannot account for the dramatic decrease of "bitch" on September 27, 2016, other than perhaps a partial loss of connection with Twitter. This figure should be interpreted with caution.

5. The 57 tweets that could be attributed to women based on gender identity stated in profiles and responses were included in the *regulatory* category. The remaining 10 with unknown genders and 34 attributed to males will be included under the *extension* category, for a total of 101 tweets coded as generic insults.

6. Eve and Pandora are the first human women who bring evil by giving into temptation—Eve by eating forbidden fruit and Pandora by opening a locked box or vase.

7. This tweet was accompanied by a picture of a woman smiling and then looking angry or bored.

8. Translated from Italian by Google Translate as "I do not know if you believe that she a fake ass bitch so shamelessly saying things about me."

9. DGAF is an acronym for "don't give a fuck."

10. Heavily retweeted link to a *Buzzfeed* video of a woman reporter being pushed out of the way while trying to get an interview with then vice presidential candidate Mike Pence.

11. "Fenna" means "gonna," likely a combination of "fixing to" and "going to."

12. STFU is an acronym for "shut the fuck up."

13. This tweet was frequently retweeted. "Lmao" is an acronym for "laughing my ass off," "smh" for "shaking my head," "std" for "sexually transmitted disease"; and "witcho" is another way to say "with your."

14. TF is an acronym for "the fuck."

15. Ten tweets could not be included here because gender identity was unknown, as in this heavily retweeted Chief Keef song lyric: "This bitch just blew my high." No one in the sample who was named identified as nonbinary.

16. The tweet linked to a picture of "manpons," a photoshopped box of tampons with the writing, "for the guys that act like little bitches."

17. Using the term "bitch" about other men seemed to fall equally among men identifying as heterosexual and gay, although this particular tweet was heavily retweeted by men identifying as gay.

18. Though it can be argued that "you guys" is not necessarily generic in that it uses the universal male for all people.

19. Variation on lyric by rapper Lil Wayne.

20. "Ride and die" means to be there for someone no matter what happens.

21. This tweet referred to a picture of actor and singer Ariana Grande.

22. Translated from Portuguese by Google Translate as "João Dória [Brazilian politician] on the radio saying that he started working at 14 years BITCH PLEASE."

23. The link associated with this tweet no longer exists so I cannot determine what "this bitch" is.

24. "A1" means "excellent."

25. "Kpop" is short for "Korean pop music."

26. AF is an acronym for "as fuck."

27. "Shook" means scared or shocked.

28. This tweet was accompanied by a picture of a woman sleeping soundly on a cloud.

29. This tweet was accompanied by four pictures of the recipient with her friends.

6

CUNT:
Silencing Women in Public

This chapter continues the analysis of misogynist words used to silence and demean women. "Cunt" is considered by many as the most offensive and abusive misogynist epithet used to label women (Baumgardner & Richards, 2000; Brontsema, 2004). It shares a similar function to the word "bitch" (to silence and discredit) and is used to identify a woman who is mean, unyielding, and unpleasant. Unlike the mainstreaming of "bitch," "cunt" is almost entirely absent in popular music and television in the United States. Some argue that this difference is because "cunt" has been considered a taboo term for hundreds of years due to its association with women's vaginas. By using "cunt" as a slur, vaginas are turned from something associated with physical pleasure and childbirth into something vulgar and offensive. Taboos around menstruation add to the taboo associated with "cunt."

The aim of this chapter is to examine the contemporary uses of "cunt" on social media and to consider the implications for gender and sexual relations and larger social inequality. Like the other misogynist slurs studied in this book, "cunt" has sexual origins. *Cunt* is defined as "vulgar slang" for "women's genitals" (*Oxford English Dictionary*, 2017). A secondary definition is an "unpleasant" or "stupid" person. *Online Etymology Dictionary* (2017) traces the origin of this word to the Middle English word *cunte* for female genitalia.

Other origins include the Latin *cunnus* (vulva), as in the contemporary *cunnilingus* ("cunnus" for vulva and "lingere" to lick) and
cuneus (wedge), and the Proto-Indo-European roots *gue* (hollow
place) and *gwen* (queen and woman). Connections are made between
cunt and the Middle English *queynte*, used as a pun for "quaint" in
Chaucer's *Canterbury Tales*. Later, Shakespeare would hint at *cunt*
using *country* in *Hamlet*.

Cunt became a taboo word by the Victorian period, previously
having appeared in names for goddesses, streets, and medical writings
during the Middle Ages (Silverton, 2009; Wajnryb, 2005). Allen
(2016) argues the transformation of *cunt* to a taboo word can be seen
in the changing pronunciation of the word *coney* for "rabbit," which
was originally pronounced "cunny" but changed to "coney" by the
nineteenth century so that it would not sound similar to "cunt."
Because of the connection between *cunt* and *quaint*, the connotation of
quaint became negative, referring to cunning, scheming, and plotting.
In 1960, Penguin Books was taken to court in the UK under a newly
passed Obscene Publications Act for *Lady Chatterley's Lover* due to its
use of "cunt" and "fuck" as well as derivatives. As evidence of changing mores, Penguin won the right to publish the book. On his website,
Hunt (n.d.) reviews the literature on "cunt" in "Cunt: A Cultural History." Hunt concludes that *cunt* is "probably the most offensive and
censored swear word in the English language," examining its contested
use in art, print, music, television, and movies (para. 13).

Similar to other pejorative words for women, "cunt" is rooted in
misogyny, expressing fears that women are tainted (as seen in taboos
about menstruation) and untrustworthy (Eve's downfall). Feminists
such as Germaine Greer (1970, 1971) have argued that the taboo surrounding "cunt" reflects women's subordination and is dependent on
the denial of women's sexuality and fear and shame associated with
the vagina. Inga Musica (2002) argues that the negativity in "cunt"
comes not only from fear and hatred of women and female bodies,
but also from the Roman Catholic Church's efforts to target powerful
and independent women. Jane (2014) recounts examples of the use of
the word "cunt" in online abuse of women who write about online
misogyny. Messages of abuse included the following: "Anita Sarkeesian is a feminist video blogger and cunt"; "Back to the kitchen,
cunt"; "Lindy West is a fat cunt who is completely unfuckable"; and
"What a fucking cunt. Kill yourself, dumb bitch" (pp. 562–564).
Recognizing the power of "cunt," a defender imitated this abuse by

referring to an online abuser of Australian actress Marieke Hardy as a "spineless little cunt" (p. 564). After harassing writer Lauren Duca repeatedly, an entrepreneur and pharmaceutical executive had his Twitter account suspended on January 8, 2017. His suspension inspired an onslaught of abuse, including a tweet of her photoshopped Twitter bio that read, "I'm a fucking cunt who stalks men and gets them banned when they troll me back."

Hunt's (n.d.) extensive history of "cunt" shows the variation in the meaning of words within different social contexts. "Cunt" continues to carry offense, but is used much more freely and in a less gendered way in the UK. It was considered racial but not gender abuse when an English footballer called another player "fucking black cunt" during a televised game in 2011 (Gavins & Simpson, 2015). Unlike "cunt" in the UK and "bitch" in the United States, "cunt" has not been incorporated into mainstream culture in the United States. Women in the UK and Australia still experience online misogyny. Fans of West Ham Football United threatened English sporting executive Karren Brady on Twitter in October 2016; however, they reserved the word "cunt" for male managers and players.

Like the other misogynist words studied here, feminists have reclaimed "cunt." Greer directly confronted the word, defining "cunt-power" as female sexual empowerment (1970). Musica (2002) similarly embraced the word "cunt" as powerful and female, arguing for it to be used as "an all new woman-centered, cuntlovin' noun, adjective, or verb" (p. 11). However, she also recognized that focusing on "cunts" can marginalize transwomen. A monologue "Reclaiming Cunt" appears in Eve Ensler's 1996 play *The Vagina Monologues*, though British writer Zoe Williams (2006) criticizes the preference for "vagina" over "cunt" in the play's title, writing "Bring on the Cunt Warriors" (para. 6). The riot grrrls in the United States also reclaimed "cunt" along with other misogynist labels (Attwood, 2007).

Findings

The keyword "cunt" was tracked on Twitter from August 17, 2016, to December 1, 2016.[1] During this period, "cunt" was used a total of 2,753,600 times. The daily average was 25,496 times, with a low of 10,660 and a high of 52,880 (see Figure 6.1). While overall the frequency of "cunt" tweets decreased during this three and a half month period, there were peaks and valleys. The figure for the last day of the period, December 1, was 22,560, which was close to the average.[2] Similar to findings for the slur "bitch," November 9, 2016, the day of the US presidential election, was the day with the highest number of "cunt" tweets. An analysis of tweets, discussed further in the section "External Events," shows the increase was due to tweets about presidential candidate Hillary Clinton.

A total of 700 tweets was randomly selected for analysis (see Appendix B for coding schemes and counts). The slightly smaller sample size is due to the fewer themes found. Data saturation was found after analyzing approximately 400 tweets. Analysis found that 83 tweets advertised pornographic websites, and 18 tweets were unclear even though coding included visual content and conversations. For instance, many examples of tweets contained one word: "cunt." In most cases, analysis of the conversation revealed the sentiment. For instance, "cunt" was a response to the tweet, *Hillary says people who chant 'USA' at Trump rallies are 'UN-American.'* A sample of 599 tweets were coded for themes. Additionally, four Facebook groups and pages and the top ten Instagram hashtags in terms of number of posts were analyzed.

Regulation (342 Tweets)

The primary use of "cunt" was to label women as disagreeable or unlikable. While some Twitter users simply included the word with someone's name or tag, others included more information, suggesting the person was annoying or unpleasant. Unlike the other slurs, when gender identity was available, a large portion of tweets referred to men. Tweets referring to users who identified as men will be included under extension uses. When gender identity of sender was available, most senders of "cunt" tweets were men. The most targeted public person was Hillary Clinton. No Facebook groups/pages or Instagram hashtags containing "cunt" fell into the category of regulating female behavior. Instagram had removed all photos for the two hashtags #cunt (23,000 posts) and #cünt (7,000 posts) as of January 1, 2017.

As with the other misogynist slurs, many of the tweets simply included the word "cunt" and a person's *name or tag* (42 tweets). Again, naming someone on Twitter means the label is publicly attached to that individual and can be removed only by the person

Figure 6.1 Keyword Mention over Time: "Cunt" (Twitter)

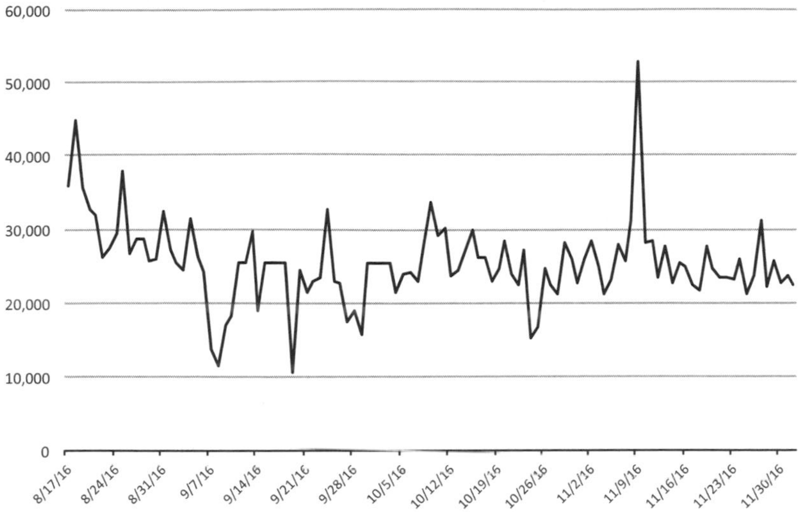

who posted the tweet or an employee of Twitter. Other information, such as the expletive "fucking" and the statement "I hate," clearly suggest insulting sentiments. Even if no one is tagged and no last name is provided (as with Jeanie below), it is possible that Twitter users in their social circle can identify them. Public labeling serves as a warning not only to the person mentioned, but for all people to avoid behaviors that may invite the label.

- *@CarrieFlies Cunt*
- *@HillaryClinton cunt*
- *JEANIE IS SUCH A FUCKING CUNT*
- *@JanetEarth I hate this cunt*

More tweets fell into the *generic insult* theme with no person named or tagged (79 tweets). Here, the additional content showed a clear attempt to enforce norms of agreeableness. Tweets in this category may also be coded under *silencing* and/or *unworthiness*. However, with no person named, numbers in this category should be interpreted with caution considering "cunt" is so often directed toward men in the UK. Tweets directed toward users who identify as men are included under *male insults*. Of more importance are the meanings attached to misogynist words. When "cunt" was directed toward users who identify as women, the intent was to express unhappiness with their behavior, serving to regulate normative gendered behavior. Like "bitch," "cunt" revealed the expectation that women should always exhibit traits of kindness and sensitivity to others (Ridgeway, 2001).

Even general statements on Twitter create a climate of misogyny (e.g., "*You are a cunt*"). Consider the reference to "sub" in the following tweet: "*You sub tweet. Talk shit bout me to the whole school. But you left him... why u mad. CUNT.*" According to *Urban Dictionary* (2017), "sub" is an abbreviation for a subliminal or underhanded comment meant to insult or embarrass someone on a public social media site. Even though no one is named, it is still possible Twitter users in a particular social circle will know who is referenced.

- *Cunt*[3]
- *Fucking cunt* 😒
- *@WeAllKnowA: We all know a jealous cunt*
- *chcę mieć koszulkę jak Kate "Fuck you cunt" właściwie to siedem - czyli na kazdy dzień tygodnia*[4]
- *why is everyone being a cunt*

Similar to the use of the word "bitch," the label "cunt" had less to do with *appearance* (12 tweets) than the sexual shaming terms "slut," "whore," and "dyke" analyzed in Chapters 2, 3, and 4). Attractiveness and body type were mentioned most often, showing that women are judged often on these factors and that attacks on a woman's appearance are considered among the harshest insults. Some tweets also mentioned overuse of makeup. Several were extremely aggressive and were also coded as *threats*. The first tweet regarding Hillary Clinton was heavily retweeted during this period:

- *@HillaryClinton she was called fat and got fat. That's hilarious! Lol sup w the mic n ear piece in ur pant suit u FUCKING wretch. You cunt*

- *will always hate that one ugly cunt of a girl for as long as I possibly can xx* 👆 🙈 [5]
- *No amount of contour or winged eyeliner will cover the fact that ur a fucking cunt hun*
- *@agathasees die fat cunt*

The slur "cunt" was less often used to suggest *promiscuity* than terms like "slut" and "whore" (4 tweets). However, due to its sting, "cunt" added intensity to tweets meant to sexually shame. The additional use of the homophobic slur "fag" will be discussed further under "Intersections." Slurs in this book tend to be distinguished by their silencing or shaming function, though it can be argued that shaming is also an attempt to silence and that all the slurs studied here attempt to regulate women's behavior, whether that behavior is related to sex or voicing an opinion.

- *Her and her thot squad are dirty asf. I'm embarrassed to even admit I was "friends" with her. She's a cunt fr*[6]
- *@carlsbro0512 this gay ass fag thinks that she is not a cunt but in reality she is a huge hoe* 👏 👏 👌 💅

Many more tweets containing "cunt" referred to *unpleasant* women (87 tweets).[7] In other words, women were not performing their gender correctly by behaving in unpleasant and displeasing ways. Descriptive terms accompanying tweets in this theme included "arrogant," "defiant," "evil," "mean," and "self-centered." Doing something as innocuous as ordering a flavored hot beverage put one at risk for the label of "cunt." However, most tweets conveyed a sentiment that was found in tweets using the slur "bitch"; women who exhibit these traits not only defied essentialist feminine norms for behavior, but in doing so, became inherently unlikable. Analysis of tweets showed expressions of hatred and disgust for women who displayed these traits. Again, Hillary Clinton topped the list among named public figures, the first tweet heavily retweeted during this period. The second tweet shows the similarities between the meanings of "bitch" and "cunt."

- *REMINDER: Hillary Clinton is hated because she IS a cunt, not because she HAS a cunt*
- *The basis behind why you're such a bitch is simple: You're a cunt*
- *@calliesally because she's a shitty person and was a total cunt to me and my friends who were nothing but nice to her.*
- *@BeEvelyn @Shanti_@EE_Zhang UGH THAT CUNT SHE UNIRONICALLY ORDERED A FLAVORED HOT BEVERAGE I'M SO DISGUSTED*
- *this old cunt pretends to be a Republican notice how she sounds no different from a Democrat*[8]

Many tweets including "cunt" referred to women as *untrustworthy* (47 tweets). In many cases, "cunt" may have been chosen to intensify the insult for women because it is considered the most offensive insult possible (Baumgardner & Richards, 2000; Brontsema, 2004). But the issue remains that untrustworthiness among women, a theme dating back to ancient times, inspired a desire to deeply offend. Note that theme of trustworthiness among women occurred often in discussions about the 2016 US presidential election. Again, Hillary Clinton figured prominently within this theme, commonly accused of untrustworthiness.

- *Nothing worse than spending $300 of your hard earned money on Food, then some cunt ahead of you using Food Stamps getting free food*
- *I hate the twat that uses my milk in common room without asking, buy some yourself you lazy cunt*
- *@HillaryClinton Lying, self serving cunt*
- *#DonaldTrumpForPresident #HilaryClinton #dogshit #cunt #smellsdead #liar #gotojail #USElection #clown*[9]

Words like "cunt" are used to demean and discredit women, rendering them *unworthy* (33 tweets). The first tweet mentions that everyone in an entire town (changed here to the common name of Springfield to protect identities) hates the target of the tweet, suggesting a possible pattern of direct ongoing cyberbullying. Tweets that called into question women's intelligence are included. Once denigrated, women can be disregarded. Again, Hillary Clinton received a large share of tweets in this theme as many tweets deemed her unqualified to be the president of the United States. Although individual tweets do not include enough information for deep analysis of sentiment, users are aware that speech has effects on the reader, so we can posit that the person chose to not only deem the target as unqualified but to denigrate the target using "cunt." Otherwise, posts could simply state, "X is unqualified for this position." The third tweet was heavily retweeted and demonstrates a view similar to that expressed in Chapter 5: *"Good pussy does come with a crazy bitch attached to it lol."*

- *bitch the entire Springfield population hates you stop trying to make yourself relevant, cunt :)*
- *@jimBell84 @ABC But this useless cunt is qualified?*[10]
- *Ever seen someone really attractive but they're single, so you assume they're either a cunt, psycho or just broken ?*
- *@MeeAnsari haha nobody would employ a useless cunt like you and especially with your ground breaking low iq*

Related to previous themes of unpleasantness, untrustworthiness, and general unworthiness, a major function of using misogynist terms is to *silence* women publicly (10 tweets). Although only 10 tweets directly silenced women through orders to "shut up" or "keep [their] mouth[s] shut," all regulatory themes serve a general silencing function. While there is a long history of silencing women by demeaning and discrediting them (Spender, 1991), unless removed, posts to social media platforms like Facebook and Twitter are permanent and widespread. Note the aggression in many of the tweets below, using terms like "shut up" and calling women "ugly" and "fat." The last tweet is also coded as a *threat*.

- *@jennylees Shut up, stinking cunt! @ivansoko22*
- *Shut the fuck up you ugly fat cunt @maryarena*
- *U can have ur own opinion about things but sometimes you should keep ur mouth shut. Theres a difference between free speech and being a cunt*
- *if you don't shut it, I'll be sending clowns after you, little cunt x x x*

Tweets included here are even more aggressive, coded as *threats* or expectations of violence directed at a particular person (28 tweets). Although analyses of single tweets cannot determine whether abuse is ongoing or actual violence is planned, the threat of violence serves to keep women frightened of deviating from normative gendered behaviors such as likability. Furthermore, many of the tweets in this category expressed a desire for people to die, indicating serious bullying behavior. The first tweet was accompanied by a picture of a text message that showed the target's name. The rest named specific people in the tweets:

- *How dare these cunt bitches say I'm mean* 🖕😑 *I'll kill em*
- *@agathasees die fat cunt*
- *@Bat777 Sad cunt, ppl like u dont even deserve to be alive. Fucking twat*
- *FUCK OUR BAD PAST WHAT BITCH BREAKING YO FUCKIN HEART ILL STABBA CUNT @livelyliv*

Extension (263 Tweets)

"Cunt" has not taken on as many varied uses as "bitch," likely because "cunt" is considered more offensive and is not used in as many contexts. Similar to the slur "bitch," the traditional meaning of "cunt" refers to women. However, it was found that most tweets extending the meaning of "cunt" were directed toward men. Almost all tweets in this theme originated in the UK or Australia. Most were used to insult men, but others were used in friendly ways. Within the UK and Australian contexts, "cunt" carries much less offense, more similar to the use of "jerk" or "asshole" in the United States. Tweets referenced public figures such as professional athletes and politicians. Some men referred to themselves as "cunts," while others referred to objects or states of being as "cunts." Two insults did not reference a particular person or gender. One originated from an Australian comedian Lewis Spears: "*Is there anything more pathetic than some cunt selfie recording themselves ripping a bong alone in their bedroom for a snapchat story?*" The other originated from a woman and was accompanied by a picture of a damaged shoe and the text: "*Look at my goddamn shoes. These are $50 shoes and some cunt wrecked them on me.*" Though using "cunt" to refer to a woman's vagina is not technically an extension of its original meaning, this theme is also considered an extension because my interest is the use of misogynist slurs and "cunt" is not a commonly used term for vaginas.

When used as a *male insult*, "cunt" overwhelmingly originated from Twitter users commenting on football and rugby matches in the UK (225 tweets). Explanations for the greater (though not complete) acceptance in England include less influence of Puritanism and the use of vulgar language to perform working-class identities, connecting "cunt" more to socioeconomic status than gender (Fogg, 2014). Tweets originating from men almost entirely criticized rival teams, unethical behavior in sports, and bad plays (discussed further under "External Events"). This use links the meaning of "cunt" to Latin and Old French words for "impotence," "powerlessness," and "weakness" (*Online Etymology Dictionary*, 2017). These qualities deviate from hegemonic norms of masculinity (Kimmel, 2000; Messner, 1999). Similar to calling a man a "bitch" or "pussy," calling a man a "cunt" is an offense because these words refer to female body parts. These terms are more insulting than calling a man a "dick" or "asshole." These examples reinforce the cultural idea that traits associated with women and femininity are inferior to those associated with men and masculinity. British male politicians were also called "cunts," though "cunt" carries less offense in the UK. Donald Trump was called a "cunt" by people within and outside the United States, to be discussed further under "External Events."

- *Fucking hate Lingard. Sorry but he is rubbish championship player. Hoped Jose would see through this fraud cunt. Clearly not yet.*
- *Overrated cunt. Spanish Gary Cahill*[11]
- *Fuck off England! Fucking Hendo you CUNT*
- *I'm that desperate to go to the midnight showing of Suicide Squad, I'm even considering going with my cunt of a brother* 😳
- *After seeing his reshuffle I reckon that horrible cunt corbyn would appoint a sinn fein secretary of defence if he could*
- *"The good ol days" @realDonaldTrump your a cunt*

When gender of the tweeter was available, women typically called men "cunts" over grievances in relationships such as cheating, laziness, abandonment or neglect of a child, and failure to pay child support. Some of these uses reinforce hegemonic masculinity while others showed a departure. Traits such as laziness and providing financial support are traditional roles for males, so deviation invited public denigration. We see how misogynist slurs serve not only to prop up femininity but also to warn men from departing from hegemonic masculinity. Publicly shaming men for cheating in a relationship deviates somewhat from traditional gender norms, as the sexual double standard results in praise for men and shame for adolescent girls and women who exhibit sexual prowess (Lyons et al., 2011; see also Chapters 2 and 3 on the online uses of "slut" and "whore").

- *@MattyFine where's the child support payments cunt*
- 😭 *enjoy, his nothing but a unfaithful cunt anyway* 😀

Tweets also included *men identifying* with the label (9 tweets). As discussed earlier, tweets did not appear intensely negative because an examination of users' accounts determined all tweets in this theme originated from users in the UK and reflect the greater cultural acceptance of the word:

- i must just be a cunt, that has to be it
- It's official I'm a cunt LG x[12]

Another theme extending the meaning was to use "cunt" to refer to an *object or state of being* (18 tweets). Extensions like this one have the potential to separate the slur from failed femininity. However, as seen with "bitch," referring to an object or state of being as "cunt" was often because it was troublesome or ineffective, reflecting the original meaning of the word.

- *This week and likely month will be a hard one for me, so I'm incredibly thankful for your support. Life can be a massive cunt at times.*
- *My ps4 is being a stupid little cunt rn*[13]
- *And now my phone has only gone and finally broken on me the shit cunt*

Although originally referring to a woman's vagina, it is no longer common in ordinary speech to use "cunt" in this way. Therefore "cunt" is included under the theme *alternative uses* (11 tweets), though using "cunt" instead of "vagina" can heighten the intensity of the statement. Using "cunt" can also be an attempt to normalize the word, perhaps resulting in a weakening of the offensiveness of the word. The last tweet refers to a song title that describes gruesome violence against women.

- *@cher im doing a project for school and need to know, wud u rather fist my cunt hole or vote for #TRUMP ?*
- *@PhilGoldin @WestHam_3 not a fan of curly cunt hair?*
- *Estar oyendo "Entrails ripped from a virgin's cunt" y PUM! publicidad de Spotify con Maluma*[14]

"Cunt" was not as popular of a term on Facebook or Instagram, likely due to decency policies and the strength of the offensiveness outside of cultural contexts in Australia and the UK. Three Facebook groups used the phrase "Cunt Mafia" (to be discussed also under the section on dissent), but none had more than 10 members. "King Cunt!" was a closed group that described itself as a group "for banter. Anything goes bar the mention of children." The description for the closed group "TresCuntsUnited" read: "If you get offended, then GTFO. We don't GAF . . . move along. This is not a group to post disgusting fetish and sex memes."[15] Other closed groups included "No RatCunts Allowed," a closed group for "dark humor" and "Southam Cunts" for "news and views," whose cover photo reads "I'm no gynecologist, but I sure know a cunt when I see one." Based on available content, this group appears centered on the town of Southam in England. These groups and pages reflect the idea that humor should not offend, yet the administrators recognize some content is considered going too far, such as posts about children, fetish, or sex memes.

Instagram hashtags fell into the extension and dissent uses. Of eight Instagram hashtags, five used "cunt" is extended ways. Posts with #cunt had been removed, but likely due to oversight or lack of resources, Instagram allowed the hashtag #cunts (99,000 posts) as of December 2016. Posts with #cunts included a wide range of posts, none of them appearing to shame or offend women. The top photos included a drawing of a vagina penetrated by a penis accompanied by erotic text and objects or people that users in the UK and Australia found irritating, including slow train service, the police, and rival football players and teams. While the word "cunt" was extended, it still carried the connotation of a woman who is annoying and unyielding. The hashtag #cuntry (9,000 posts) was used to mean "country," but also was used by gay men to tag themselves in rustic settings about a quarter of the time. Hashtag #cuntsfucked (6,000 posts) means being "incredibly intoxicated" and contained predominantly photos of men in the UK. The hashtag #cuntseverywhere (4,000 posts) contained a variety of photos, many humorous memes, and most others depicting men in the UK. Hashtag #cuntmuffin (3,000 posts) means "failure," and posts more commonly came from the UK but also the United States, suggesting a broadening of the term that could weaken its derogatory content.

Dissent (126 Tweets)

Efforts to reappropriate "cunt" include Greer's (1970) "The Politics of Female Sexuality" and Musica's (2002) *Cunt: A Declaration of Independence*, both arguing for the reclamation of the word to mean something positive and powerful, necessary for eradicating negative cultural attitudes toward the vagina and women in general. However, others doubt the ability to transform "cunt" due to its history as one of the most taboo words (Baumgardner & Richards, 2000). Following the argument of Brontsema (2004), the choice is not between positive or negative, but rather a dialectical relationship in which the positive power results from the negative taboo. In a 2006 interview, Greer admits she has adjusted her position, preferring "cunt" to retain its taboo so that it may be used as a powerful political weapon (Barnes, 2006). In the dissent category, we see examples of Twitter users rejecting, reclaiming, critiquing, educating, defending, and using "cunt" as a friendly term.

Because of the taboo surrounding "cunt," Twitter users *rejected the label* (19 tweets). Reasons given include denying that they are unyielding and unpleasant women. Rejection of this kind reinforces the meaning of "cunt" as a difficult and unpleasant woman while simultaneously providing users with the agency to define themselves. Unlike previous words, the greater offense led to several people unhappily identifying with the label, as evidenced by language, emoticon, and emoji. A representative example is the tweet "*I'm really a cunt* :(." It is also possible that the second and third tweets contain some humor. The last tweet originated from the UK.

- *Doesn't make you a cunt. Makes you one of the strongest and sassiest girl I know* ❤❤
- *I'm really not a cunt. I'm actually very sweet. Ask anyone. Not her. Don't ask her either. NO! Especially not her. Just take my word for it*
- *Changed my mind. Im not a cunt they are*
- *I used to think I was better than people who liked sports or misspelt words. Then I realised I was just being a cunt*

While "cunt" has not had the same history of positive reclamation in popular culture as "bitch," Twitter users harnessed "cunt" as a *positive label* (28 tweets). Musica (2002) writes that "when viewed as a positive force in the language of women . . . the negative power of 'cunt' falls in upon itself" (p. xxvi). Tweets suggest that "cunt" and "bitch" share traits, such as meanness and evilness. Like Zoe Williams (2006) and the riot grrrls (Attwood, 2007), these women are rejecting these traits as negative and instead reclaiming them as signs of strength and pride:

- *Been such a lil cunt all day* 😼
- *I'm feelin like a mega cunt tonight* 😴🅝
- *When someone crosses me I become a vicious cunt. Lol*
- *Bitch? Hoe? Cunt? Whore? Slut? Dude I'm all of that sorry* 😂😴🙆💁😂

Despite "cunt" being considered one of the most taboo words in the English language, it was used occasionally in *friendly* tweets among women (9 tweets), though to a lesser extent than the other terms. This use has the potential to remove the derogation, although, like positive reclamation, using "cunt" in a friendly way does not necessarily completely transform the term. In fact, the original definition might provide an edge desired among these users.

- *My best friends a cunt* 😀
- *@Ilina_lazarov aww love you cunt* 🖤

Twitter users used the platform to *directly critique* the use of "cunt" and the taboo surrounding the word (26 tweets). This critique shows the ability for the platform to provide agency around discourse and inter-action around conflicting ideologies. Many of the direct critiques related to the 2016 US presidential election, noting the recognition that misogynist attitudes were normalized during the election. The election will be discussed in more detail in the "External Events" section.

- *@sle1795 why is cunt your go to insult* 😒 *it makes you all sound so trashy*
- *@Cant_catch_me @DocJim @Willow86 I thought calling Sarah that word was deplorable. Drunk moron maybe. But cunt never*
- *raise your hand if you've ever been called a cunt because you wrote about a concurring opinion in a federal circuit...*
- *Never ever thought I would see the word "cunt" as part of a Republican (the party of "family values") presidential cam-paign slogan*[16]

Related to direct critiques, Twitter users employed the platform to *educate* others on the use of "cunt," particularly around the 2016 US presidential election (33 tweets). In light of charges of fake news stories on social media, education allows people to raise issues about sources and evidence for political positions. One user both critiqued the use of "cunt" and provided education by tweeting "*a cunt is a vagina*," likely hoping to shed light on the origins of the word and its connection to misogyny. The user who complained about talk show host Joy Behar calling a rape victim "trash" missed a major point about misogynist language when referring to Behar as a "cunt." Leading up to the election, the most retweeted "cunt" tweet was the first example:

- *This guy, at the rally with his wife and three kids, in his "She's A Cunt, Vote For Trump" shirt*[17]

- *@johnmccain2016 you called your wife a "cunt" yet you care about you daughters and women #liar #trumpwins*
- *@alexishere @dylanner a cunt is a vagina*
- *This is incredible. Confronting. And true. Do me a favor and read it before you call me a "dumb cunt," k? #ImWithHer*[18]
- *@candincarter The stupid cunt @JoyVBehar that works for you just called a rape victim "trash", your show is fucken pathetic*

A new theme emerged in which Twitter users *defended* the use of the slur "cunt" (11 tweets). It is likely that people felt the need to offer arguments in support of the use of "cunt" but not the other slurs studied in this book due to the greater taboo of "cunt" and lower reclamation. Defending the use of "cunt" might contribute to its reclamation. However, it also shows the debate over the significance of language for cultural attitudes, with some claiming slurs cannot cause injury and others claiming slurs significantly influence cultural attitudes. People who condemned the use of injurious words were deemed sensitive and overly emotional, a sentiment captured by the first tweet below. Additionally, this theme captured current debates about free speech on the Internet, with some wanting less censorship on social media platforms and others wanting more. These debates are addressed more fully in Chapter 7.

- *I miss the old Twitter now everyone's a sensitive cunt over everything*
- *@GrammarGod @flyyyy @musique21 @NeoConPaul not shut up CUNT. see yr to liberal to find that word funny, FUCK YER FEELINGS*
- *@StephenWalters @MrStevenCree @SamHeughan Here in California we say C U Next Tuesday. Well some do, I just say Cunt. Cause I like it*
- *If you are offended by the word "cunt" or "fuck", I'll do you a favor and tell you to stay clear of me. #girlswithfoulmouths #nofucksgiven*

Compared to the other slurs studied, fewer Facebook pages and groups featured "cunt" in their titles, likely due to the taboo and decency standards on the site. One Facebook page featured "cunt" in a reclaimed way: "CUNTMAFIA" referred to a musical group from New York. The creator writes that they did not want to use the name to be "trendy" or "watered down," but to reflect the use in the punk and vogue scene. "Cunt" was used in positive, reclaimed ways on Instagram. The hashtag #cunty (23,000 posts) was also used by the LGBTQIA community to post pictures of the underground queer ballroom scene in New York City in which people compete for prizes by walking and posing in the dance style known as voguing. Other photos featured women tagging themselves to suggest an attitude similar to "bitch" but even stronger and also occasionally humorously. This usage suggests some reclaiming of the word, despite its description as the most offensive word for women. The hashtag #cuntlife (7,000 posts) was used predominantly as a form of positive self-identification. Roughly half of the posts contained hashtags referencing gay identities. A small portion used "cunt" to identify themselves as unpleasant and unyielding women, again by choice and with pride. The hashtag #cuntface (5,000 posts) also involved self-identification to refer to an expression akin to "resting bitch face" from Chapter 5. When gender identity was available in accompanying hashtags and profile information, most self-identifying pictures featured women, but the hashtag was also used by and about people who identified as male and/or queer.

External Events

The 2016 US presidential election dominated Twitter usage of "cunt" during the period under investigation. While most tweets were directed toward Hillary Clinton, Donald Trump was also called a "cunt" by Twitter users inside and outside of the United States. In the random sample, 15 tweets mentioned Hillary Clinton by name and all expressed negative sentiments. Tweets about Clinton included: "*It is nothing but last ditch effort from the (((establishment))) and @HillaryClinton, that corrupted cunt who will continue to sell Amerika*" and "*Such a cunt. LISTEN: Hillary Freak Out. Makes Vile Move When She Finds Bible in Limo #pjnet #TeaParty #NRA.*"[19] Tweets reflected the ancient belief that women are deceitful and cannot be trusted. Melania Trump was also targeted: "*D.C. welcomes Melania Trump, 'First Cunt and Madam-in-Chief of the United States.*'" Tweets also targeted Donald Trump, reflecting the idea that calling a man a word for vagina is particularly harsh: "*If Trump insists on continuing to call Clinton 'Crooked Hillary', I push that we start calling him 'Cunt Donald*'" and "*man i feel sorry for america, imagine having a racist, sexist, spoilt disrespectful brat of a cunt as your next possible president.*" None of the other presidential nominees or third-party candidates were referred to as "cunts" in this sample.

Mention of other political events included a comment attributed to Senator John McCain; the vote for Britain to exit from the European Union, known as "Brexit"; and an ethics scandal in UK football. This heavily retweeted tweet about McCain linked to several news articles claiming he had referred to his wife as a "cunt": "'*At least I don't plaster on the makeup like a trollop, you cunt.*' - *John McCain to his wife Cindy, in public.*" The outrage at McCain potentially calling his wife a "cunt" in public shows the taboo associated with the word, and the reference to "trollop" reflects sexual shaming, referring to a woman who is perceived as promiscuous.

The lower taboo in the UK led to the use of "cunt" in relation to Brexit, such as "*@brexittruths you are a cunt as look at the exchange rate! You have won fuck all by doing this!*" Several events in UK football and soccer, including an ethics scandal, led to an increase in managers, players, and referees being called "cunts": "*Fuck Allardyce, Greedy Cunt. Think about how hard you worked for your £350 pw and then try sympathise with a greedy millionaire.*" We saw earlier that players who made bad plays or were on rival teams were often called "cunts": "*Why do they always play Young against us? Shit cunt plays like a prime Ronaldo every time.*" Professional footballers were called "cunts" for appearing ungrateful or greedy. Examples included, "*Star on Sunday reporting newcastle to buy back Debuchy, fuck him, jaanmatt is much better! Money grabbing cunt! #nufc #afc*" and "*Sturridge is the most selfish cunt going.*" While these may be regulating masculinity performances, the greater acceptance in the UK means the slur carries less offense and thus the regulatory function is less forceful.

"Cunt" was not used nearly as often as "bitch" in popular culture (see Chapter 5). There were two references to "cunt" related to music. In both cases, "cunt" was used to refer to men (i.e., Kid

Cudi's song "Judgmental Cunt" and the rap collaboration "Cunt $wab Mafia"). "Cunt swab" is an insult similar to douchebag, often used when a man fails to successfully perform masculinity. While this usage reflects an extension of the word, traditional binary gender norms are not challenged.

Intersections

Very few racial, religious, or homophobic slurs accompanied "cunt" on Twitter. The black slang "nigga" was occasionally used as a neutral counterpart for men: "*You went write back to this nigga you're a cunt*" and "*you're also a selfish CUNT but you my nigga doe.*"[20] There were more tweets drawing attention to racism, showing Twitter as a platform to address injustice. However, in these three examples, tweeters did not make connections between racism and misogyny: "*Fuckin racist cunt*";[21] "*@AnaMaria you need to learn to be less of a racist cunt*"; and "*@CamillaMLopez @Tumelo_M @Zander95 you are a ridiculous racist cunt, go take shots of bleach, read a real history book then go die.*" It is possible that one racial slur occurred, though it targeted Hillary Clinton: "*@TeamTrump @realDonaldTrump you got my 100%support! Fuck that dirt cunt@HillaryClinton.*" The tweeter may have meant "dirty," intending to use "cunt" to demean and discredit her. However, *Urban Dictionary* (2017) defines "dirt cunt" as a pejorative for a black woman or a black woman's vagina, revealing a hierarchy in which vaginas are still offensive, but white supremacy intersects with gender to consider white women's vaginas less offensive than black women's. Another tweet used the pejorative "Paki" to refer to people from Pakistan: "*this paki needs to stop prank calling me and go pray to allah to forgive him for being a cunt.*" Two examples of homophobic slurs used "cunt" in this sample: "*@BTurner3012 hey fuck you idiot I don't give a fucking finnark*[22] *what u think u little cock sucking cunt*" and "*@dannyboy88 this gay ass fag thinks that she is not a cunt but in reality she is a huge hoe* 🍆🍆👋." Both tweets were used to demean men by calling them "cocksuckers" and "fags." The second tweet suggests that a man is being taken advantage of by a woman, so "fag" is being used to label men who fail to successfully perform hegemonic masculinity, consistent with ethnographic research by Pascoe (2012).

Conclusion

"Cunt" is considered by many to be the most offensive and misogynist slur against women (Baumgardner & Richards, 2000; Brontsema, 2004). Though it is similar to "bitch" in that it refers to gender performance, it did not occur as commonly on Twitter, likely due to its greater taboo status. As a result, it was also reclaimed less in popular culture. Although "cunt" has some variations, such as "cunty," newer meanings emerged on Instagram such as "cuntfucked," "cuntlife," and "cuntmuffin." Nevertheless, "cunt" did not have as varied uses as other misogynist slurs. Because of the greater offense, social media sites such as Facebook and Instagram did not permit content that used "cunt" in an offensive way toward women.

Consistent with expectations, "cunt" was primarily used to regulate women's behavior. Both "bitch" and "cunt" reflect gendered beliefs about women's agreeableness and trustworthiness. Women were called "cunts" for behaving in ways considered unlikable, unpleasant, untrustworthy, and unworthy. Slurs such as "bitch" and "cunt" are rooted in a patriarchal society that expects women to be pleasant and hidden from public discourse (Beard, 2014; Spender, 1991). Hillary Clinton figured prominently in tweets. She was accused mostly of being untrustworthy and unworthy, not only of becoming president of the United States, but also as a woman and a person. Furthermore, she was criticized for expressing strong views in public.

To successfully perform heterofemininity, which is assumed to be white and affluent, women must not only be likable but also reserved and not opinionated. When women expressed an opinion, particularly in public spheres such as politics, "cunt" was used to definitively discredit and silence without productive dialogue or informed counterarguments. "Cunt" then serves to remind women to refrain from engaging in public discourse. Essentialist beliefs about gender mean that women and men are evaluated differently. To succeed in spheres such as academia, business, and politics, women then are caught in a bind where to be successful might mean being less likable (Bowles, Babcock, & Lai, 2007; Eagly, Makhijani, & Klonsky, 1992; Gregory, 2016; Rudman & Glick, 2001). Like the use of all misogynist slurs, the effect is to deny women's humanity and right to participate in all sectors of society.

The high rate of naming and generic insults on Twitter leads to a general climate of hostility toward women. Even when a specific woman is not named, the message to refrain from speaking freely in public forums is sent to all women. The use of "cunt" in gendertrolling shows a concerted effort to silence women through derogatory labeling. While this research does not look at threats over time, the data contain instances of single threats of violence against women on Twitter. New policies around harassment seem to be addressing these issues, for many of the tweeters' accounts had been suspended as of January 1, 2017. The effectiveness of institutional policies is discussed in more detail in Chapter 7.

Cultural context matters. "Cunt" is more accepted in the UK, where a large portion of tweets were directed toward professional male athletes. While greater acceptance in ordinary conversation carries potential for weakening the meaning of "cunt," it tended to refer to men who had lost control or failed. This use reinforces the notion that masculinity means constant independence, power, and success particularly in sports (Kimmel, 2000; Messner, 1999). Though it is an extension to apply "cunt" to men, and the connotation is less harsh, the derogation is intact. It is unclear whether people in the United States, particularly those who follow UK football, will pick up the term, or if negative reactions by people in the United States will cause people in the UK to avoid using it. Potential for greater disruption lies in new phrasings of "cunt," such as "cuntlike" and the use of "cunty" within the LGBTQIA community. It is possible that use of "cunt" as a nongendered insult is catching on in the United States, though, like "pussy," much of the offense lies in its association with women's bodies.

Even more transformative potential lies in forms of dissent on Facebook, Instagram, and Twitter. Women and men defended the label "cunt," arguing for its normalcy. Women educated others on the use of the word, positively identified with the term, and offered direct critiques, though "cunt" has not been reclaimed as much as "bitch." "Dyke" and "slut" also showed more positive identification than "whore," with connections to education and activism. Feminists argue that the greater taboo of "cunt" lies in its direct connection to women's vaginas. To end misogyny, deeply held attitudes toward women's bodies must change (Greer, 1971; Musica, 2002). In addition, structural change must occur. The denigration of women's bodies is supported by policies that limit women's access to health care, control over fertility, and freedom from sexual violence. In Chapter 7, I will return to the question of whether misogynist terms like "cunt" can be reclaimed using the master's tools (Lorde, 1984) and the relationships among language, structural change, and women's rights.

Notes

1. "Cunt" was tracked for a shorter time than the other misogynist terms studied. It became clear while researching online abuse of women and analyzing social media that "cunt" was an important concept to study, particularly due to the increase in the use of "bitch" and "cunt" on Twitter leading up to the 2016 US presidential election.

2. Data are unable to explain the major falls in use of "cunt" in September; it may have been due to losing connection with Twitter or drops in overall Twitter activity. Counts should be interpreted with caution.

3. Further investigation revealed this tweet was in response to the tweet, *"Hillary says people who chant 'USA' at Trump rallies are 'UN-American.'"*

4. Translated from Polish by Google Translate as "I want a shirt like Kate, 'Fuck you cunt' actually seven—that is, on each day of the week."

5. X means a kiss.

6. "Asf" is an acronym for "as fuck," and "fr" for "for real."

7. Two were not included here because information about gender identity was unavailable.

8. This tweet was a comment on a tweet by Republican strategist and political commentator Ana Navarro that read, *"Dear GOP: Congrats! We nominated a misogynist, racist, vulgar, lying, ignorant, mad man as our nominee. Oh, and he breaths like Darth Vader."*

9. This tweet was heavily retweeted and accompanied by two pictures: one of a fly landing on Clinton during a debate and one of flies on excrement.

10. This tweet was in response to a tweet expressing support for Hillary Clinton.

11. This tweet was accompanied by a photo and stats for Spanish professional football player Sergio Ramos.

12. This tweet was from Liam Gallagher (LG), the singer for the band Oasis, in response to criticism that he formerly tweeted: *"Solo record are you fucking tripping dickhead im not a cunt LG x."*

13. "Rn" is an acronym for "right now."

14. This tweet refers to a song title by a death metal band called Cannibal Corpse, translated from Spanish by Google Translate as "Listening to 'Entrails ripped from a virgin's cunt' and PUM! Advertising Spotify with Maluma."

15. GTFO is an acronym for "get the fuck out," and GAF is an acronym for "give a fuck."

16. This tweet was in response to the "She's a Cunt, Vote for Trump" t-shirt.

17. This tweet was accompanied by a photo of the man wearing the "She's a Cunt, Vote for Trump" t-shirt and standing with a woman and two children at a Trump rally.

18. This tweet linked to a *Daily Kos* article defending Hillary Clinton against attacks.

19. This tweet was accompanied by a link to a news article by *Conservative Tribune* in which a Secret Service agent claimed Hillary Clinton was rude and once hit another Secret Service agent with a Bible.

20. "Doe" is an alternative word for "though."

21. This tweet was in response to a photo by @whitemotivation of a woman accompanied by the caption "I love my White skin, my ancestors, my people, our history, culture, accomplishments & how absolutely amazing we are." Many responded with charges of racism and reminders that black lives matter.

22. It is unclear what "finnark" means.

7

Transformation and Dissent on Social Media

Misogynist slurs are used thousands of times a day on social media. Systematic research confirms that online, users perceived as women experience a particular form of abuse that employs threats of sexual violence and misogynist slurs (Citron, 2014; Demos, 2016b; Jane, 2014; Mantilla, 2015). The use of misogynist slurs online can be considered ambient or passive sexual harassment in that both create a hostile environment. Online sexual harassment has become so common that groups such as the United Nations are calling for a "world-wide wake-up call" (Broadband Commission for Sustainable Development, 2015). While harassment of white women in public positions has received the most media attention, women of color experience both misogynist and racist abuse. Online harassment is associated with negative effects on mental health and educational outcomes. Not isolated to online interactions, trolling and publishing personal information has caused some women to limit online activity, cancel public appearances, and change physical addresses.

My work in this book expands upon existing research by examining terms primarily used to shame women sexually ("dyke," "slut," and "whore) and terms primarily used to silence women ("bitch" and "cunt"). Inductive qualitative analysis of content from social media platforms Facebook, Instagram, and Twitter revealed that women have been labeled "bitch," "cunt," "dyke," "slut," and "whore" when they deviate from heterofeminine performances. These slurs serve a public regulatory function, warning women to conform to gender and sexual norms. Analysis also revealed that misogynist slurs were used in ways that extended their meaning, including referring to men as "bitches" and using "bitch" as an intensifier, as in "It's Britney bitch." Although many of these tweets depended on the misogynist meanings found in regulatory uses, extensions possess the power to disrupt gender and sexual norms. Holding the most power for disruption were themes related to dissent. Analysis found resistance and transformation of gender and sexual norms in the form of reappropriation, critical discourse, and political organization around feminist issues.

The varied uses of misogynistic slurs on social media raise important questions about the relationships between language and culture, social media, gender relations, and structural gender inequality. Language enables much of what happens in the social world, such as marking people as deviant or outsiders and justifying differential treatment. Narratives shape our understanding of the world and are crucial to the creation and maintenance of structural inequality. With respect to gender, using "he" for all people made men the subject and women the "other," and the pronouns "he" and "she" enforce binary gender identities. The hashtag #wordsmatter refers to a pledge in the media to stop using the word "illegal" to describe undocumented immigrants. At the time of this publication, many public figures, media outlets, and educational institutions signed this pledge, and the Associated Press changed its stylebook (Define American, 2016).

At the structural level, gender and sexual inequality are supported by institutions, such as schools and corporations, and economic, religious, and political systems. Despite advancements in higher education and labor force participation, progress toward gender equality is uneven across sectors of society. The earnings gap has stalled, and women are underrepresented in politics (Cotter, Hermsen, & Vannemann, 2011). In addition, women continue to experience high rates of intimate partner violence, and rape continues to be underreported and unpunished (UN Statistics Division, 2015). Accompanied by sustained efforts at the institutional and structural levels, disruptions in misogynist language have the potential to reverberate back to the social structure, transforming gender relations and gender and sexual inequality.

Online sexual harassment reflects a cultural bias in which women are deemed inferior and traits associated with women are feared, hated, and suppressed. Rooted in a patriarchal society, women are expected to be passive, pleasant, and hidden from public discourse

(Beard, 2014; Spender, 1991). Misogynist language enforces binary and essentialist gender and sexual identities and roles. Words like "dyke," "slut," and "whore" remain feared insults for adolescent girls and women and are used to shame women who are perceived as masculine, promiscuous, and untrustworthy (Attwood, 2007; Kreager & Staff, 2009, Lyons et al., 2011; Payne, 2010). "Bitch" and "cunt" are used to demean women who are perceived as disagreeable and unaccommodating (Brontsema, 2004; Kleinman, Ezzell, & Frost, 2009). Misogynist terms intersect with class and race to target working-class women and women of color for not conforming to hegemonic femininity (Armstrong et al., 2014; Hill Collins, 1990, 2004).

By shining a light on everyday misogyny, we can observe gender relations and consider ways to make the Internet a more welcoming place for women. Given the importance of the Internet for social interaction, what happens on the Internet has far-reaching consequences for social relations. Around the world, people spend an average of 100 minutes browsing social media every day (Global Web Index, 2016). Social media platforms such as Twitter are critical for understanding contemporary social interaction and inequality. Misogyny existed long before the Internet, and the Internet has not necessarily increased sexual abuse toward women (boyd, 2014). However, posts to public social media sites such as Twitter reach large audiences. Reliance on the Internet also makes it difficult to escape potential harassment. It is impossible to determine how many women refrain from interacting online or entering technological fields due to a climate of misogyny. Jane (2014) predicts that online misogyny is likely to become more common and would be considered unacceptable if occurring in another domain.

I began writing this conclusion the day after participating in the 2017 Women's March on Washington, D.C. The march was originally organized to protest misogynist statements made during the 2016 presidential campaign and later expanded to address climate change, LGBTQIA rights, immigrant rights, Islamophobia, police brutality, public education, and racial inequality. Misogynist language permeated the presidential campaign, some of it coming from then president-elect Donald Trump's Twitter account, including, "*Did Crooked Hillary help disgusting (check out sex tape and past) Alicia M become a U.S. citizen so she could use her in the debate?*"[1] People reacted strongly to recordings made public by the *Washington Post* in which Trump claimed to kiss women and grab their genitals without consent (Fahrenthold, 2016).[2] Misogyny was documented at rallies for Trump, including "Trump that Bitch" t-shirts and the heavily retweeted photo of a man wearing a shirt that read "She's a Cunt Vote for Trump." Twitter users were particularly upset that the man wearing this shirt appeared to be standing with a woman and young children.

Continuing into 2017, Kim Weaver dropped out of the race for Iowa's Fourth Congressional District after online harassment included death threats. Television anchor Mika Brzezinski of MSNBC was another target of misogynist tweets emanating from the president's Twitter account. Australian actress Marieke Hardy was trolled by a pharmaceutical executive and entrepreneur whose Twitter account has since been suspended. As I finish this conclusion, that same man used Facebook to harass Hillary Clinton during the tour for her forthcoming book *What Happened*, offering $5,000 to anyone who could "grab a hair" from her head. Donald Trump shared a doctored GIF of his golf ball knocking Hillary Clinton down. This image was accompanied by the hashtag #CrookedHillary, depicting not only violence but the continued emphasis on her supposed untrustworthiness. After football player Colin Kaepernick kneeled during the National Anthem in protest of police brutality, Trump used the phrase "son of a bitch" to criticize Kaepernick and other football players who "disrespected the flag." Recognizing the gendered aspect to the phrase "son of a bitch," poet and writer Jeffers (2017) reminds us that racial norms define respectable female sexuality as white and animalize black children and their mothers, including white women who consort with black men. Numerous men in high-profile positions in varied fields, such as entertainment, politics, and technology, are being accused of sexual harrassment and assault.

Summary of Findings

"Bitch" was, by far, the most common misogynist slur on Twitter, averaging 418,665 tweets a day. "Slut" was the second most-used misogynist term on Twitter at 37,646 average uses a day. "Cunt" occurred 25,496 times a day, followed by "whore" at 21,018. "Dyke" was the least common term, used 2,720 times a day. Though "bitch" and "cunt" were used in similar ways, the difference in frequency was due to the high extensions of "bitch" and the greater taboo associated with "cunt" in some cultural contexts (Baumgardner & Richards, 2000; Brontsema, 2004). "Slut" and "whore" were used in similar ways, but the association of "whore" with prostitution serves as a harsher insult (Pheterson, 1993; Pomeroy, 1995). People actively engage with the world through social media; consequently, results are dependent on the period under investigation. All misogynist terms measured on Twitter through November 2016 showed a spike in use on November 9, the day the results of the 2016 US presidential election were announced. Hillary Clinton was the most common public figure named in misogynist tweets.

Regulation

Qualitative analysis revealed that apart from "bitch," misogynist slurs were primarily intended to regulate women's behavior. "Dyke" contained the largest portion of regulatory tweets even though there were also high numbers of dissenting tweets showing its reclamation. All slurs served as a public scarlet letter, used to *name or tag* people who identified or were perceived as women, as in *"We all know a slut named @Tina_Lee."* Before social media, a girl might be labeled a "slut" in school, but the label reaches farther and lasts longer when someone is publicly named or tagged on Twitter. All slurs included *generic insults* that served to remind women of the consequences of heterofeminine digressions, as in *"ur just a rude bitch."*

Appearance was a major area of regulation, with all slurs marking women as failing to display heterofemininity, which often meant having short hair and wearing baggy clothing, as in *"I hate how bitches think getting the dyke chop as a haircut is cute like nah im not tryna date you with that haircut."* For "slut" and "whore," tweets often referenced body weight and modest clothing: *"@angelica_94: Fat whore lol"* and *"I'm not saying your shorts should say 'Whore' on the bum...but your labia's showing."* All misogynist words, with the exception of "cunt," regulated women's *demeanor*. Women were often called "dykes" for exhibiting what society considers masculine traits such as athleticism, outspokenness, and toughness, demonstrated in the tweet *"I hate when women basketball players walk around actin like dudes. get your dyke ass on somewhere else."* Slurs were used to remind women to behave in controlled manners: *"If your a girl and you go out every weekend and get smashed then your a slut."*

An emphasis on traditional ideals of femininity upholds hegemonic masculinity by making traits such as athleticism, risk-taking, and outspokenness seem to belong naturally to men's domain (Connell & Messerschmidt, 2005; Schippers, 2007). Therefore, misogynist slurs do as much to reproduce and maintain heteromasculine norms as heterofeminine norms. Misogynist tweets also reinforced racial and class-based sexual hierarchies, as in "*@msmaddie fuck you whore you white trash.*" Although racial identity was not always available, tweets containing "hoe" and "THOT" were accompanied by slang more commonly used in the African American community such as "nigga," as shown in "*RT if your girl a hoe be honest nigga.*"

Except for "dyke," misogynist terms were used to denote *untrustworthiness* with respect to sexual and other behaviors, reflecting ancient views of women as inherently deceitful. "Bitch" served this function often, as in "*Nobody Likes A Home Wrecking Ass Bitch. Stay In Your Lane 👍.*" Women were called "bitches" and "cunts" for behaving in ways considered *unpleasant*, as in "*@calliesally because she's a shitty person and was a total cunt to me and my friends who were nothing but nice to her.*" Feminine norms dictate that women should be silent and agreeable (Spender, 1991). "Bitch" included the additional theme of *dominant* or *agentic* behavior, as in this tweet: "*There's a difference between a slut and a bitch... A slut will sleep with anyone. A bitch will sleep with anyone... But you.*"

The primary uses of "slut" and "whore" (as well as some examples of "bitch" and "cunt") regarded *promiscuity*, being *unfaithful*, or expressing *any sexual interest* at all. Gender scholars recognize that the gender system depends, in part, on the control of women's sexuality through ideas about deviant sexual behavior, sexual violence, and laws about marriage and family (Lorber, 1994). Women are considered the more virtuous sex who must act as the moral custodians of men's behavior (Vance, 1992). Tweets criticized women who failed to control sexual desires, such as "*@angelina slut...goes from guy to guy and doesn't care.*"

The connection between "whore" and prostitution (Pheterson, 1993) resulted in more references to *sex work* and a new theme of *gold digger*, including "*@jennyfergirl she's a golddigging fake whore with collagen lips and fake tits and fugly face.*" As opposed to being too available, "dykes" were criticized for being *unavailable* as in this tweet posted by a user identifying as male: "*I hate seeing a beautiful ass dyke.*" Compulsory heterosexuality demands that women remain available and attractive to men (Rich, 1980). However, women who were too available were called "sluts" and "whores," making women's reputations dependent on their relationships to men. "Dyke" tweets also introduced another unique theme of *sin/immorality*, primarily attributed to religious edicts: "*@WBCSaysRepent: Taking the Lord's name in vain means using God's name to promote vanity and sin. 'The Lord led me to my dyke lover.'*"

All misogynist terms were used to mark women who deviate from heterofeminine norms as *unworthy*, particularly in terms of their relationships with men, as in the tweet, "*Can't turn a whore into a housewife.*" These claims of unworthiness define sexual desire as men's purview and determine women's worth through adherence to gender norms and relationships to men. A new theme of *silencing* emerged from the slurs considered more offensive, "cunt" and "whore," reflecting the idea that women should be agreeable and not express opinions (Beard, 2014). One example of silencing is the tweet "*Shut the fuck up you ugly fat cunt @maryarena.*" Most disturbing, all misogynist terms analyzed in this book included examples of *threats*, consistent with the experiences of women bloggers and gamers. The current research does not look at continued threats over time; however, even one-time insults create a climate of hostility around gender and sexual freedom and serve as warnings to others to remain in line with heterofeminine norms. Due to perceived toughness and masculine styles, the label "dyke" was associated with the most threats of physical violence from men, as in "*dyke bitches get beat up too.*"

External events influenced the frequency and use of misogynist slurs. Although there is not a total count for the period under investigation, Hillary Clinton was the most commonly targeted public figure, and peaks in the use of misogynist terms were due to an increase in tweets about her. Tweets referred primarily to perceptions of Clinton as *unpleasant, untrustworthy,* and *unworthy.* A representative example was, "*Hillary is a whore who's been sold out to Saudi 💰. Every decision revolves around donations to Clinton Foundation.*" Investigations have revealed that hundreds of fake Facebook and Twitter accounts originating in Russia were set up before the US presidential election to spread false information. It is difficult to tell how many of the tweets about Hillary Clinton came from fake accounts, but a postelection survey found that fake news tilted in favor of Donald Trump and content was shared more than 30 million times (Allcott & Gentzkow, 2017). Volunteers and bots continue to spread misinformation to undermine trust in elections and influence their outcomes in countries other than the United States, including France, India, the Netherlands, the Philippines, and the UK (Vaidhyanathan, 2017).

Besides Hillary Clinton, almost all of the celebrity women referred to as one of the misogynist slurs identify or are perceived as immigrant, non-European, or African American. This group includes Amber Rose, Ariana Grande, Azealia Banks, Melania Trump, Selena Gomez, Kim Kardashian, and to a lesser extent her sisters Khloe and Kourtney Kardashian and Kendall and Kylie Jenner. Tweets often included mentions of their real or imagined ethnicity, showing the intersection of gender and race-ethnicity. For example, "*@melania-trump is a whore. Sloveian slut. Call girl who wants women to be raped by her husband. She only wants money, gold digging immigrant.*" Although members of the LGBTQIA community are harassed at high levels, this sample did not include a high number of additional homophobic terms. The low occurrence of homophobic terms was most likely because of the reclamation of "dyke" and the current focus on terms generally reserved for women. However, that did not stop Twitter users from enforcing heteromasculinity by directing misogynist terms such as "bitch" and "cunt" toward men.

Symbolic interactionists have long noted the effect of others' impressions on individuals (Goffman, 1959), and the stage on which one performs heterofemininity has become even more public. Social media users display their gender and sexuality for others to comment on and critique through tweets, Facebook groups and pages, and Instagram hashtags. Women who do not conform to heterofeminine norms are deemed unworthy, particularly of male attention. Consequently, women's worth is defined solely in relation to men, perpetuating the idea that women are not autonomous beings with control over their bodies. Unwillingness to accept women's voices and sexual agency has consequences for basic human rights and full participation in spheres such as politics. In a special issue of *Sexualities*, Plante and Fine (2017) recognize the role of reputation in sexual shaming and gendered social control. They argue that sexual reputations are central to social interaction, can cause harm to individuals, and halt progressive social change. Surveillance and restrictions on women's rights are compounded by classism, racism, and structural inequality. White, middle-class, educated women are not inherently marked as domineering or overly sexual and can more easily discard the image of "bitch" or "slut."

This study found less public shaming and silencing of women on Facebook and Instagram compared to Twitter. The difference is likely due to Facebook's stricter terms of use and more rigorous monitoring. Twitter's greater anonymity and character limit reduce the opportunities for thoughtful conversation. However, the current research examined only public data and cannot compare private use of misogynist slurs across the three social media platforms.

Extension

In addition to the expected regulatory functions, misogynist slurs were used online to extend meanings beyond labels for women who deviate from heterofeminine norms. Extensions have the potential to disrupt misogynist meanings. As words get revised or thrown around casually, the potential for lost pejorative power arises. "Bitch" was the only misogynist term that had a higher frequency of extension than regulation themes and was used in more varied ways than the other terms. The high frequency of extensions of "bitch" is likely due to its incorporation into popular culture and its weaker connection to women's bodies and sexuality. "Bitch" was the only term used as an *intensifier* as in *"bitch, please."* Intensifiers add force to a statement, and though force comes from the negative connotation of "bitch," it is less tied to gender or sexuality, as in *"Just posted a photo @ South Beach, Miami (Bitch!)."* However, it was also used to express exasperation, suggesting a connection to the themes of agreeableness and trustworthiness, as in *"Nothing I hate more than when I ask a customer how they're doing and they just start ordering. BITCH ANSWER MY DAMN QUESTION."*

"Bitch" was also used in two *colloquial phrases*, "son of a bitch" and "resting bitch face." While "son of a bitch" insults a man by insulting his mother, it is thrown about so casually that it is not always perceived as an insult. For instance, someone might say it when they stub their toe. In this way, "son of a bitch" is more of an exclamation. The idea of a "resting bitch face" exposes the idea that women should always appear cheerful. "Bitch" has also become a verb for *complaining*, as in *"If you vote I don't wanna hear you bitch."* "Bitch" along with "cunt" and "slut" were used to refer to inanimate objects or states of being, as in *"Payback is a bitch."* Similar to the use of intensifiers, using "bitch" to complain or refer to a negative state or inanimate object alters its meaning but retains its negative connotation.

"Bitch" (and one tweet containing "dyke") commonly served as a counterpart for *woman* or *girlfriend* as in *"I miss having a ride or die bitch."* Linguists use the term "neutral counterpart" if the word "bitch" can be replaced with "woman" or "girlfriend" and retain its meaning. Anderson and Lepore (2013), Ashwell (2016), and Kleinman, Ezzell, and Frost (2009) do not consider "bitch" neutral because it implies that all women are "bitches." However, the speakers do not seem to be calling their girlfriends "bitches" in the traditional sense of the word. "Bitches" referred to women or girlfriends without the intent to convey negative sentiment. Though this appears to be a neutral use of "bitch," the question remains as to why the terms "woman" or "girlfriend" were not used.

Higher occurrences of racial slang that accompanied "bitch" and "dyke" suggest greater use as neutral counterparts in the African American community. In-group uses of modified slurs show the need to be sensitive to the meanings of words within cultural contexts (Francesca, 2010). While all misogynist terms were used to *insult men*, the higher use of "cunt" in the UK is due to historical and socioeconomic factors where "cunt" is more akin to "jerk" or "asshole" (Hunt, n.d.). The variation in the meaning of "cunt" again shows the need for sensitivity to cultural contexts. Being on a rival team, making bad plays, or displaying greed or lack of sportsmanship resulted in labeling men as "cunts" as in "*Fucking hate Lingard. Sorry but he is rubbish championship player. Hoped Jose would see through this fraud cunt. Clearly not yet.*" The greater acceptance of "cunt" in the UK explains why it is the only misogynist slur that men applied to themselves, as in this tweet from Liam Gallagher of the band Oasis: "*It's official I'm a cunt LG* x." "Cunt" showed more variation in use on Facebook and Instagram, such as the adjectives "cunty" (used more frequently on Twitter by users identifying as gay males) and "cuntfucked," "cuntlife," and "cuntmuffin." It remains to be seen whether "cunt" will become more accepted due to it being less offensive in Australia and the UK. Fans of UK football who interact online could adopt "cunt" as a slang through exposure even if "cunt" is considered taboo where they live.

When "slut" and "whore" were applied to men, the slurs retained their original meanings as having more than the accepted number of sexual partners. However, applying the slurs to men shows some weakening of the sexual double standard. Having many sexual partners has long been considered natural and culturally desirable for men. Therefore, sometimes "man" had to precede the word to make the meaning clearer, as in "*My cousin is a man whore!*" When "bitch" or "dyke" were applied to men, these terms were used to insult men who were not performing masculinity successfully, reinforcing gender norms consistent with research on masculinity (Connell, 2005; Kimmel, 2000; Messner, 1999). Furthermore, using terms associated with women intensifies the insult, as when calling men "gay" or "fag" (Pascoe, 2012). The new concept of "fuck boy" brings into focus men's sexuality in a way not previously done. "Slut" and "whore" were also used to humiliate the submissive in an SM relationship, showing the sexual derogation associated with the terms.

A common extension of "whore" on Facebook, Instagram, and Twitter was the phrase "attention whore." Facebook groups used "whore" to refer to anything in which someone has an *inordinate interest*, such as shoes or books. It is perhaps the derogatory content of "whore" that makes tweets like *"Because I'm a selfie whore.😈"* sound cool and edgy. However, many of the new meanings reflected the original misogyny. "Whore" was chosen for this use because whores are viewed as lacking control and having insatiable desires. Furthermore, pejorative words may make desirable slang because of their negative connotations. But repeated use of extensions in non-sexual ways may weaken the derogatory content by separating words from their original meanings.

Dissent

Themes included under the category of dissent hold the most power to create ruptures in meanings, draining slurs of their pejorative power and potentially transforming cultural attitudes about gender and sexuality. Studies of adolescents confirm resistance and reframing of female sexuality online (Kelly, Pomerantz, & Currie, 2006; Stokes, 2007) and off-line (Ringrose & Renold, 2012). However, not all forms of dissent carry the same potential for social change regarding sexuality. Some forms of dissent, like resistance, can be thought of as passive and, therefore, less effective relative to revolutionary action that creates new meanings and practices.

The terms "dyke" and "slut" were used most often in dissenting ways. "Dyke" was used often as a form of *positive self-identification*, while "slut" was often used in *direct critiques*. All misogynist terms were used as forms of *positive identities* (also known as *reappropriation* or *reclamation*). The reclamation of "dyke" was well underway on social media sites, captured by the commonly retweeted *"Be all the dyke you can be. Namaste."* In-group uses of black slang suggest that "dyke" may be more reclaimed in the African American community. However, some women who identified as lesbians disapproved of the label "dyke," coded as *direct critiques*. Despite feminist efforts by Greer (1971) and others to reclaim the words "cunt" and "whore" as positive and powerful, these words were less reclaimed due to the greater stigmas attached to vaginas and prostitution.

All slurs apart from "cunt" were used in *celebratory* ways. Again, this usage is likely due to the greater taboo associated with "cunt" in cultural contexts such as in the United States. Celebratory uses carry disruptive power by changing the connotation from negative to positive. However, they can also reinforce the original meanings of misogynist slurs. For example, celebratory tweets about "sluts" and "whores" often celebrated their sexual availability, reinforcing the labeling of women based on sexual activity, as in "*I want to sleep with a slut.*" "Dykes" were celebrated by members of the in-group and heterosexual men who saw having sex with "dykes" as a conquest. Celebrating "bitches" did not significantly alter the meaning, but the word took on a positive connotation of strength, such as when preceded by "bad" as in "*@WeAllKnowA: We all know a bad bitch named Shaniqua.*"

Friendly uses are similar to *positive-identification* and *celebration* in that words are transformed to have a positive connotation, though the extent to which they are separated from their original meanings is unclear. All misogynist terms were used this way, although "cunt" less often due to its lower cultural acceptance. Findings were consistent with Sutton's (1995) discovery that women use "slut" endearingly. For instance, "*happy birthday, ya slut* 🍷 💃" is friendly, though the tweet does not reveal whether the recipient is considered a "slut." Repeated use outside of original contexts carries the potential to separate misogynist words from their derogation.

All slurs contained examples of tweets *rejecting the label.* Rejecting labels shows the potential for social media to provide agency. These users of social media did not allow themselves to be labeled, potentially standing up to abusers. However, rejecting a label offers limited opportunity for disruption in its meaning. Consider this representative tweet: "*How can I be a slut if I only slept with one guy?*" The denial reinforces the idea that a "slut" is a woman who has had multiple sex partners and should not be applied to someone who has followed gendered sexual norms by having sex with only one partner. Ashwell (2016) argues that since gendered slurs generally do not have neutral correlates, denying that someone is a "slut" means this person is not part of a deviant group. "Cunt" was the only term that was *directly defended* on Twitter, though it was defense of the use of the word rather than its underlying meaning, as in this tweet: *"If you are offended by the word "cunt" or "fuck", I'll do you a favor and tell you to stay clear of me. #girlswithfoulmouths #nofucksgiven."* Twitter users also debated the use of slurs on social media, with some wanting a more civil environment and others wanting absolute freedom of speech. Both sides demonstrated the capacity for the exchange of ideas.

Direct critiques, education, and *political organizing* hold the most potential to challenge stigma attached to deviance from heterofeminine norms. The current sample did not include examples of people using "bitch" in these ways, perhaps because of its greater incorporation into mainstream language. Though not included in this sample, conversations about the use of "bitch" to describe assertive women are happening online and off-line (Cottle, 2016; Friend, 2015). The rest of the slurs included examples of *direct critiques* and *education*, consisting of themes that could be considered a form of revolutionary action. "Slut" was used more often in critiques and education, primarily because of the phrase "slut-shaming" entering the public vernacular. With the creation of this phrase, a complex problem is condensed into something people can more easily use to challenge norms around women's sexuality. By tweeting a phrase such as *"destroy gender roles and slut shaming 2k16,"* conversations about gender and sexuality become public.

Critiques of "dyke" showed that while many reclaimed "dyke," others found the term offensive, as in *"The slurs 'faggot', dyke' 'tranny' and 'queer' have to stop. It's offensive and it's gross."* Other tweets recognized greater acceptance when slurs were used by members of the in-group, as in *"lesbians be using tf outta the word 'dyke' but wanna get offended & upset as soon as a straight mf call em one.😒"* People used Twitter to *educate* others about the injury caused by using misogynist slurs as well as the hypocrisy: *"Cuz you're a dumbass if you're a dyke and make fun of another dyke for wearing a fuckin skirt. You're literally doing what straight ppl do."*

People used Twitter to *directly critique* misogyny, shown in this common retweet: *"This guy, at the rally with his wife and three kids, in his 'She's A Cunt Vote For Trump' shirt."* People directly challenged the ideas underlying misogynist slurs: *"The idea of being a slut/hoe/whore is a manmade social construct intended to limit a woman's sexuality.*" Feminist blogs and magazines such as *Bitch* and *Feministing* also used Facebook and Twitter to post articles challenging sexual shaming. "Slut" was the only term used to organize political activity, with the exception of one "dyke" tweet. Political organizing was primarily due to "slut walks" in which women march to protest a rape culture that denies women complete control over their bodies and fails to punish rapists. The first one was in Ontario in 2011 although "Take Back the Night" marches started in the 1970s.[3] The organization of an annual SlutWalk in Los Angeles by Amber Rose since 2015 has brought great media attention to the event, in part due to her celebrity status. Since then, walks have been organized around the world. One tweet included "dyke" as in *"So this Saturday, Chicago's Dyke March celebrates 20 years—lots of people not recognised by standard (white) left will be there.*" Many more examples of organizing events and community-building for women who identify as "dykes" appeared on Facebook, such as "Dyke Marches" and "Dykes on Bikes."

Summary

All misogynist terms studied here served regulatory uses online, reminding women at the level of interaction to remain in line with the heterogender norms of agreeableness, deference, monogamy, pleasantness, romance, and trustworthiness. Social media content that targets women's bodies, clothing, and other behaviors suggests that women's behavior is carefully and consistently scrutinized online. From a sociological perspective, misogynist language not only reflects but also shapes and reinforces essentialist gender norms, institutions, and structures that sort women and men into different roles. Although all misogynist terms have sexual origins, "slut" and "whore" have the most to do with feminine heterosexuality. The misogynist terms "bitch" and "cunt" have the most to do with feminine gender norms. "Dyke" relates to both gender and sexual norms. Misogynist terms are also used to remind men to remain in line with masculine norms of behavior. The meanings of misogynist slurs are extended to describe inanimate objects and serve as intensifiers, suggesting potential for the meanings of words to change. Holding even more potential for social change are direct critiques of misogyny, education in the form of feminist articles, and organization of political action such as marches addressing women's rights.

Language and Society

Debate exists over the ability to reclaim or reappropriate previously injurious words. Some view the reclamation of "slut" and "whore" as impossible because the terms' meanings are too deeply rooted in patriarchy (Gwynne, 2013; Tanenbaum, 2000, 2015). Others argue that a consumerist culture markets girls' sexual agency for profit and has co-opted ideas such as "girl power" that appear to be feminist but in fact operate as new forms of social control (McRobbie, 2008). Kleinman, Ezzell, and Frost (2009) argue that reclaiming words like "bitch" fails to provide women with real power or change the meaning for people who hold negative opinions.

Alternately, reclamation can construct new identities that do not conform to traditional notions of heterofemininity. Feminists such as Annie Sprinkle and Maria Beatty (1992), Germaine Greer (1971), the riot grrrls (Attwood, 2007), and Margo St. James (1987) have argued for reclaiming the misogynistic terms included in this book. bell hooks (1997) sees the potential for liberation in reclaiming speech by creating counterhegemonic worldviews. Drawing from language philosophy, J. L. Austin (1962) and Judith Butler (1997) argue that certain kinds of speech acts (illocutionary and felicitous[4]) hold the power to shape reality, and that only by occupying and being occupied by injurious terms can we oppose them. This discourse, Butler argues, must be returned in a different form that challenges more than just the meanings of language: "Within the very signification that is 'queer,' we read a resignifying practice in which the desanctioning power of the name 'queer' is reversed to sanction a contestation of the terms of sexual legitimacy" (1993: 232).

Reclaimed words can be thought of as reversing the political charge by creating a value change (i.e., assertive women are good, and women are free to have sex whenever and with whomever they want). However, not all forms of reappropriation disrupt underlying meanings. Choosing to use the word "slut" for oneself or one's friends in a friendly and playful way removes some of the stigma but does not challenge the underlying idea that women who have had more than the acceptable number of sexual partners exist in a category called "slut." It is possible that as reappropriation becomes widespread, as seen in this sample with "dyke," slurs will lose their offensive intensity (Anderson & Lepore, 2013). Words tied to movements for social change, such as "feminist," may hold the most potential to challenge patriarchy (Kleinman, Ezzell, & Frost, 2009).

Online direct critiques and education may directly challenge heterofeminine norms for behavior and sexuality. The meanings of pejorative words are vague and contextual, and thus are open to change. For instance, what counts as "more than an appropriate" number of sexual partners in Ashwell's (2016) definition of a "slut" (p. 235)? Meanings of misogynist terms are also flexible. Etymologies tell us that some slurs originally held positive meanings, suggesting that positive connotations can be taken back. "Bitch" was originally associated with followers of the Greek goddess Diana. Its former power was warped to make attributes associated with women negative. "Cunt" referred to vaginas, but came to represent something offensive and used to denigrate women. Change might come more slowly for words that have long and deep-rooted histories like "whore," but even the injury of "cunt," considered by many to be the most injurious of words about women, depends on context and connotation. Men are called "cunts" for any annoying behavior in the UK, where the term is more akin to "asshole" or "jerk."

Misogynist slurs have been mainstreamed and altered in many ways, including being used as intensifiers and reclaimed for commentary and art as in Bitch Media (*Bitch* magazine) and *Slut: The Musical*. Members of in-groups use words such as "nigga" and "queer" with less or no derogation. Disagreement may continue over reclamation, as seen in this sample over the use of "dyke." It is also difficult to predict which words will become fully reclaimed and which will not. Jeong (2017) reports that the club Dykes on Bikes has been denied a trademark due to laws that define "dyke" as disparaging lesbians, while simultaneously women are proudly proclaiming themselves "dykes" online and off-line.

Holding more transformative potential, new phrases have entered the public vernacular that use misogynistic slurs to directly critique the heterofeminine norms that produced them, such as "slut-shaming" and "bad bitch." Reclaiming slurs does not necessarily require a complete loss of the negative meaning. Brontsema (2004) argues that "to take up *queer* is at once to recognize and revolt against homophobia" (p. 4, emphasis in original). "Queer" could only effectively fight homophobia by highlighting homophobia. Rather than adopting a binary argument in which misogynist terms are either separable or inseparable from their injurious power, the relationship is dialectical in that the pejoration of a slur such as "dyke" is embraced in order to become transformative. In doing so, words like "dyke" claim "a political fierceness and anti-assimilationism that *lesbian* lacks, the latter seen to appeal to male, heterosexual, white, middle-class taste" (Brontsema, 2004: 14, emphasis in original). Ashley (1982) argues that the reclamation of "dyke" by lesbians since the 1970s performed "verbal karate" by turning a tool of the oppressor into one's own weapon (p. 126).

Reclaiming derogatory terms is a worthy cause because it rebels against speech meant to injure, moving toward the possibility of self-emancipation. The question remains whether discursive actions can supply new meanings around gender and sexuality that reverberate back to the social structure. Attacks on voice and bodily autonomy are part of a larger culture and set of practices that threaten women's reproductive rights, inadequately address sexual violence, and devalue women's work. Rejecting linguistic idealism means that language cannot transform social relations without accompanying shifts in patriarchal social norms, relations, and structures (Ashwell, 2016; Butler, 1990; White, 2002). Social media platforms are uniquely situated to transform attitudes about gender and sexuality, gender relations, and oppressive social structures by raising awareness, reframing narratives, and building community.

Social Media and Social Change

The Internet is complex, and some aspects of it contribute to democratic participation while others encourage abuse. Features of social media platforms such as anonymity, distance, and access to a broad audience may increase abusive speech by reducing empathy, opportunity costs, and identification by law enforcement. Online interactions mirror power relations off-line, allowing the powerful to dictate the style of dialogue. Drawing from Jurgen Habermas's (1989) notion of the public sphere, Matthew Hindman (2009) argues that the Internet would have to give greater voice to ordinary citizens and challenge the monopoly of traditional and new political elites to increase democratic participation. Studying millions of web pages on six diverse political topics, Hindman found that a small group of white, highly educated, male professionals were vastly overrepresented in online opinions and that people clustered around the top few information sources, such as Google. Writer and documentarian

Astra Taylor (2014) makes a similar observation: "While it's true that anyone with an Internet connection can speak online, that doesn't mean our megaphones blast our messages at the same volume. Online, some speak louder than others" (p. 4). Currently, Facebook dominates social media, though platforms such as Snapchat[5] are growing in popularity.

There is also a transformative aspect to the Internet, one in which power and identity themselves are "under attack" (Cavanagh, 2007: 14). Social media networks have the potential to be used as new forms of civic participation by people who lack the power to operate through the political system (Sassen, 2002). New channels for civic participation allow for new constructions of the self and unprecedented participation and voice. Despite their limitations, social media remain promising venues for disrupting existing power relations.

It is still unclear if language on social media can further social justice projects in ways that transform social relations and structures. Avoiding determinist theories means that the Internet neither causes nor is entirely unimportant for social movements. Contrary to concerns over weak ties and arguments about the ineffectiveness of "clicktivism" and "slacktivism," social media contributed to movements such as the Arab Spring uprisings (Howard & Hussain, 2013), Black Lives Matter (Eligon, 2015; Ware, 2016), and Occupy Wall Street (Penney & Dadas, 2013). Social media contributed to these movements through hashtags and memes that increased awareness, the digital circulation of information outside mainstream channels, and the facilitation of organizing through online communications. In 2012, the "binders-full-of-women" meme[6] raised awareness of the underrepresentation of women in politics and a lack of knowledge by the public of gender inequality (Rentschler & Thrift, 2015).

Much work is being conducted at the intersection of race and gender to protest police brutality against black people. In addition to #BlackLivesMatter, #SayHerName was created to raise awareness of police brutality against black women specifically. Hashtags serve to create counter media images and remind the community of self-care, including #BlackGirlMagic, #BlackManJoy, #CareFreeBlackKids2k16, and #HeyBlackGirl (Finley, 2016). Other hashtags raise awareness of body shaming, reproductive rights, and violence against women, including #metoo #freethenipple, #shoutyourabortion, and #yesallwomen.

Feminist online responses and advice-giving provide support and solidarity and can be considered political activity (Gould, 2010; Nussbaum, 2010). In response to Donald Trump's comments about touching women without their consent, writer Kelly Oxford tweeted on October 7, 2016, *"Women, tweet me your first assaults. they aren't just stats. I'll go first: Old man on city bus grabs my 'pussy' and smiled at me, I'm 12."* Within a day, Oxford had received millions of responses. Patterns of reporting sexual assault show that women feel empowered when others come forward. By providing information, holding rapists accountable, and building networks, Rentschler (2014) and Valenti (2013) argue that online activity has allowed women to respond to rape culture in a way that law enforcement, schools, and the media have not. Women took to social media to share their experiences of being silenced on the days that Senator Elizabeth Warren was prevented from speaking on the floor of the Senate, Senator Kamala Harris was interrupted during Senate hearings, Representative Maxine Waters reclaimed her time during congressional hearings, and a board member at Uber commented that women talk too much. This online activity led to posts of empirical research educating the public that men talk more often and longer in public than women, women are consistently interrupted more often than men, and women who express anger are viewed unfavorably (Brescoll, 2011; Brescoll & Sonnenfeld, 2014; Tannen, 1990). Gender-fluid and transgender adolescents use blogs and social media sites, such as Instagram and YouTube, to learn about themselves and meet others, helping to overcome suicidal thoughts, depression, and anxiety (Wortham, 2016). I concur with Brickell (2012) in that "we need to draw attention to power, name it as such, and examine its multiple dimensions and complexities" (p. 38), including instances of dominance and harassment as well as pleasure and freedom. The increase in online misogyny has put gender issues at the forefront and even educated people on what the word "misogyny" meant.

Online activities are particularly effective at inciting social change when picked up by television and newspaper media outlets, celebrities and politicians become involved, and activities connect to or inspire civic engagement through demonstrations, donations, and lobbying efforts. According to Ware (2016), the hashtag campaign #BlackLivesMatter has done more than anything else to make racial inequality a part of the national conversation, bringing together diverse groups under one larger mission, gaining the attention of politicians, and inspiring protests and boycotts across the country. The world has been exposed to the reality of police brutality through the streaming of live videos on Facebook, including the fatal shooting of Philando Castile. The 2014 Ice Bucket Challenge, in which people shared videos of themselves dumping buckets of ice over their heads to raise awareness of ALS (amyotrophic lateral sclerosis), was criticized as ineffective. However, a press release from the ALS Association (2016) credits a scientific breakthrough to donations received from the challenge. With one tweet of a press statement, four adolescent girls organized a 1,000-person protest against gun violence and police brutality in Chicago's Millennium Park. Their hashtag #BLMChiYouth trended on Twitter, and the protest was picked up by local and national news stations (Chang, 2016). Clothing company Billabong changed the images of women on their website after writer Karen Knowlton's blog about the objectification of women on its landing page went viral. The Women's March on Washington, D.C., originated from a Facebook post. Participation by diverse and seasoned activists created an international event (Friedman, 2017). According to political scientists Erica Chenoweth and Jeremy Pressman, 3.3 million people may have attended Women's Marches in the United States, making it the largest protest in US history (Frostenson, 2017).

All posts or tweets of the misogynist words studied here (except "bitch") exhibited some form of education, such as informing people about misogyny, sharing testimonials, and offering advice. Social media data collected in the current work showed that "slut" was tied to off-line social movements such as SlutWalks, which originated in Toronto in 2011 and have since gone global. Having a celebrity such as Amber Rose organize the Los Angeles SlutWalk increased media attention. However, the attention on young white women in the Toronto SlutWalk shows that claiming public spaces is perhaps more appealing and effective for people "just outside of hegemonic femininity" (Currans, 2012: 96). How class, race, sexuality, and gender conformity intersect with feminist access to public space, including on the Internet, is important future work. Though this sample did not contain education about "bitch," social media users educated others about the harm of double standards and rigid gender and sexual norms by posting arguments and reposting feminist content from online magazines and public figures.

What Can We Do?

If social media platforms are to contribute to feminist social change, they must be a place where women feel safe expressing ideas. Community, institutional, and legal efforts can improve the climate on social media platforms. Even though online threats of violence are against the law, those who have been targets of severe abuse complain that cases are mishandled by law enforcement (Citron, 2014; Mantilla, 2015). This calls for the clarification of laws and education of law enforcement personnel. Users complain that reports of abuse are also mishandled by social media. A 2016 survey found that 90 percent of reported complaints of abuse went unheeded on Twitter (Warzel, 2016). It is not just users applying pressure. As this book goes to press, new laws and government sanctions are being proposed to hold platforms like Facebook, Google, and YouTube responsible for regulating violent speech and images.

Social media platforms are responding to this pressure. Facebook recently added a tool to report posts more easily and guidelines for spotting fake news. Facebook is also improving its artificial intelligence DeepText to become better at identifying abusive and deceptive content. Because of its high data volume, Facebook also added more human moderators to review reports of harassment and abuse. Instagram uses humans and filters to identify and remove offensive comments and hashtags. Twitter has made it easier to block and report abuse, and users are now prohibited from setting up multiple accounts, posting private information about other people, and impersonating someone else. "The Twitter Rules" prohibit direct and indirect violent threats, harassment, hateful conduct, and attacks against people based on race, ethnicity, national origin, sexual orientation, gender, gender identity, religious affiliation, age, disability, and disease (Twitter Rules, 2017). Facebook and Instagram's Terms of Service have been considered exemplary for years because they include language about offensive content and bullying (Citron, 2014).

For less severe cases, such as offensive content and bullying, community standards and terms of use raise debates over who, if anyone, should decide what is considered offensive. Many feel strongly that the government should not have the sole power to define offensiveness, particularly as it relates to sexuality (Butler, 1997; Foucault, 1978/1990). The First Amendment of the Constitution of the United States protects freedom of speech from government interference.[7] As private corporations, websites such as Twitter are within their rights to create terms of use that prohibit abusive behavior. Like newspaper editors and television news producers, media companies make choices about our interactions with content. Influencing content through software, along with other decisions made by private companies, is still consistent with early declarations that the Internet should be free from outside forces and set up its own forms of self-governance (Barlow, 1996). In debates over freedom of speech, even the most permissive of positions such as that of John Stuart Mill (1859/1962) claim that people should have complete liberty with the sole exception of harming others.

Limiting online participation due to abusive behavior is a major social cost. Women who complain about abuse are often accused of being too sensitive or threatening free speech and the Internet's independence. Smith (2016a) argues that "the nature of 'speech' changes with the advent of new technology, and our intuitive notion of 'freedom of speech' will eventually have to change along with it" (para. 16). Complaints of suppression of conservative news and high-profile suspensions of abusers have caused some people to seek social media platforms that promise no censorship, such as Gab[8] (Barrett, 2016). The removal of white supremacist websites and pages after a "Unite the Right" rally in Charlottesville, Virginia, and the murder of protestor Heather Heyer on August 12, 2017, has intensified the debate over freedom of speech on the Internet. CEOs of social media companies are beginning to realize that harassment should not necessarily be given the protections of "free speech," as it limits other users' freedom of speech for fear of harassment, or worse, it drives users from their sites.

Chemaly (2013) and Citron (2014) argue that community standards are subjective and male-biased. They accuse Facebook of removing photos of women breastfeeding, menstruating, and wearing revealing clothing, but the latter only if women are considered unattractive by employees. Male bias in standards has been attributed to a lack of awareness and diversity within the technology industry. The phrase "who guards the guardians"[9] seems appropriate here. Organizations and users of social media can influence website policies. In 2014, feminist groups exerted pressure and started petitions for Facebook to remove pages promoting rape and domestic violence, and Twitter began working with the nonprofit organization Women, Action, and the Media to examine the problem of sexual harassment (Mantilla, 2015).

The large number of individuals using social media suggests there will rarely be full agreement on what counts as offensive speech or harm. Moral standards change, and the concept of offensiveness is fluid. Consequently, it is up to users of social media to apply pressure when there is noncompliance with standards. Community efforts to monitor sites should remain rigorous and adaptable.

To assess the limitations of free speech on social media platforms, users must know the rules (Kaminski & Klonick, 2017). The leaked internal rules for restricted speech on Facebook revealed, for example, that "someone shoot Trump" should be removed by moderators because Trump is in a protected category, while "to snap a bitch's neck, make sure to apply all your pressure to the middle of her throat" should not be removed because it is not considered a credible threat (Hopkins, 2017: para. 11).

Creating a more inclusive environment on social media platforms still requires accompanying cultural and structural change. Censorship does not prevent people from speaking about sexuality in a repressive way (Foucault, 1978/1990). Users can circumvent terms of use by creating fake accounts after suspension and evade banned words by spelling words differently or making up new words with the same meaning. Awareness campaigns organized by the Cyber Civil Rights Initiative (2017), Discourse of Online Misogyny (Hardaker, 2014), and the United Nations (Broadband Commission for Sustainable Development, 2015) recognize that the first step to changing attitudes is sensitization programs that educate parents and children on what constitutes online abuse and its effects. In addition, these programs provide resources and training for law enforcement. In June 2017, David's Law passed in Texas, making harassment, bullying, and cyberbullying a criminal offense. Named after San Antonio teenager David Molak, who committed suicide after relentless cyberbullying, this law also requires schools in Texas to include cyberbullying when discussing bullying policies, notify parents if their child is bullying or bullied, cooperate with law enforcement if threats are made, and offer counseling services.

Some of the most important examples of resistance and support comes from feminist blogs and magazines such as *Bustle*, *Bitch*, *Feministe*, *Feministing*, and *Jezebel*. Women who have experienced online abuse are writing about their experiences and creating guides that teach others how to stay safe on the Internet, such as "Speak Up and Stay Safe(r): A Guide to Protecting Yourself from Online Harassment" (Sarkeesian, Friedman, & Bracey Sherman, 2016), Anita Sarkeesian's nonprofit Feminist Frequency, and "Anita Sarkeesian's Guide to Internetting While Female" (2015). These guides include information on identifying and blocking trolls, removing and restricting the sharing of personal information, turning off geolocation when posting to social media, trusting interpretations of experiences, and, above all, reporting harassment. Zoë Quinn is the CEO of Crash Override, a website with tools and services for avoiding and addressing online harassment. Quinn has written about their online experiences in the book *Crash Override: How Gamergate (Nearly) Destroyed My Life, and How We Can Win the Fight Against Online Hate* (2017). The book offers an important structural element to explanations for online harassment, including content-neutral algorithms and politics. Third party apps such as Block Together can share block lists. Feminist digital activists are sharing methods to assess risks and options to protect themselves, such as masking Internet protocol (IP) addresses, using encryption, and creating strong passwords. Awareness campaigns should not just target women. It is victim blaming when we tell only women how to avoid abuse. We should include everyone in campaigns to discourage online abuse, a concept learned in anti–sexual violence programs (Flood, 2011). Anti-abuse educational programs in schools can educate all students, teachers, and administrators about online abuse and the importance of taking reports of abuse seriously.

Awareness campaigns have even more effect on society when people act and that action receives attention. The Who Needs Feminism campaign went viral with people posting pictures of themselves with signs reading "*#Ineedfeminism because . . .*" followed by such statements as "*I don't view equality as a radical concept*" and "*1/3 of 10 years old girls biggest worry is their body.*" Seidman (2013) reported that the campaign raised participants' awareness of gender and sexual privilege. Seidman considered the #Ineedfeminism campaign a new model of political activity for the twenty-first century that combined earlier forms of political organizing with new media. Promising new research looks at how community engagement can be created online, potentially reducing abusive interactions. Humor is a promising style for engaging with abusive speech, according to Susan Benesch of the Berkman Klein Center for Internet and Society at Harvard University and Massachusetts Institute of Technology (MIT) doctoral candidate Jonny Sun (known on Twitter as Jomny Sun), the creator of the humorous aliebn[10] account (Lichtenstein, 2017). Sun uses the term "urban landscapes" to describe popular places on social media that function like landmarks where people can meet to create meaningful engagement (Lichtenstein, 2017: para. 23).

Conclusion

Silencing and sexual shaming are significant feminist issues and speak to larger concerns for social justice. The use of terms such as "bitch" and "cunt" aims to silence and discourage women from writing online or taking on public positions of power (Beard, 2014; Spender, 1991). Payne (2010) argues that "the virulence of *slut* and the diminishing of a girl's cultural capital that accompanies being so labeled, makes clear to all the association between a woman's worth as a human being and her sexual practices" (pp. 317–318, emphasis in the original). Social media content reveals restrictive and impossible limitations on women, showing the ambiguities and complexities of gender performances. If clothing is too loose, women are "dykes." If clothing is too tight, women are "sluts" and "whores." If women reject male attention, they are called "bitch," "cunt," or "dyke." If they actively seek male attention, they are a "slut" or "whore." Misogynist slurs also tell us a great deal about hegemonic masculinity. Men are called "bitches" and "dykes" if they fail to perform heteromasculinity, similar to the use of "fag" in Pascoe's (2012) research.

The goal of the research presented in this book is to contribute to our awareness of the effects of everyday online misogynist language. Contemporary misogyny can be theorized as a reaction or backlash to increased rights for women (Faludi, 1991, 2011). Silencing and shaming rail against this social change. Everyday online misogyny during 2016, and the fact that Hillary Clinton was named more on Twitter than any other public figure, make clear that doubts about women's trustworthiness and value persist and tolerance is low for women's opinions, particularly as they relate to feminist issues. According to the report "The Impact of 'Modern Sexism' on the 2016 Presidential Election," 36.2 percent of people can be categorized as "modern sexists" (Maxwell & Shields, 2017). Items on the Modern Sexism scale include believing "most women interpret innocent remarks or acts as being sexist," "when women lose to men in a fair competition, they typically complain about being discriminated against," and "discrimination against women is no longer a problem in the United States" (Maxwell & Shields, 2017: para. 15). Angie Maxwell, one of the authors of the report, is quoted as saying, "Modern Sexism is really about animosity and distrust toward successful women . . . you think they're trying to get favors and they're pretending about inequality . . . it's distrust, it's animosity, it's resentment and frustration" (as cited in Onion, 2017: para. 12). Maxwell concludes: "Working women have gone from 'incapable' to 'sly and corrupt.' I'm not sure it's an upgrade" (para. 12).

Conversely, opinion polls show growing support for gender and sexual rights (Pew Research Center, 2015). Hillary Clinton became the first woman nominee for US president. Awareness of misogynist workplace cultures in technology and media have led to the firings of Roger Ailes and Bill O'Reilly from Fox News, Harvey Weinstein of The Weinstein Company, and James Damore from Google, as well as the stepping down of Travis Kalanick as chief executive of Uber. High profile cases may encourage other women to come forward. However, Fox News and Uber took action only after pressure from advertisers and investors. Pressure on universities is leading to a reevaluation of responses to sexual harassment and sexual assault complaints, including at American University, Columbia University, and University of California, Berkeley. In a setback, Education Secretary Betsy DeVos formally withdrew guidance developed during the Obama administration for handling sexual assaults in schools.

The goal of this research is not just to encourage the use of more humane language on social media, but to clarify how online misogyny both constitutes and is constituted by structural gender inequality and reflects and perpetuates essentialist ideas about gender, race, class, and sexuality, limiting self-expression and perpetuating inequality. As constructs that constantly need accomplishing through repeated social interactions and power structures, gender and sexuality are open to transformation through online and off-line narratives and political action. The gender system is inherently unstable, and by exploring microruptures central to the heterogendered matrix, the process of doing gender emerges (Butler, 1990; Renold & Ringrose, 2008). Efforts to reestablish gender and sexual norms and inequality are also occurring at the structural level, including new laws permitting discrimination in the workplace and private businesses, proposed restrictions on reproductive rights, and alarming acts of harassment and violence against the LGBTQIA community, particularly transwomen of color (James et al., 2016: 201–208; National Coalition of Anti-Violence Programs, 2016).[11] These policies and actions disproportionately affect women of color, low-income women, and women living in rural areas.

Social transformation in gender and sexuality requires moving away from binary notions of girls and women as "either savvy sexual agents or objectified sexualized victims" (Renold & Ringrose, 2011:

404). Agency is more complicated than domination or subordination. Gender and sexual expression cannot be viewed solely as matters of personal choice. Gender and sexual norms also reflect white, middle-class, heterosexual, cisgender identities. Though Hillary Clinton was the most frequent target of misogynist slurs, she was running for the highest political position in the United States. Women of color are shamed and silenced for any kind of sexual expression or public appearance, revealing the assumption of whiteness and economic affluence in heteronormative constructions of femininity. Michelle Obama had to endure sexist and racist attacks while serving as first lady. In a speech to the Women's Foundation of Colorado, she revealed the emotional burden that racial online attacks caused, likening each to tiny cuts (White, 2017). Remaining positive, Obama told young girls that the cuts can heal and that girls and women can help each other survive their first wounds. Consequently, discussions of gender and sexual agency must recognize structural limitations created by intersecting axes of domination such as class, race, nationality, homophobia, and transphobia. This research was limited by a focus on online misogyny directed toward people perceived as women. Future research should consider abuse of people perceived as transgender, nonbinary, and gender nonconforming.

The ability to share information and the plurality of voices mean that social media platforms are in a position to bring about social change. The varied uses of misogynist slurs on social media, particularly education and direct critiques, hold the potential to transform cultural attitudes about gender and sexuality. The data gathered show that social media users create alternative narratives around hetero-feminine behavior and sexuality by redefining, reappropriating, and critiquing misogynist slurs. Social media users contribute to new meanings for words like "bitch" and "whore" that have served as derogatory terms for women for centuries.

The goal of raising awareness of online misogyny is to bring greater attention to issues of sexual harassment and threats of violence. Online discourse can prevent the reversal of gender and sexual rights by providing education on the effects of misogynist ideas and supplying direct critiques of oppressive narratives and policies. Social media can be used to organize collective action in the hopes of inspiring social change, providing a link between language and social structure. Change may be slow and sometimes reverse course, but we can continue to utilize social media platforms to further global projects for social justice.

Notes

1. This tweet refers to Hillary Clinton and actor and 1996 Miss Universe winner Alicia Mochado.

2. The *Washington Post* obtained a 2005 recorded conversation between Donald Trump and television host Billy Bush in which Trump says, "You know I'm automatically attracted to beautiful—I just start kissing them. It's like a magnet. Just kiss. I don't even wait. And when you're a star, they let you do it. You can do anything. . . . Grab them by the pussy. You can do anything" (Fahrenthold, 2016).

3. Take Back the Night began as a protest against the threat of violence women experience walking at night and has evolved into international marches, rallies, and vigils to protest all violence with an emphasis on rape, intimate partner violence, and sexual abuse in the home.

4. As opposed to looking at whether a speech act is true, Austin (1962) develops the concept of illocutionary, what is meant in a speech act, and whether the speech act has met a set of felicity conditions, including whether the speaker believes a future act will be detrimental to the hearer.

5. Snapchat is a mobile app developed in 2011 that allows users to send photos and videos that disappear 10 seconds after being viewed.

6. The "binders-full-of-women" meme originated from a statement by Mitt Romney during the second US presidential debate in 2012 that he went to women's groups to find more women for his cabinet and they brought him "binders full of women."

7. The First Amendment reads: "Congress shall make no law respecting an establishment of religion, or prohibiting the free exercise thereof; or abridging the freedom of speech, or of the press; or the right of the people peaceably to assemble, and to petition the Government for a redress of grievances" (Constitute Project, 2017).

8. Gab is a social networking platform launched in 2016 that promises no censorship, only filtering options.

9. The question "Who guards the guardians?" is often used to refer to the guardians in Plato's *Republic* and a poem by Juvenal.

10. Jonathan Sun's Twitter account, @jonnysun, has over 120,000 followers and features absurd and touching humor from an "aliebn confuesed abot humamn lamgauge."

11. According to the National Coalition of Anti-Violence Programs (2016), 2016 was the deadliest year on record for LGBTQ and HIV-affected communities with seventy-seven homicides, including predominantly Latinx lives lost in the Pulse Nightclub shooting in Orlando, Florida, in June.

APPENDIX A:
Methodology

I used digital trace data to shed light on contemporary interactions involving gender and sexuality. The term *digital trace data* is defined as evidence of human and human-like activity that is logged and stored digitally (Howison, Wiggins, and Crowston, 2011). Rogers (2009) defines data from sources such as Facebook, Instagram, and Twitter as native digital data, unlike virtual methods such as online surveys that simply use the Internet to carry out research. Facebook, Instagram (now owned by Facebook), and Twitter are the three most popular social media platforms.[1] Data gathered from random national samples of people in the United States and published by the Pew Research Center (Duggan, 2015) found that Facebook was the most popular of the social media platforms. The report indicated that 72 percent of online adults use Facebook, 28 percent use Instagram, and 23 percent use Twitter. Usage has increased for all since their conceptions, though it has leveled off in recent years for Twitter.

Although Twitter is preceded by other microblogs, its popularity and immediacy is unprecedented. According to Internet Live Stats (2016), around 6,000 tweets per second are posted on Twitter, resulting in 500 million tweets per day. Twitter users can also send direct messages, but the primary use is the 140-character "tweet" sent publicly. Users can also share images, videos, and web address URLs, and original tweets can be replied to, retweeted, and favorited. Twitter's follow and hashtag (#) mechanisms serve to group information around topics and among people with common interests. Similarly, hashtags on Instagram caption and group photos and videos. As on Twitter, Instagram users follow people and are followed.

Facebook is primarily used to interact with and share content with friends, but my focus on public interactions around gender and sexuality required an examination of misogynist terms in the titles of groups and pages. Facebook pages and groups are designed for people to expand their connections beyond friends. Pages allow public figures and organizations to create a public presence. Groups allow people to come together around a common interest or cause. People can interact and share content, and groups can be publicly available or private with invitation-only membership.

Data Collection

Like traditional sociological methods, Social Media Management Software (SMMS) recognizes large amounts of social media data, also referred to as "big data," in a process known as monitoring or social listening. Using misogynist terms derived from the literature, SMMS HootSuite (http://hootsuite.com) streamed, archived, and provided analytics on data captured from Twitter containing keywords "bitch," "cunt," "dyke," "ho," "hoe," "queer," "rape," "slut," "slut-shame/shaming," and "whore." SMMS programs such as Hoot-Suite were designed for marketing purposes, but they work well for the social sciences.

For this research, Twitter, Facebook, and Instagram can be considered research sites. Analysis focuses on Twitter because of data availability. A random sample of dates between January 2016 and December 2016 was selected.[2] Within each date, 50–100 random tweets were selected for analysis. The goal was to analyze a minimum of 700 tweets for each word, stopping after reaching data saturation. More tweets containing "bitch" and "slut" were analyzed because they contained a wider range of uses than the other terms.

HootSuite has the benefit of accessing 100 percent of public tweets. Therefore, it does not have the same problems of representativeness as publicly available Streaming APIs (Driscoll & Walker, 2014). However, even though Twitter has millions of users, the ability to monitor all tweets would not be representative of all people, let alone all online interactions. Thus, the sample size, though collected randomly, is very small compared to the population of tweets. Each chapter provides a total number of tweets, how many were analyzed, and how many were omitted due to the inability to reliably code or because of irrelevance, such as the last name "Dyke" or programs called "bots" that automatically post to Twitter. Some interruptions occurred in keyword tracking when connection with HootSuite was lost and the keyword "slut" exceeded HootSuite's data allowance with its data provider, so keyword counts should be interpreted with caution. In addition, though daily averages are not dependent on the number of days tracked, they could be affected by the period under investigation. For instance, the lower daily average for "slut" counts compared to Demos (2016b) could be due to spikes in use during the twenty-three days they tracked "slut" in April and May 2016 and my inability to track tweets after September 5, 2016, due to increased volume. I also used Hootsuite's and Twitter's search features to examine the content of tweets on peak days. To present counts over time and total counts, missing data were filled with the average for the period the slur was tracked. The samples are small, but this research is primarily concerned with the qualitative meaning attached to tweets.

HootSuite's streaming function was used to examine Facebook data, although the more manageable amount of data on Facebook and Instagram and the importance of groups and pages in Facebook and hashtags in Instagram permitted use of the platforms' search functions. Facebook data include the first 50–100 pages and groups containing the term under investigation. Note that the sample contains only user-generated content; Facebook creates pages for common themes, taking content from Wikipedia.com. When publicly available, content was examined for each page and group. For Instagram, samples include the top hashtags appearing in searches. Instagram's algorithm for defining top hashtags includes multiple factors, such as number of likes and speed of engagement.

Data Analysis

Qualitative content analysis explores the ways misogynist slurs are used in tweets, Facebook groups and pages, and Instagram hashtags. Traditional qualitative methods such as content and discourse analysis can apply to digital communications (Ackland, 2013; Hine, 2005). Analysis of tweets, hashtags, and groups/pages is much like the search for themes in traditional unobtrusive analysis of qualitative data. Content analysis is an established method in the social sciences and is appropriate for the study of the meaning of words and conversations (Krippendorff, 2004). Content analysis is concerned with the importance of what is communicated and why and with what effect. Similar to other content analysis studies, units of analysis are randomly selected tweets, Facebook pages and groups, and Instagram hashtags. The units of analysis are driven by the options written into the platforms (the ways users interface with the platform) and search mechanisms within those platforms.

The analysis follows an inductive approach, allowing sentiment or themes to emerge. Since the data have already been selected for manifest content (misogynist slurs), coding is concerned with the underlying meaning or latent content. Data were organized into themes using the qualitative analysis software NVivo (http://www .qsrinternational.com). See Table B.1 in Appendix B for themes and their definitions. Within each theme, representative tweets and tweets showing the range of uses are presented. Other than presenting tweets in italics and with bulleted points, and enclosing Facebook pages and groups in quotes for readability, all content is presented exactly as it appears on Facebook, Instagram, and Twitter, including misspellings and punctuation errors.

A major contribution of this methodology is the use of human coding rather than a computer algorithm. Researchers at Demos (2016b) used a proprietary natural-language processing program to code "slut" and "whore" tweets as aggressive, self-identification, and other. Computer algorithms have the benefit of allowing researchers to analyze millions of texts, and researchers checked the reliability and validity of their program against person-coded tweets. A large portion of tweets could not be coded by the algorithm, and 19 percent of aggressive tweets were coded incorrectly when checked against human analysis (p. 6). The following is an example provided by Demos (2016b): the tweet "*@kygirl2675 you're a whore because you took pictures in a bathing suit. Nope*" would likely be coded as aggressive by the computer program, but it is not completely clear whether the user is saying "nope" to the person taking pictures in a bathing suit or "nope" to the idea that this image qualifies her as a whore. Furthermore, due to the inductive approach, this study can add new themes such as "appearance" to refer to posing in a bathing suit.

Though words like "bitch" and "slut" or their equivalents in other languages are widely understood, meaning is created within a particular context, so "slut" can be used to express anger that someone has many sexual partners or anger that "slut" is used to shame someone who has many sexual partners. Therefore, a careful and holistic coding practice is necessary. Interpretation was greatly enhanced by reading entire conversations and examining other information, such as linked photos, videos, punctuation, and emoji to find additional clues regarding sentiment. A common example is the tweet "*Cunt I hate her so much.*" This tweet is negative, and by accessing Twitter users' pages, it was discovered that the tweet captioned a picture of Hillary Clinton. "*No I'm a bitch*" was in response to a photo of a question: "*do u ever just wanna meet the opposite sex version of u.*" An algorithm might code the tweet "*I'm having a bad day, wish I could find a slut*" as shaming instead of celebratory.

Interpretation was also enhanced by searching the Internet for proper names (for example, many of the "cunts" on Twitter referred to male UK football and rugby players), song lyrics, and acronyms (such as UP for the state Uttar Pradesh in India). Information such as slang could be clarified using websites such as *Urban Dictionary*, though entries are user-generated and there may be disagreements. Definitions with the highest ratings and agreement with other sources were used. Human coding also meant misspellings could be interpreted, as long as they were not misspellings of the main keywords. This research was limited to English words, though searches capture much of the content on Twitter because English is the dominant language (Lehman, 2014). Furthermore, English versions of the words under examination were found in tweets written in other languages, including Arabic, Bulgarian, Chinese, Dutch, Filipino, Hindi, French, Indonesian, Italian, Japanese, Polish, Portuguese, Spanish, and Vietnamese. Google Translate was used to interpret portions of text written in languages other than English, though translations were not always accurate or intelligible and attempts were made to clarify with native speakers.

Comparing the findings for "slut" with algorithms for sentiment analysis, my sample contained less pornography: almost 41 percent compared to 56 percent (Demos, 2016b). HootSuite also computes sentiment for keywords, offering more categories than Demos and websites such as socialmention.com, which calculated only 10 percent of "slut" mentions on social media as negative, dramatically lower than my findings. HootSuite found 56 percent of tweets were negative, including "anger/loathing," "humiliation/shame," "sadness/grief," and "fear/uneasiness." Remaining codes were positive (44 percent), including "enjoyment/elation," "affection/friendliness," "amusement/excitement," and "contentment/gratitude" (see Figure A.1).

Figure A.1   Sentiment Analysis for Tweets Using "Slut"

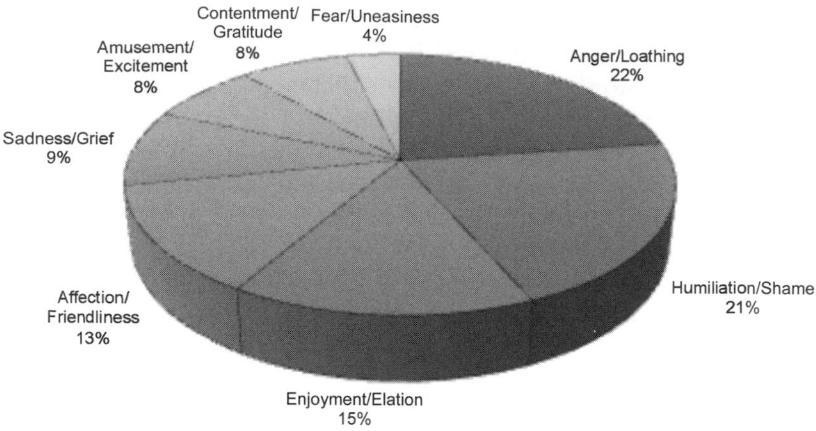

Contentment/ Gratitude 8%
Fear/Uneasiness 4%
Amusement/ Excitement 8%
Anger/Loathing 22%
Sadness/Grief 9%
Affection/ Friendliness 13%
Humiliation/Shame 21%
Enjoyment/Elation 15%

Source: HootSuite.

Limitations

Though Facebook, Instagram, and Twitter have millions of users, social media users do not represent all people (boyd & Crawford, 2011), skewing younger, more affluent, and more educated than the general US population (Brenner & Smith, 2013). Human coding takes time, resulting in small samples. However, even if all tweets could be coded, frequent users would be oversampled. Data exclude private social media interactions, but this research is concerned with the public regulation of gender and sexual norms. Content relevant to this study may be missing due to unintentional and intentional misspellings such as "b*tch" as well as censorship of content.

Using an etic or outsider approach to digital data has its drawbacks. Though meaning of language is typically inferred by the listener or reader, this analysis was unable to measure how many people read a post, nor could it directly ask social media users what they intended when they posted misogynist slurs. Richer understandings of intent can be gained from supplementing digital data with surveys and interviews (Marwick and boyd, 2011). For example, consider the tweet: *"My mother called my sister a slut."* Does the speaker agree or disagree with this action, and if there is disagreement, is it because the mother used the slur or because she applied it to her sister?

Internet researchers argue for a blurring of the distinction between off-line and online, pointing out that computer-mediated interactions are not inferior or insignificant and often occur in combination with face-to-face interactions (Orgad, Bakardjieva, & Gajjala, 2009; Zhao, 2006). People who use social media are embodied and their computers and mobile devices exist in their off-line worlds. In the absence of nonverbal cues such as facial expressions, social media users attempt to clarify their meaning with acronyms, emoji, and Internet slang such as "lol." Directly asking questions about socially undesirable attitudes may obtain dishonest responses because of interviewer effects. Finally, interviewees may be crafting selves just as much as public social media users. Qualitative interviews of social media users could greatly enhance our understanding of the motivations and effects of online sexual harassment.

It is important to debate issues of data quality and to ask what it is that online data tells us (Rogers, 2013). The plurality of voices expressing sentiments around gender and sexuality is measured in a format that is less top-down than other media outlets such as newspapers. However, I accessed only public social media data. Data were also limited by what the social media platforms allowed and what can be archived (boyd & Crawford, 2011), hence my emphasis on Twitter over Facebook and Instagram due to the archiving function in Hoot-Suite. I also limited my analysis to text and photos, unlike Demos (2016b), which also analyzed metadata such as how many people received the tweet and from where the tweet was sent.[3] Researchers must exercise caution when inferring public opinion from Twitter (Freelon, 2014). When people retweet, use hashtags, or include @-mentions, it does not mean they are subscribing to the idea (Driscoll & Walker, 2014). For this research, it is less important whether the tweeter carries the belief or the claim is true, but the way in which people frame gender and sexuality and the potential impact on social media, so the performative aspect of posting online is part of the empirical and theoretical analysis.

Nevertheless, it is useful to understand the various motivations for tweeting, creating a Facebook group or page, or constructing or using a hashtag. Generally, social media users are influenced by their audience, what others post, and how others react to their posts through likes, views, shares, and comments. Users are concerned with how others interpret them, engaging in a similar kind of impression management identified by Goffman (1959) in face-to-face interactions.

Hogan (2010) argues that the concepts of "performance" and "frontstage/backstage" do not work as well for online interactions, preferring instead "exhibition" or a "curated" self, both involving choices of what to share. Drawing from Foucault, Orenstein (2010, 2012) characterizes the Internet as a virtual panopticon in which people select and frame content with the goal to please or impress a certain crowd. Facebook users, for instance, can select favorite movies and books to cultivate an identity, and Instagram is individually curated. On Twitter, presentation of self occurs more through text but also includes links, photos, and videos.

Interviews reveal that people using public social media imagine their audiences (Marwick & boyd, 2011). They may be considering how one specific person receives their post even when they choose to post publicly rather than to send a direct message, or they imagine a more generalized audience of people with similar interests. Considering the multitude of potential motivations and audiences, people choose what they post, resorting to what Hogan (2010) calls the "*lowest common denominator* of what is normatively acceptable" (p. 383, emphasis in the original). This choice makes publicly revealing personal information and using potentially offensive language perhaps more surprising. Smith (2016b) blames abusive language on format choices. Short messages make it harder to develop nuanced arguments and easier to misinterpret what others say, and the anonymity of user accounts provides safety for online abusers.

Analysis is limited by reliance on a single coder's interpretation. It should be remembered that all researchers are interpreters of data. Coding occurred in four rounds to increase the reliability of coding within and across keywords. In some cases, codes changed in later rounds as new patterns and uses were clarified. Examples are provided so that the reader may assess the coding scheme (see Table B.1 in Appendix B). Data that could not be reliably coded after three or four rounds were labeled "unclear." Coding continued until data saturation was reached and no new themes were found (for total tweets coded and counts see Table B.2 in Appendix B). I hope that disagreements and alternate interpretations can lead to fruitful discussions and the advancement of social theory.

Though data include publicly available social media data, native digital methods also raise ethical issues (Bruckman, 2002). Not all people mentioned in tweets have public accounts, nor do all public users of social media expect their tweets to be compiled and put in print (boyd & Crawford, 2011; Driscoll & Walker, 2014). Furthermore, people posting publicly may be imagining a small audience (Ackland, 2013; Marwick & boyd, 2011). All names and Twitter handles are replaced by pseudonyms, other than public figures and organizations such as media outlets. Any similarity to existing Twitter names is coincidental.

Notes

1. In 2016, Snapchat passed Twitter in daily active users (Frier, 2016), though overall usage remained lower and Snapchat is less useful here because it is a closed network unavailable to the wider Internet.

2. Some slurs like "slut" were archived earlier (Levey, 2015), while others like "bitch" began in 2016. While not discussed fully here, the keyword "rape" was tracked on Twitter from January 1, 2016, to March 31, 2016, and again beginning in August 1, 2016. A full qualitative analysis is forthcoming.

3. See Bruns and Burgess (2012) for other Twitter data available, such as location and user ID.

APPENDIX B:
Coding Scheme
and Twitter Counts

Table B.1 Themes and Definitions

Themes	Definitions
Regulation	
Any sex/sexual interest	Expressing desire, initiating sexual encounters, expressing pleasure
Appearance	Physical description, usually body and clothing
Demeanor	Broad category including cheap, drug user, out of control, unstable
Domineering	Lacks deference and obedience
Generic slur	Text includes slur but no additional information
Gold digger	A woman who uses men for financial gain
Immoral/sin	Sin or moral depravity
Naming	References a specific person's name or @username
Promiscuity	More sexual partners than appropriate, indiscriminate, overly sexual
Sex worker	Woman who engages in commercial sex
Silencing	Attempt to stop someone from voicing opinion
Threat	Mentions violence or hope for accident or illness
Unavailable	Uncooperative or unyielding
Unfaithful/untrustworthy	Infidelity or dishonesty
Unpleasant	Disagreeable, displeasing, appalling, or nasty
Unworthy	Inferior, unintelligent, or unsuitable for anyone's time or attention
Extension	
Alternative uses	Used in a novel way, not coded elsewhere
Intensifier	Exclamation, strengthens statement
Celebratory	Expressing desire and appreciation
Colloquial phrases	Combinations of words used in ordinary language

continues

190

Table B.1   Continued

Themes	Definitions
Complaining	Overly expressing dissatisfaction or annoyance
BDSM	Bondage, dominance, submission, and masochism
Inordinate interest	Overly into or desiring something
Male identification	Men adopting the slur
Male insult	Threatening men, men with many sexual partners, unfaithful
Object or state of being	A thing or situation
Woman or girlfriend	Replacement for a person identified as a woman or girlfriend
Dissent	
Defending the label	Providing an argument in support of the use of the slur
Direct critiques	Questioning or rejecting the meaning or basis of a slur
Education	Providing information or links opposing the slur
Friendly	Used affectionately and endearingly among people in a social circle
Organization	Using social media as a platform for collective action
Positive self-identification	Reclamation or proudly appropriating the slur
Rejecting the label	Challenging association with the slur
Omitted	
Unclear/irrelevant	Sentiment cannot be determined, originated from a bot, unrelated to gender or sexuality
Pornography	Advertisement or link to pornographic video or webcam site

Table B.2   Twitter Results for Individual Slurs

Themes	Bitch	Cunt	Dyke	Slut	Whore
Regulation	442 (42.5%)[a]	342 (57.1%)	636 (80.4%)	751 (58.3%)	378 (63.2%)
Any sex/sexual interest				24	21
Appearance	11	12	95	106	26
Demeanor	13		185	31	43
Domineering	21				
Generic slur	57	79	38	113	66
Gold digger					6
Immoral/sin			10		
Naming	49	42	124	243	77

continues

Table B.2   Continued

Themes	Bitch	Cunt	Dyke	Slut	Whore
Promiscuity	14	4		84	40
Sex worker				6	18
Silencing		10			6
Threat	52	28	142	29	18
Unavailable			24		
Unfaithful/ untrustworthy	117	47		32	14
Unpleasant	62	87			
Unworthy	46	33	18	83	43
Extension	474 (45.6%)	263 (43.9%)	83 (10.5%)	63 (5.0%)	153 (25.6%)
Alternative uses		11			
Intensifier	101				
Colloquial phrases	16				
Complaining	12				
BDSM				10	13
Inordinate interest				3	79
Male identification		9			
Male insult	188	225	82	43	61
Object or state of being	48	18		7	
Woman or girlfriend	109		1		
Dissent	147 (14.1%)	126 (21.0%)	326 (41.2%)	459 (35.7%)	108 (18.1%)
Celebratory	25		81	63	14
Defending the label		11			
Direct critiques		26	40	201	19
Education		33	30	41	1
Friendly	16	9	31	57	24
Organization			1	15	
Positive self- identification	75	28	115	42	23
Rejecting the label	31	19	28	40	27
Total tweets analyzed	1,040	599	791	1,287	598
Omitted					
Unclear/irrelevant	56	18	121	154	35
Pornography	54	83	54	989	201
Total tweets coded	1,150	700	966	2,430	834
Average daily tweets	418,665	25,496	2,720	37,646	21,018

Note: a. Percentages do not add up to 100 percent because themes are not mutually exclusive.

References

Ackland, Robert. 2013. *Web Social Science: Concepts, Data and Tools for Social Scientists in the Digital Age.* London: Sage.

Adamczyk, Amy. 2017. *Cross-National Public Opinion About Homosexuality: Examining Attitudes Across the Globe.* Oakland: University of California Press.

Allcott, Hunt, and Gentzkow, Matthew. 2017. Social Media and Fake News in the 2016 Election. *Journal of Economic Perspectives* 31(2): 211–236.

Allen, Keith. 2016. Pragmatics in Language Change and Lexical Creativity. Retrieved from https://springerplus.springeropen.com/articles/10.1186/s40064-016-1836-y.

The ALS Association. 2016. ALS Ice Bucket Challenge Donations Lead to Significant Gene Discovery. Retrieved from http://www.alsa.org/news/media/press-releases/significant-gene-discovery-072516.html.

Anderson, Luvell, and Ernie Lepore. 2013. Slurring Words. *Noûs* 47(1): 25–48.

Archer, Margaret. 1995. *Realist Social Theory: The Morphogenetic Approach.* Cambridge: Cambridge University Press.

Armstrong, Elizabeth A., Laura T. Hamilton, Elizabeth M. Armstrong, and J. Lotus Seeley. 2014. "Good Girls": Gender, Social Class, and Slut Discourse on Campus. *Social Psychology Quarterly* 77(2): 100–122.

Armstrong, James D. 1997. Homophobic Slang as Coercive Discourse Among College Students. In Anna Livia and Kira Hall (eds.). *Queerly Phrased: Language, Gender, and Sexuality.* Pp. 326–334. New York: Oxford University Press.

Ashley, Leonard R. N. 1982. Dyke Diction: The Language of Lesbians. *Maledicta* 6: 123–162.

Ashwell, Lauren. 2016. Gendered Slurs. *Social Theory and Practice* 42(2): 228–239.

Attwood, Feona. 2007. Sluts and Riot Grrrls. *Journal of Gender Studies* 16(3): 233–247.

Austin, J. L. 1962. *How to Do Things with Words.* Oxford: Oxford University Press.

Bamberg, Michael. 2004. Form and Functions of "Slut Bashing" in Male Identity Constructions in 15-year-olds. *Human Development* 47(6): 331–353.

Barak, Azy. 2005. Sexual Harassment on the Internet. *Social Science Computer Review* 23(1): 77–92.

Barnes, Anthony. 2006, January 21. The C Word*. Retrieved from http://www
.independent.co.uk/news/uk/home-news/the-c-word-340215.html.

Barlow, John Perry. 1996. Declaration of Independence of Cyberspace.
Retrieved from https://www.eff.org/cyberspace-independence.

Barrett, Grant. 2013. A Wordnado of Words in 2013. December 21. Retrieved
from http://www.nytimes.com/2013/12/22/opinion/sunday/a-wordnado-of
-words-in-2013.html.

Barrett, James. 2016. New Social Media Network "Gab" Promises No Censorship,
Draws Alt-Right Users Banned by Twitter. December 12. Retrieved from
http://www.dailywire.com/news/11521/new-social-media-site-gab-promises
-no-censorship-james-barrett.

Baumgardner, Jennifer, and Amy Richards. 2000. *Manifesta: Young Women,
Feminism, and the Future*. New York: Farrar, Straus and Giroux.

Bay-Cheng, Laina Y. 2015a. Living in Metaphors, Trapped in a Matrix: The
Ramifications of Neoliberal Ideology for Young Women's Sexuality. *Sex
Roles* 73(7): 332–339.

———. 2015b. The Agency Line: A Neoliberal Metric for Appraising Young
Women's Sexuality. *Sex Roles* 73(7): 279–291.

Beard, Mary. 2014. The Public Voice of Women. *London Review of Books* 36(6):
11–14.

Bechdel, Alison. 2016. Dykes to Watch Out For. Retrieved from http://dykes
towatchoutfor.com.

Berger, Peter, and Thomas Luckmann. 1966. *The Social Construction of Reality:
A Treatise in the Sociology of Knowledge*. Garden City: Doubleday.

Bettie, Julie. 2014. *Women Without Class: Girls, Race, and Identity*. Oakland:
University of California Press.

Bitch Media. 2015. Retrieved from https://bitchmedia.org/about-us.

Blackwell, Bonnie. 2004. How the Jilt Triumphed over the Slut: The Evolution
of an Epithet, 1660–1780. *Women's Writing* 11(2): 141–161.

Blumer, Herbert. 1969. *Symbolic Interactionism: Perspective and Method*.
Englewood Cliffs, NJ: Prentice-Hall.

Bowles, Hannah Riley, Linda Babcock, and Lei Lai. 2007. Social Incentives for
Gender Differences in the Propensity to Initiate Negotiations: Sometimes It
Does Hurt to Ask. *Organizational Behavior and Human Decision Processes*
103(1): 84–103.

boyd, danah. 2014. *It's Complicated: The Social Lives of Networked Teens*. New
Haven, CT: Yale University Press. Kindle Edition.

boyd, danah, and Kate Crawford. 2011. Six Provocations for Big Data. Paper
presented to *A Decade in Internet Time: Symposium on the Dynamics of the
Internet and Society*. Oxford: Oxford Internet Institute.

Brenner, Joanna, and Aaron Smith. 2013. 72% of Online Adults Are Social Networking Site Users. Retrieved from http://www.pewinternet.org/2013/08/05
/72-of-online-adults-are-social-networking-site-users.

Brescoll, Victoria. 2011. Who Takes the Floor and Why: Gender, Power, and Vol-
ubility in Organizations. *Administrative Science Quarterly* 56(4), 622–641.

Brescoll, Victoria, and Jeffrey Sonnenfeld. 2014. Women as Bosses Still Face
Bias. February 21. Retrieved from https://dealbook.nytimes.com/2014/02
/21/women-as-bosses-still-face-bias.

Brickell, Chris. 2012. Sexuality, Power and the Sociology of the Internet. *Current
Sociology* 60(1): 28–44.

Broadband Commission for Sustainable Development. 2015. Combatting Online
Violence Against Women and Girls: A Worldwide Wake-Up Call. ITU/
UNESCO Report. Retrieved from http://www.broadbandcommission.org
/publications/Pages/bb-and-gender-2015.aspx.

Brock, André. 2012. From the Blackhand Side: Twitter as a Cultural Conversation. *Journal of Broadcasting & Electronic Media* 56(4): 529–549.

Brontsema, Robin. 2004. A Queer Revolution: Reconceptualizing the Debate over Linguistic Reclamation. *Colorado Research in Lingustica* 17(1): 1–17.

Brown, Adriane. 2016. "She Isn't Whoring Herself Out Like a Lot of Other Girls We See": Heteronormative Propriety and "Authentic" American Girlhood on Taylor Swift Fan Forums. In Nancy L. Fisher and Steven Seidman (eds.). *Introducing the New Sexuality Studies.* Pp. 400–411. London: Routledge.

Bruckman, Amy. 2002. Studying the Amateur Artist: A Perspective on Disguising Data Collected in Human Subjects Research on the Internet. *Ethics and Information Technology* 4(3): 217–231.

Bruns, Axel, and Jean Burgess. 2012. Notes Towards the Scientific Study of Public Communication on Twitter. *Australian Research Council Centre of Excellence for Creative Industries and Innovation.* Brisbane, Australia: Queensland University of Technology.

Butler, Judith. 1990. *Gender Trouble: Feminism and the Subversion of Identity.* New York: Routledge.

———. 1991. Imitation and Gender Insubordination. In Diana Fuss (ed.). *Inside/Out: Lesbian Theories, Gay Theories.* Pp. 13–31. New York: Routledge.

———. 1993. *Bodies that Matter: On the Discursive Limits of "Sex."* New York: Routledge.

———. 1997. *Excitable Speech: A Politics of the Performative.* New York: Routledge.

Califia, Pat. 1994. Macho Sluts. Boston: Alyson.

Camp. Elizabeth. 2013. Slurring Perspectives. *Analytic Philosophy* 54(3): 330–349.

Canaan, Joyce. 1986. Why a "Slut" Is a "Slut": Cautionary Tales of Middle Class Teenage Girls' Morality. In Hervé Varenne (ed.). *Symbolizing America.* Pp. 184–208. Lincoln: University of Nebraska Press.

Caputi, Jane. 2004. *Goddesses and Monsters: Women, Myth, Power, and Popular Culture.* Madison: The University of Wisconsin Press.

CASS Briefings. 2013. Researching Online Abuse: The Case of Trolling. ESRC Centre for Corpus Approaches to Social Sciences, Lancaster University, UK.

Cassidy, Wanda, Chantal Faucher, and Margaret Jackson. 2013. Cyberbullying Among Youth: A Comprehensive Review of Current International Research and Its Implications and Application to Policy and Practice. *School Psychology International* 34(6): 575–612.

Cavanagh, Allison. 2007. *Sociology in the Age of the Internet.* Berkshire, UK: Open University Press.

Centers for Disease Control. 2014. Lesbian, Gay, Bisexual, and Transgender Health. Retrieved from http://www.cdc.gov/lgbthealth/youth.htm.

Chang, Bettina. 2016. How Four Teenage Girls Organized This Week's Huge Silent Protest. July 14. Retrieved from http://www.chicagomag.com/city-life/July-2016/Black-Lives-Matter-Chi-Youth-Sit-In-Rally.

Chapkis, Wendy. 1997. *Live Sex Acts: Women Performing Erotic Labor.* New York: Routledge.

Chasmer, Jessica. 2016. Guardian Columnist Quits Twitter over "Rape and Death Threat" Against 5-year-old Daughter. July 27. Retrieved from http://www.washingtontimes.com/news/2016/jul/27/jessica-valenti-guardian-columnist-quits-twitter-o.

Chauncey, George. 1994. *Gay New York: Gender, Urban Culture, and the Makings of the Gay Male World, 1890–1940.* New York: Basic Books.

Chemaly, Soraya. 2013. The Digital Safety Gap and the Online Harassment of Women. March 30. Retrieved from http://www.huffingtonpost.com/soraya -chemaly/women-online-harassment_b_2567898.html.

Citron, Danielle Keats. 2009. Law's Expressive Value in Combating Cyber Gender Harassment. 108 *Michigan Law Review* 373.

———. 2014. *Hate Crimes in Cyberspace*. Cambridge: Harvard University Press.

CNN. 2017. Reddit Troll "Violentacrez" Speaks Out. Retrieved from http://www .cnn.com/videos/us/2012/10/19/ac-pkg-griffin-reddits-villain.cnn.

Collier, Kate L., Henny M. W. Bos, and Theo G. M. Sandfort. 2013. Homophobic Name-Calling Among Secondary School Students and Its Implications for Mental Health. *Journal of Youth and Adolescence* 42(3): 363–375.

Connell, R. W. 1987. *Gender and Power: Society, the Person, and Sexual Politics*. Stanford: Stanford University Press.

———. 2005. *Masculinities*. Cambridge: Polity Press.

Connell, R. W., and James W. Messerschmidt. 2005. Hegemonic Masculinity: Rethinking the Concept. *Gender & Society* 19(6): 829–859.

Conrad, Browyn Kara. 2006. Neo-Institutionalism, Social Movements, and the Cultural Reproduction of a Mentalité: Promise Keepers Reconstruct the Madonna/Whore Complex. *The Sociological Quarterly* 47(2): 305–331.

Constitute Project. 2017. US Constitution. Retrieved from https://www.constitute project.org/constitution/United_States_of_America_1992.

Cotter, David, Joan Hermsen, and Reeve Vanneman. 2011. Reframing Gender Inequality: Explaining the Stalled Gender Revolution. November 3. Work in Progress. Retrieved from https://workinprogress.oowsection.org/2011/11/03 /reframing-gender-equality-explaining-the-stalled-gender-revolution.

Cottle, Michelle. 2016. The Era of "The Bitch" Is Coming. August 17. Retrieved from https://www.theatlantic.com/politics/archive/2016/08/the-era-of-the -bitch-is-coming/496154.

Crawford, Kate. 2009. Following You: Disciplines of Listening in Social Media. *Continuum: Journal of Media & Cultural Studies* 23(40): 525–535.

Crawford, Mary, and Danielle Popp. 2003. Sexual Double Standards: A Review and Methodological Critique of Two Decades of Research. *Journal of Sex Research* 40(1): 13–26.

The Crunk Feminist Collective. 2017. SlutWalks v. Ho Strolls. May 23. Retrieved from https://crunkfeministcollective.wordpress.com/2011/05/23 /slutwalks-v-ho-strolls.

Currans, Elizabeth. 2012. Claiming Deviance and Honoring Community: Creating Resistant Spaces in U.S. Dyke Marches. *Feminist Formations* 24(1): 73–101.

Cyber Civil Rights Initiative. 2017. Retrieved from https://www.cybercivil-rights.org.

Dahlberg, Lincoln. 2001. Computer-Mediated Communication and the Public Sphere: A Critical Analysis. *Journal of Computer-Mediated Communication*. Retrieved from http://jcmc.indiana.edu/vol7/issue1/dahlberg.html.

de Beauvoir, Simone. 1949/1989. *The Second Sex*. New York: Vintage Books.

Define American. 2016. #Words Matter. Retrieved from https://defineamerican .com/campaigns/wordsmatter.

Demos. 2016a. New Demos Study Reveals Scale of Social Media Misogyny. Retrieved from https://www.demos.co.uk/press-release/staggering-scale-of -social-media-misogyny-mapped-in-new-demos-study.

———. 2016b. The Use of Misogynist Terms on Twitter. Retrieved from https:// www.demos.co.uk/wp-content/uploads/2016/05/Misogyny-online.pdf.

Dewey, Caitlin. 2016. Every 10 Seconds Someone on Twitter Calls a Woman a Slut or Whore. May 26. Retrieved from https://www.washingtonpost.com /news/the-intersect/wp/2016/05/26/every-10-seconds-someone-on-twitter -calls-a-woman-a-slut-or-whore/?utm_term=.6d5a5a1415fd.

DiMaggio, Paul, Eszter Hargittai, W. Russell Neuman, and John P. Robinson. 2001. Social Implications of the Internet. *Annual Review of Sociology* 27: 307–336.

Ditmore, Melissa. 2011. *Prostitution and Sex Work*. Santa Barbara: Greenwood.

Driscoll, Kevin, and Shawn Walker. 2014. Working Within the Black Box: Transparency in the Collection and Production of Big Twitter Data. *International Journal of Communication* 8: 1745–1764.

Duggan, Maeve. 2015. The Demographics of Social Media Users. August 19. Retrieved from http://www.pewinternet.org/2015/08/19/the-demographics -of-social-media-users.

Eagly, Alice H., Mona G. Makhijani, and Bruce G. Klonsky. 1992. Gender and the Evaluation of Leaders: A Meta-analysis. *Psychological Bulletin* 111(1): 3–22.

Easton, Dossie, and Catherine A. Liszt. 1998. *The Ethical Slut: Guide to Infinite Sexual Possibilities*. San Francisco, CA: Greenery Press.

Eder, Donna, Catherine C. Evans, and Stephen Parker. 1995. *School Talk: Gender and Adolescent Culture*. New Brunswick, NJ: Rutgers University Press.

Eligon, John. 2015. One Slogan, Many Methods: Black Lives Matter Enters Politics. November 18. Retrieved from http://www.nytimes.com/2015/11/19 /us/one-slogan-many-methods-black-lives-matter-enters-politics.html.

Ellafante, Ginia. 2016. Poor, Transgender and Dressed for Arrest. September 30. Retrieved from http://www.nytimes.com/2016/10/02/nyregion/poor-transgender -and-dressed-for-arrest.html.

Encyclopedia.com. 2017. Bulldagger. Retrieved from http://www.encyclopedia .com/social-sciences/encyclopedias-almanacs-transcripts-and-maps/bulldagger.

Fahrenthold, David A. 2016. Trump Recorded Having Extremely Lewd Conversation About Women in 2005. October 8. Retrieved from https://www .washingtonpost.com/politics/trump-recorded-having-extremely-lewd -conversation-about-women-in-2005/2016/10/07/ 3b9ce776-8cb4-11e6-bf8a -3d26847eeed4_story.html?utm_term=.ce6dd06cfcfd.

Faludi, Susan. 1991. *Backlash: The Undeclared War Against American Women*. New York: Crown.

———. 2011, *Stiffed: The Betrayal of the American Man*. Reprint Edition. HarperCollins e-books.

Filipovic, Jill. 2016. The Men Feminists Left Behind. November 5. Retrieved from http://www.nytimes.com/2016/11/06/opinion/campaign-stops/the-men -feminists-left-behind.html.

Fine, Michelle. 1988. Sexuality, Schooling, and Adolescent Females: The Missing Discourse of Desire. *Harvard Educational Review* 58(1): 29–53.

Finley, Taryn. 2016. Black Twitter Countered Tragedy with These 6 Uplifting Hashtags. July 13. http://www.huffingtonpost.com/entry/black-twitter -countered-tragedy-with-these-6-uplifting-hashtags_us_5783a034e4b0 c590f7ea090a.

Fjær, Eivind Grip, Willy Pedersen, and Sveinung Sandberg. 2015. "I'm Not One of Those Girls": Boundary-Work and the Sexual Double Standard in a Liberal Hookup Context. *Gender & Society* 29(6): 960–981.

Flood, Michael. 2011. Involving Men in Efforts to End Violence Against Women. *Men and Masculinities* 14(3): 358–377.

Fogg, Ally. 2014. How to Confuse an American: The Politics of the C-word. Retrieved from http://freethoughtblogs.com/hetpat/2014/05/12/how-to -confuse-an-american-the-politics-of-the-c-word.

Foucault, Michel. 1978/1990. *The History of Sexuality, Volume 1: An Introduction.* New York: Vintage Books.

Francesca. 2010. The Rap: More than Just Hip-Hop. *Word: The Online Journal on African American English.* Retrieved from https://africanamericanenglish .com/2010/04/17/the-rap-more-than-just-hip-hop.

Franklin, Karen. 2000. Antigay Behaviors Among Young Adults: Prevalence, Patterns, and Motivators in a Noncriminal Population. *Journal of Interpersonal Violence* 15(4): 339–362.

Freelon, Deen. 2014. On the Interpretation of Digital Trace Data in Communication and Social Computing Research. *Journal of Broadcasting & Electronic Media* 58(1): 59–75.

Freeman, Jo. 1968. The BITCH Manifesto. Retrieved from www.jofreeman.com /joreen/bitch.htm.

Friedman, Sarah. 2017. Who Started the Women's March on Washington? This Hawaii Grandmother's Mission Spread Like Wild Fire. January 20. Retrieved from https://www.bustle.com/p/who-started-the-womens-march-on-washington -this-hawaii-grandmothers-mission-spread-like-wild-fire-32015.

Friend, Nina. 2015. How Women 15 to 50 Feel About the Word "B*tch." June 4. Retrieved from http://www.huffingtonpost.com/2015/06/04/women-on-the -word-bitch-ages-15-to-50_n_7512490.html.

Frier, Sarah. 2016. Snapchat Passes Twitter in Daily Usage. June 2. Retrieved from https://www.bloomberg.com/news/articles/2016-06-02/snapchat-passes -twitter-in-daily-usage.

Frostenson, Sarah. 2017. The Women's Marches May Have Been the Largest Demonstration in US History. January 22. Retrieved from http://www.vox .com/2017/1/22/14350808/womens-marches-largest-demonstration-us -history-map.

Fuss, Diana (ed.). 1991. *Inside/Out: Lesbian Theories, Gay Theories.* New York: Routledge.

Garcia, Lorena. 2012. *Respect Yourself, Protect Yourself Latina Girls and Sexual Identity.* New York: New York University Press.

Gardiner, Becky, Mahana Mansfield, Ian Anderson, Josh Holder, Daan Louter, and Monica Ulmanu. 2016. The Dark Side of Guardian Comments. April 12. Retrieved from https://www.theguardian.com/technology/2016/apr/12/the -dark-side-of-guardian-comments.

Gavins, Joanna, and Paul Simpson. 2015. Regina v John Terry: The Discursive Construction of an Alleged Racist Event. *Discourse & Society* 26(6): 712–732.

Geek Feminism Wiki. n.d. Lewis' Law. Retrieved from http://geekfeminism.wikia .com/wiki/Lewis%27_Law.

Giddens, Anthony. 1984. *The Constitution of Society.* Oakland: University of California Press.

Gladwell, Malcolm. 2010. Small Change: Why the Revolution Will Not Be Tweeted. October 4. Retrieved from http://www.newyorker.com/magazine /2010/10/04/small-change-malcolm-gladwell.

Global Web Index. 2016. Home Page. Retrieved from http://insight.global webindex.net/social.

Goffman, Erving. 1959. *The Presentation of Self in Everyday Life.* New York: Doubleday.

Goldberg, Michelle. 2015. Feminist Writers Are So Besieged by Online Abuse That Some Have Begun to Retire. February 20. Retrieved from https:// www.washingtonpost.com/opinions/online-feminists-increasingly-ask-are -the-psychic-costs-too-much-to-bear/2015/02/19/3dc4ca6c-b7dd-11e4-a200 -c008a01a6692_story.html?utm_term=.b9991671627f.

Gotell, Lise, and Emily Dutton. 2016. Sexual Violence in the "Manosphere": Antifeminist Men's Rights Discourses on Rape. *International Journal for Crime, Justice and Social Democracy* 5(2): 65–80.

Gottfried, Jeffrey, and Elisa Shearer. 2016. News Use Across Social Media Platforms 2016. Pew Research Center Report. May 26. Retrieved from http://www.journalism.org/2016/05/26/news-use-across-social-media-platforms-2016.

Gould, Deborah. 2010. On Affect and Protest. In Janet Staiger, Ann Cvetkovich, and Ann Reynolds (eds.). *Political Emotions: New Agendas in Communication.* Pp. 18–44. New York: Routledge.

Greer, Germaine. 1970. The Politics of Female Sexuality. *Oz* 29 (July): 10–11.

———. 1971. *The Female Eunuch.* London: London Book Club Associates.

Gregory, Michele Rene. 2016. *The Face of the Firm: Corporate Hegemonic Masculinity at Work.* New York: Routledge.

Griffin, Christine. 1982. *The Good, the Bad and the Ugly: Images of Young Women in the Labour Market* [Occasional Paper]. London: Centre for Contemporary Cultural Studies.

Guerra, Kristine. 2016. Judge Apologizes for Asking Accuser in Rape Case Why She Couldn't Keep her Knees Together. September 12. Retrieved from https://www.washingtonpost.com/news/worldviews/wp/2016/09/12/judge-apologizes-for-asking-accuser-in-rape-case-why-she-couldnt-keep-her-knees-together/?utm_term=.da5012a447db.

Gwynne, Joel. 2013. Slutwalk, Feminist Activism and the Foreign Body in Singapore. *Journal of Contemporary Asia* 43(1): 173–185.

Habermas, Jurgen. 1989. *The Structural Transformation of the Public Sphere: An Inquiry into a Category of Bourgeois Society.* Cambridge: MIT Press.

Hardaker, Claire. 2014. *Discourses of Online Misogyny.* DOOM Project: Corpus Approaches to Social Science. Retrieved from http://cass.lancs.ac.uk/?p=1250.

Heilman, Madeline E. 2001. Description and Prescription: How Gender Stereotypes Prevent Women's Ascent up the Organizational Ladder. *Journal of Social Issues* 57(4): 657–674.

Hess, Amanda. 2014a. Why Women Aren't Welcome on the Internet. January 6. Retrieved from https://psmag.com/why-women-aren-t-welcome-on-the-internet-aa21fdbc8d6#.8587ngx7l.

———. 2014b. A *Thot* Is Not a *Slut*: The Popular Insult Is More About Race and Class Than Sex. October 16. Retrieved from http://www.slate.com/blogs/xx_factor/2014/10/16/a_thot_is_not_a_slut_on_popular_slurs_race_class_and_sex.html.

Hill, Catherine, and Holly Kearl. 2011. Crossing the Line: Sexual Harassment at School. Washington, DC: AAUW Report.

Hill Collins, Patricia. 1990. *Black Feminist Thought: Knowledge, Consciousness, and the Politics of Empowerment.* New York: Routledge.

———. 2004. *Black Sexual Politics: African Americans, Gender, and the New Racism.* New York: Routledge.

Hills, Rachel. 2015. *The Sex Myth: The Gap Between Our Fantasies and Reality.* New York: Simon & Schuster.

Hindman, Matthew. 2009. *The Myth of Digital Democracy.* Princeton: Princeton University Press.

Hinduja, Sameer, and Justin W. Patchin. 2010. Bullying, Cyberbullying, and Suicide. *Archives of Suicide Research* 14(3): 206–221.

———. 2012. Cyberbullying: Neither an Epidemic nor a Rarity. *European Journal of Developmental Psychology* 9(5): 539–543.

Hine, Christine. 2005. Internet Research and the Sociology of Cyber-Social-Scientific Knowledge. *Information Society* 21(4): 239–248.

Hogan, Bernie. 2010. The Presentation of Self in the Age of Social Media: Distinguishing Performances and Exhibitions Online. *Bulletin of Science, Technology, & Society* 30(6): 377–386.

Hom, Christopher. 2008. The Semantics of Racial Epithets. *Journal of Philosophy* 105(8): 416–440.

hooks, bell. 1997. *Teaching to Transgress: Education as the Practice of Freedom.* New York: Routledge.

Hopkins, Nick. 2017. Revealed: Facebook's Internal Rulebook on Sex, Terrorism and Violence. May 21. Retrieved from https://www.theguardian.com/news/2017/may/21/revealed-facebook-internal-rulebook-sex-terrorism-violence.

Howard, Philip N., and Muzammil M. Hussain. 2013. *Democracy's Fourth Wave? Digital Media and the Arab Spring.* Oxford: Oxford University Press.

Howison, James, Andrea Wiggins, and Kevin Crowston. 2011. Validity Issues in the Use of Social Network Analysis with Digital Trace Data. *Journal of the Association for Information Systems* 12(2). Retrieved from http://aisel.aisnet.org/jais/vol12/iss12/2.

Hughes, Geoffrey. 2006. *Encyclopedia of Swearing: The Social History of Oaths, Profanity, Foul Language, and Ethnic Slurs in the English-Speaking World.* Armonk, NY: M. E. Sharpe.

Humphreys, Lee, Phillipa Gill, Krishnamurthy Balachander, and Elizabeth Newbury. 2013. Historicizing New Media: A Content Analysis of Twitter. *Journal of Communication* 63(3): 413–431.

Hunt, Matthew. n.d. Cunt: A Cultural History of the C-Word. Retrieved December 31, 2016, from http://www.matthewhunt.com/cunt/index.html.

Internet Live Stats. 2016. Twitter Usage Statistics. Retrieved from www.internetlivestats.com/twitter-statistics (accessed November 14, 2016).

Jacquet, Jennifer. 2015. *Is Shame Necessary? New Uses for an Old Tool.* London: Allen Lane.

James, Sandy E., Jody L. Herman, Susan Rankin, Mara Keisling, Lisa Mottet, and Ma'ayan Ana. 2016. *The Report of the 2015 U.S. Transgender Survey.* Executive Summary. Washington, DC: National Center for Transgender Equality. Retrieved from http://www.transequality.org/sites/default/files/docs/usts/USTS Full Report - FINAL 1.6.17.pdf.

Jane, Emma Alice. 2014. "Back to the Kitchen, Cunt": Speaking the Unspeakable About Online Misogyny. *Continuum: Journal of Media & Cultural Studies* 28(4): 558–570.

Jeffers, Honorée Fanonne. 2017. Teachable Racial Moment: A Black History Lesson Behind "Son of a Bitch." September 23. Retrieved from http://honoreejeffers.com/blog/2017/09/23/teachable-racial-moment-a-black-history-lesson-behind-son-of-a-bitch/.

Jeong, Sarah. 2017. Should We Be Able to Reclaim a Racist Insult—as a Registered Trademark? January 17. Retrieved from https://www.nytimes.com/2017/01/17/magazine/should-we-be-able-to-reclaim-a-racist-insult-as-a-registered-trademark.html?_r=0.

Kaminski, Margot E., and Kate Klonick. 2017. Facebook, Free Expression and the Power of the Leak. June 27. Retrieved from https://www.nytimes.com/2017/06/27/opinion/facebook-first-amendment-leaks-free-speech.html.

Kelly, Deidre M., Shauna Pomerantz, and Dawn H. Currie. 2006. No Boundaries? Girls' Interactive, Online Learning About Femininities. *Youth & Society* 38(1): 3–28.

Kettrey, Heather Hensman. 2016. What's Gender Got to Do with It? Sexual Double Standards and Power in Heterosexual College Hookups. *Journal of Sex Research* 53(7): 754–765.

Kimmel, Michael. 2000. *The Gendered Society*. New York: Oxford University Press.

Kleinman, Sherryl, Matthew B. Ezzell, and A. Cory Frost. 2009. Reclaiming Critical Analysis: The Social Harms of "Bitch." *Sociological Analysis* 3(1): 47–68.

Kofoed, Jette, and Jessica Ringrose. 2012. Travelling and Sticky Effects: Exploring Teens and Sexualized Cyberbullying Through a Butlerian-Deleuzian-Guattarian Lens. *Discourse: Studies in the Cultural Politics of Education* 33(1): 5–20.

Kreager, Derek A., and Jeremy Staff. 2009. The Sexual Double Standard and Peer Acceptance. *Social Psychology Quarterly* 72(2): 143–164.

Krippendorff, Klaus. 2004. *Content Analysis: An Introduction to Its Methodology*. Thousand Oaks, CA: Sage.

Laville, Sandra. 2016. Research Reveals Huge Scale of Social Media Misogyny. May 26. Retrieved from https://www.theguardian.com/technology/2016/may/25/yvette-cooper-leads-cross-party-campaign-against-online-abuse.

Le Espiritu, Yen. 2000. We Don't Sleep Around Like White Girls Do: Family, Culture, and Gender in Filipina American Lives. *Signs* 26(2): 415–440.

Lehman, Brian. 2014. The Evolution of Languages on Twitter. March 10. Retrieved from https://blog.gnip.com/twitter-language-visualization.

Levey, Tania G. 2015. Online Sexual Shaming: An Analysis of Misogynistic Keywords on Twitter. Paper presented at the meeting of the American Sociological Association, August, Chicago, IL.

Levin, Sam. 2017. Facebook Promised to Tackle Fake News. But the Evidence Shows It's Not Working. May 16. Retrieved from https://www.theguardian.com/technology/2017/may/16/facebook-fake-news-tools-not-working.

Lichtenstein, Jesse. 2017. A Whimsical Wordsmith Charts a Course Beyond Twitter. *New York Times Magazine*. June 15. Retrieved from https://www.nytimes.com/2017/06/15/magazine/a-whimsical-wordsmith-charts-a-course-beyond-twitter.html?_r=0.

Lorber, Judith. 1994. *Paradoxes of Gender*. New Haven, CT: Yale University Press.

Lorde, Audre. 1984. *Sister Outsider: Essays and Speeches*. New York: Crossing Press.

Lucal, Betsy. 1999. What It Means to Be Gendered Me: Life on the Boundaries of a Dichotomous Gender System. *Gender and Society* 13(6): 781–797.

Lyons, Heidi, Peggy C. Giordano, Wendy D. Manning, and Monica A. Longmore. 2011. Identity, Peer Relationships, and Adolescent Girls' Sexual Behavior: An Exploration of the Contemporary Double Standard. *Journal of Sex Research* 48(5): 437–449.

Maas, Megan K., Cindy L. Shearer, Meghan M. Gillen, and Eva S Lefkowitz. 2015. Sex Rules: Emerging Adults' Perceptions of Gender's Impact on Sexuality. *Sexuality and Culture* 19(4): 617–636.

MacKinnon, Catharine A. 1989. *Toward a Feminist Theory of the State*. Cambridge: Harvard University Press.

Madden, Mary, Amanda Lenhart, Sandra Cortesi, Urs Gasser, Maeve Duggan, Aaron Smith, and Meredith Beaton. 2013. Teens, Social Media, and Privacy. Pew Research Center Report. Retrieved from http://pewinternet.org/Reports/2013/Teens-Social-Media-And-Privacy.aspx.

Manovich, Lev. 2011. Trending: The Promises and Challenges of Big Social Data. In Matthew K. Gold (ed.). *Debates in the Digital Humanities*. Pp. 460–475. Minneapolis: The University of Minnesota Press.

Mantilla, Karla. 2015. *Gendertrolling: How Misogyny Went Viral*. Santa Barbara: Praeger.

Marcotte, Amanda. 2013. "Men's Rights" and "Revenge Porn" Sites Seethe with Anger over Women's Autonomy. December 16. Retrieved from https://rewire .news/article/2013/12/16/mens-rights-and-revenge-porn-sites-seethe-with -anger-over-womens-autonomy.

Marwick, Alice E., and danah boyd. 2011. I Tweet Honestly, I Tweet Passionately: Twitter Users, Context Collapse, and the Imagined Audience. *New Media & Society* 13(1): 114–133.

Maxwell, Angie, and Todd Shields. 2017. The Impact of "Modern Sexism" on the 2016 Presidential Election. Report from the Diane D. Blair Center of Southern Politics and Society. Retrieved from https://blaircenter.uark.edu/the-impact -of-modern-sexism.

Maynard, Douglas W. 1988. Language, Interaction, and Social Problems. *Social Problems* 35(4): 311–334.

McAuliffe, Naomi. 2014. This Was the Year Sexist Language Declined and Fell (and Moved Online). December 31. Retrieved from https://www.theguardian .com/commentisfree/2014/dec/31/sexist-language-online-twitter-rape-threats -gamergate-misogynist.

McRobbie, Angela. 2008. Young Women and Consumer Culture: An Intervention. *Cultural Studies* 22(5): 531–550.

Messerschmidt, James W. 2011. The Struggle for Heterofeminine Recognition: Bullying, Embodiment, and Reactive Sexual Offending by Adolescent Girls. *Feminist Criminology* 6(3): 203–233.

Messner, Michael A. 1999. Becoming 100 Percent Straight. In Coakley, Jay, and Peter Donnelly (eds.). *Inside Sports*. Pp. 104–110. Abingdon, UK: Routledge.

Mill, John Stuart. 1859/1962. *On Liberty*. London: J. W. Parker and Son.

Miller, Sarah H. 2016. "How You Bully a Girl": Sexual Drama and the Negotiation of Gendered Sexuality in High School. *Gender & Society* 30(5): 721–744.

Millett, Kate. 1970. *Sexual Politics*. Garden City, NY: Doubleday.

Mills, Jane. 1991. *Womanwords: A Vocabulary of Culture and Patriarchal Society*. London: Virago.

Morahan-Martin, Janet. 2000. Women and the Internet: Promise and Perils. *CyberPsychology and Behavior* 3(5): 683–691.

Musica, Inga. 2002. *Cunt: A Declaration of Independence*. Expanded and Updated Second Edition. New York: Seal Press.

Nagle, Jill (ed.). 1997. *Whores and Other Feminists*. New York: Routledge.

National Coalition of Anti-Violence Programs. 2016. *Lesbian, Gay, Transgender, Queer, and HIV-Affected Hate Violence in 2016*. Retrieved from https://avp .org/resources/reports.

New York Times. 2017. This Week in Hate. January 29. Retrieved from www .nytimes.com/column/this-week-in-hate.

Nielson, Joyce McCarl, Glenda Walden, and Charlotte A. Kunkel. 2000. Gendered Heteronormativity: Empirical Illustrations in Everyday Life. *The Sociological Quarterly* 41(2): 283–296.

NoHomophobes.com. 2016. Home Page. Retrieved from http://www .nohomophobes.com.

Nussbaum, Martha C. 1999. *Sex and Social Justice*. Oxford: Oxford University Press.

———. 2010. Objectification and Internet Misogyny. In Saul Levmore and Martha C. Nussbaum (eds.). *The Offensive Internet: Speech, Privacy, and Reputation*. Chapter 6. Cambridge: Harvard University Press. Kindle Edition.

Nyboe, Lotte. 2004. "You Said I Was Not a Man": Performing Gender and Sexuality on the Internet. *Convergence: The International Journal of Research into New Technologies* 10(2): 62–80.

Onion, Rebecca. 2017. Bad News: We're Sexist. June 7. Retrieved from http://www.slate.com/articles/double_x/doublex/2017/06/new_research_on _role_of_sexism_in_2016_election.html.

Online Etymology Dictionary. 2017. Retrieved from http://www.etymonline .com.

Orenstein, Peggy. 2010. I Tweet, Therefore I Am. July 30. Retrieved from http://www.nytimes.com/2010/08/01/magazine/01wwln-lede-t.html?_r=2.

———. 2012. Foucault and Social Media: Life in a Virtual Panopticon. Retrieved from https://philosophyforchange.wordpress.com/2012/06/21 /foucault-and-social-media-life-in-a-virtual-panopticon.

Orgad, Shani, Maria Bakardjieva, and Radhika Gajjala. 2009. How Can Researchers Make Sense of the Issues Involved in Collecting and Interpreting Online and Offline Data? In Annette Markham and Nancy Baym. *Internet Inquiry: Conversations About Method.* Pp. 33–67. Thousand Oaks: Sage.

Oxford English Dictionary. 2017. Retrieved from http://www.oed.com.

Pascoe, C. J. 2012. *"Dude, You're a Fag": Adolescent Masculinity and Fag Discourse.* Berkeley: University of California Press. E-book.

Payne, Elizabethe. 2010. Sluts: Heteronormative Policing in the Stories of Lesbian Youth. *Educational Studies* 46(3): 317–336.

Penney, Joel, and Caroline Dadas. 2013. (Re)Tweeting in the Service of Protest: Digital Composition and Circulation in the Occupy Wall Street Movement. *New Media & Society* 16(1): 74–90.

Pew Research Center. 2014. Online Harassment. October. Retrieved from http://www.pewinternet.org/2014/10/22/online-harassment.

———. 2015, June. Support for Same-Sex Marriage at Record High, but Key Segments Remain Opposed. Retrieved from http://www.people-press.org /files/2015/06/6-8-15-Same-sex-marriage-release1.pdf.

Pheterson, Gail. 1993. The Whore Stigma: Female Dishonor and Male Unworthiness. *Social Text* 37: 39–64.

Plante, Rebecca F., and Gary Alan Fine. 2017. Sexuality and Reputation: An Introduction. *Sexualities* 20(7): 767–771.

Pomeroy, Sarah. 1995. *Goddesses, Whores, Wives, and Slaves: Women in Classical Antiquity.* New York: Schocken Books. E-Book.

Poole, Emily Katherine. 2013. Hey Girls, Did You Know? Slut-Shaming on the Internet Needs to Stop. *University of San Francisco Law Review* 48(221): 1–40. Retrieved from https://ssrn.com/abstract=2400703.

Queen, Carol. 1997. Sex-Radical Politics, Sex Positive Thought, and Whore Stigma. In Jill Nagle (ed.). *Whores and Other Feminists.* Pp. 125–135. New York: Routledge.

Quinn, Zoë. 2017. *Crash Override: How Gamergate (Nearly) Destroyed My Life, and How We Can Win the Fight Against Online Hate.* New York: PublicAffairs.

Reid, Julie A., Sinikka Elliott, and Gretchen R. Webber. 2011. Casual Hookups to Formal Dates: Refining the Boundaries of the Sexual Double Standard. *Gender & Society* 25: 545–568.

Renold, Emma, and Jessica Ringrose. 2008. Regulation and Rupture: Mapping Tween and Teenage Girls' Resistance to the Heterosexual Matrix. *Feminist Theory* 9(3): 313–338.

———. 2011. Schizoid Subjectivities?: Re-theorizing Teen Girls' Sexual Cultures in an Era of "Sexualization." *Journal of Sociology* 47(4): 389–409.

Rentschler, Carrie A. 2014. Rape Culture and the Feminist Politics of Social Media. *Girlhood Studies* 7(1): 65–82.

Rentschler, Carrie A., and Samantha C. Thrift. 2015. Doing Feminism in the Network: Networked Laughter and the "Binders Full of Women" Meme. *Feminist Theory* 16(3): 329–359.

Rich, Adrienne. 1980. Compulsory Heterosexuality and Lesbian Existence. *Signs* 5(4): 631–660.

Richardson, Laurel. 2004. Gender Stereotyping in the English Language. In Richardson, Laurel, Verta Taylor, and Nancy Whittier (eds.). *Feminist Frontiers*, Sixth Edition. Pp. 89–94. New York: McGraw-Hill.

Ridgeway, Cecilia L. 2001. Gender, Status, and Leadership. *Journal of Social Issues* 57(4): 637–655.

Ringrose, Jessica, and Emma Renold. 2010. Normative Cruelties and Gender Deviants: The Performative Effects of Bully Discourses for Girls and Boys in School. *British Educational Research Journal* 36(4): 573–596.

———. 2012. Slut-Shaming, Girl Power, and "Sexualisation": Thinking Through the Politics of the International SlutWalks with Teen Girls. *Gender and Education* 24(3): 333–343.

Ringrose, Jessica, Laura Harvey, Rosalind Gill, and Sonia Livingstone. 2013. Teen Girls, Sexual Double Standards and "Sexting": Gendered Value in Digital Image Exchange. *Feminist Theory* 14(3): 305–323.

Rivers, Caryl, and Rosalind C. Barnett. 2015. *The New Soft War on Women: How the Myth of Female Ascendance Is Hurting Women, Men—and Our Economy*. New York: Jeremy P. Tarcher/Penguin.

Rogers, Richard. 2009. *The End of the Virtual: Digital Methods*. Amsterdam: Amsterdam University Press.

———. 2013. *Digital Methods*. Cambridge: MIT Press.

Ronson, Jon. 2015. *So You've Been Publicly Shamed*. New York: Riverhead Books.

Rosin, Hanna. 2012. *The End of Men: And the Rise of Women*. New York: Riverhead Books.

Rubin, Gayle. 1992. Thinking Sex: Notes for a Radical Theory of the Politics of Sexuality. In Carol S. Vance (ed.). *Pleasure and Danger: Exploring Female Sexuality*. Pp. 267–319. London: Pandora.

Rudman, Laurie A., and Peter Glick. 2001 Prescriptive Gender Stereotypes and Backlash Toward Agentic Women. *Journal of Social Issues* 57(4): 743–762.

Ruether, Rosemary Radford. 1974. Misogynism and Virginal Feminism in the Fathers of the Church. In Rosemary Radford Reuther (ed.). *Religion and Sexism: Images of Women in the Jewish and Christian Traditions*. Pp. 150–183. New York: Simon & Schuster.

Sandberg, Sheryl, and Anna Maria Chávez. 2014. Sheryl Sandberg and Anna Maria Chávez on "Bossy," the Other B-Word. March 8. Retrieved from http://www.wsj.com/articles/SB10001424052702304360704579419150649284412.

Sanders, Teela. 2004. The Risks of Street Prostitution: Punters, Police and Protesters. *Urban Studies* 41(9): 1703–1717.

Sarkeesian, Anita. 2015. Anita Sarkeesian's Guide to Internetting While Female. February 2. Retrieved from http://www.marieclaire.com/culture/news/a13403/online-harassment-terms-fight-back.

Sarkeesian, Anita, Jaclyn Friedman, and Renee Bracey Sherman. 2016. Speak Up and Stay Safe(r): A Guide to Protecting Yourself from Online Harassment. Retrieved from https://onlinesafety.feministfrequency.com/en.

Sassen, Saskia. 2002. Towards a Sociology of Information Technology. *Current Sociology* 50(3): 365–388.

Schippers, Mimi. 2007. Recovering the Feminine Other: Masculinity, Femininity, and Gender Hegemony. *Theory & Society* 36(1): 85–102.

Schmitz, Rachel M., and Emily Kazyak. 2016. Masculinities in Cyberspace: An Analysis of Portrayals of Manhood in Men's Rights Activist Websites. *Social Sciences* 5(2): 1–16.

Schneider, Christopher J. 2011. Culture, Rap Music, "Bitch," and the Development of the Censorship Frame. *American Behavioral Scientist* 55(1): 36–56.

Schulz, Muriel. 1975. The Semantic Derogation of Woman. In Barrie Thorne and Nancy Healy (eds.). *The Language of Sex: Difference and Dominance.* Pp. 64–75. Rowley, MA: Newbury House.

Seidman, Rachel F. 2013. Who Needs Feminism? Lesson from a Digital World. *Feminist Studies* 39(2): 549–562.

Shirky, Clay. 2008. *Here Comes Everybody: The Power of Organizing Without Organizations.* New York: Penguin.

Silverschanz, Perry, Lilia M. Cortina, Julie Konik, and Vicki J. Magley. 2008. Slurs, Snubs, and Queer Jokes: Incidence and Impact of Heterosexist Harassment in Academia. *Sex Roles* 58(3): 179–191.

Silverton, Peter. 2009. *Filthy English: The How, Why, When and What of Everyday Swearing.* London: Portobello.

Sinclair, Katerina O., Sheri Bauman, V. Paul Poteat, Brian Koenig, and Stephen T. Russell. 2012. Cyber and Bias-Based Harassment: Associations with Academic, Substance Use, and Mental Health Problems. *Journal of Adolescent Health* 50(5): 521–523.

Smith, Aaron. 2011. Twitter Update 2011. June 1. Retrieved from http://pewinternet .org/Reports/2011/Twitter-Update-2011.aspx.

Smith, Noah. 2016a. Freedom of Speech in the Digital Age. October 6. Retrieved from http://noahpinionblog.blogspot.com/2016/10/freedom-of-speech-in-digital -age.html.

———. 2016b. Trolls Are Crippling Twitter. November 4. Retrieved from https:// www.bloomberg.com/view/articles/2016-11-04/trolls-are-crippling-twitter.

Spender, Dale. 1991. *Women of Ideas and What Men Have Done to Them.* London: Pandora.

———. 1995. *Nattering on the Net: Women, Power and Cyberspace.* North Melbourne: Spinifex Press.

Sprinkle, Annie, and Maria Beatty. 1992. *The Sluts & Goddesses Video Workshop or How to Be a Sex Goddess in 101 Easy Steps.* Video.

Statistica. 2017. Most Famous Social Network Sites Worldwide as of April 2017, Ranked by Number of Active Users (in Millions). Retrieved from https://www.statista.com/statistics/272014/global-social-networks-ranked -by-number-of-users.

Steinblatt, Jacob, and Leon Markovitz. 2016. Sexist Haters Call Melania Trump "Bitch" 443 Times. July 19. Retrieved from http://www.vocativ.com /342355/along-with-plagiarism-claims-melania-trump-was-hit-with-regular -ol-sexism.

St. James, Margo. 1987. The Reclamation of Whores. In Laurie Bell (ed.). *Good Girls/Bad Girls: Feminists and Sex Trade Workers Face to Face.* Pp. 81–87. Toronto: Seal Press.

Stokes, Carla E. 2007. Representin' in Cyberspace: Sexual Scripts, Self-Definition and Hip Hop Culture in Black Adolescent Girls' Homepages. *Culture, Health and Sexuality* 9(2): 169–184.

Sutton, Laurel A. 1995. Bitches and Skanky Hobags. In Kira Hall and Mary Bucholtz (eds.). *Gender Articulated: Language and the Socially Constructed Self.* Pp. 279–296. New York: Routledge.

Tanenbaum, Leora. 2000. *Slut! Growing up with a Bad Female Reputation.* New York: Perennial.

————. 2015. *I Am Not a Slut: Slut-Shaming in the Age of the Internet*. New York: Harper-Collins.

Tannen, Deborah. 1990. *You Just Don't Understand: Women and Men in Conversation*. New York: Ballantine Books.

Taylor, Astra. 2014. *The People's Platform: Taking Back Power and Culture in the Digital Age*. New York: Metropolitan Books.

Theriault, Anne. 2014. The Men's Rights Movement Taught Elliot Rodger Everything He Needed to Know. July 25. Retrieved from http://m.huffpost.com/ca/entry/5386818.

Thurlow, Crispin. 2001. Naming the "Outsider Within": Homophobic Pejoratives and the Verbal Abuse of Lesbian, Gay and Bisexual High-School Pupils. *Journal of Adolescence* 24(1): 25–38.

Tirrell, Lynne, 2012. Genocidal Language Games. In Ishani Maitra and Mary Kate McGowan (eds.). *Speech and Harm: Controversies Over Free Speech*. Pp. 174–221. Cambridge: Cambridge University Press.

Tolman, Deborah L. 2002. *Dilemmas of Desire: Teenage Girls Talk About Sexuality*. Cambridge: Harvard University Press.

————. 2012. Female Adolescents, Sexual Empowerment and Desire: A Missing Discourse of Gender Inequity? *Sex Roles* 66(11–12): 746–757.

Trottier, Daniel, and Christian Fuchs. 2014. Theorising Social Media, Politics and the State: An Introduction. In Daniel Trottier and Christian Fuchs (eds.). *Social Media, Politics and the State: Protests, Revolutions, Riots, Crime and Policing in the Age of Facebook, Twitter and YouTube*. Pp. 3–38. New York: Routledge.

Twitter Rules. 2017. Retrieved from https://support.twitter.com/articles/18311#.

Twitter Terms of Service. 2016. Retrieved from https://twitter.com/tos?lang=en#us.

UN Statistics Division. 2015. Violence Against Women. In *The World's Women: Trends and Statistics*. Retrieved from http://unstats.un.org/unsd/gender/chapter6/chapter6.html.

Urban Dictionary. 2017. Retrieved from www.urbandictionary.com.

Vaidhyanathan, Siva. 2017. Facebook Wins, Democracy Loses. September 8. Retrieved from https://www.nytimes.com/2017/09/08/opinion/facebook-wins-democracy-loses.html?mcubz=1.

Valenti, Jessica. 2013. I Have a Theory. October 17. Retrieved from http://jessicavalenti.com/post/64156129338/i-have-a-theory.

————. 2016. Insults and Rape Threats. Writers Shouldn't Have to Deal with This. April 14. Retrieved from https://www.theguardian.com/commentisfree/2016/apr/14/insults-rape-threats-writers-online-harassment.

Vance, Carole S. 1992. *Pleasure and Danger: Exploring Female Sexuality*. London: Pandora.

Wajnryb, Ruth. 2005. *Expletive Deleted: A Good Look at Bad Language*. New York: Free Press.

Ware, Lawrence. 2016. The Politics of Being Woke. July 14. Retrieved from http://www.theroot.com/articles/culture/2016/07/the-politics-of-being-woke.

Warner, Michael. 1993. *Fear of a Queer Planet*. Minneapolis: University of Minnesota Press.

Warzel, Charlie. 2016. 90% of the People Who Took BuzzFeed News' Survey Say Twitter Didn't Do Anything When They Reported Abuse. September 22. Retrieved from https://www.buzzfeed.com/charliewarzel/90-of-the-people-who-took-buzzfeed-news-survey-say-twitter-d.

West, Candace, and Don H. Zimmerman. 1987. Doing Gender. *Gender & Society* 1(2): 125–151.

West, Lindy. 2015. What Happened When I Confronted my Cruellest Troll. February 2. Retrieved from https://www.theguardian.com/society/2015/feb/02/what-happened-confronted-cruellest-troll-lindy-west.

White, Abbey. 2017. Michelle Obama on the Toll of Racism and Sexism: "Small, Tiny Cuts ... Every Single Day." July 27. Retrieved from https://www.vox.com/identities/2017/7/27/16050576/michelle-obama-racism-sexism-white-house.

White, Emily. 2002. *Fast Girls: Teenage Tribes and the Myth of the Slut.* New York: Berkley Books.

Williams, Zoe. 2006. The Feminist Mistake. June 14. Retrieved from https://www.theguardian.com/commentisfree/2006/jun/14/comment.gender.

Williams Crenshaw, Kimberlè. 1993. Beyond Racism and Misogyny: Black Feminism and 2 Live Crew. In Mari J. Matsuda, Charles R. Lawrence III, Richard Delgado, and Kimberlè Crenshaw (eds.). *Words that Wound: Critical Race Theory, Assaultive Speech and the First Amendment.* Pp. 111–116. Boulder, CO: Westview Press.

Willis, Ellen. 1992. *No More Nice Girls: Countercultural Essays.* Middletown, CT: Wesleyan University Press.

Wollstonecraft, Mary. 1792/1988. *A Vindication of the Rights of Woman.* New York: Norton.

Wortham, Jenna. 2016. For Gay and Transgender Teens, Will It Get Better? September 8. Retrieved from https://www.nytimes.com/2016/09/11/magazine/for-gay-and-transgender-teens-will-it-get-better.html?_r=0.

Worthen, Meredith G. F. 2014. The Cultural Significance of Homophobia on Heterosexual Women's Gendered Experiences in the United States: A Commentary. *Sex Roles* 71(3–4): 141–151.

Wurtzel, Elizabeth. 1998. *Bitch: In Praise of Difficult Women.* New York: Doubleday.

Zakaria, Rafia. 2015. Sex and the Muslim Feminist: On Refusing to Equate Sexual Pleasure with Freedom. November 13. Retrieved from https://newrepublic.com/article/123590/sex-and-the-muslim-feminist.

Zhao, Shanyang. 2006. The Internet and the Transformation of the Reality of Everyday Life: Toward a New Analytic Stance in Sociology. *Sociological Inquiry* 76(4): 458–474.

Index

About the Book

Women who use social media are often subjected to blatant sexual harassment, facing everything from name calling to threats of violence. Aside from being disturbing, what does this abuse tell us about gender and sexual norms? And can we use the Internet to resist, even transform, destructive misogynistic norms?

Exploring the language of shaming and silencing women in the cybersphere, Tania Levey addresses these questions and also considers how online attempts to regulate women's behavior intersect with issues of race, ethnicity, and class.

Tania G. Levey is associate professor of sociology at York College, City University of New York.